Toronto Medieval Texts and Translations 2

THE COURT OF SAPIENCE

The medieval English allegorical poem, the *Court of Sapience*, was written in the middle of the fifteenth century by an unknown author. It is best described as an encyclopaedia: in the allegory the poet describes the nature and activities of wisdom in all its aspects. He includes a moving account of the fall of man and his restoration by divine wisdom; then he leads his dreamer through a landscape where all the traditional beauties of nature are catalogued and assigned their properties. The visit to the castle of Sapience, inhabited by all the branches of learning and the seven restorative virtues, completes the poem as we have it.

The first edition was an early production of Caxton's press, and it was reprinted by his successor, Wynkyn de Worde. This is a new edition of Caxton's text of the poem. Variant readings from the extant manuscripts have been supplied, and a glossary is added. The poet's sources and ideas have been investigated in detail and are discussed in the lengthy introduction and extensive commentary.

The poem is an attractive work in itself, and has been admired by C.S. Lewis and other modern critics. It is also a valuable witness to the taste of the early Tudor period.

E. RUTH HARVEY is a member of the Department of English, Victoria University, University of Toronto.

TORONTO MEDIEVAL TEXTS AND TRANSLATIONS

General Editor: Brian Merrilees

Edited by E. RUTH HARVEY

The Court of Sapience

UNIVERSITY OF TORONTO PRESS
Toronto Buffalo London

© University of Toronto Press 1984
Toronto Buffalo London
Reprinted in paperback 2017
ISBN 978-0-8020-5628-3 (cloth)
ISBN 978-1-4875-9148-9 (paper)

Canadian Cataloguing in Publication Data

Main entry under title:
The Court of Sapience

(Toronto medieval texts and translations, ISSN 0821-4344; 2)
Bibliography: p.
Includes index.
ISBN 978-0-8020-5628-3 (bound) ISBN 978-1-4875-9148-9 (pbk.)

I. Harvey, E. Ruth, 1944–   II. Series.

PR1965.C68 1983   821'.2   C83–098430–5

This book has been published with the help of grants from the Canadian Federation for the Humanities, using funds provided by the Social Sciences and Humanities Research Council of Canada, and from the Publications Fund of University of Toronto Press.

Contents

Acknowledgments

In the library of the Warburg Institute the *Court of Sapience* stands on the shelf with the medieval encyclopaedias, where I first met it many years ago. This happy insight into the real nature of the poem and the instruction I received from Dame Frances Yates in the survival of classical learning have guided my work with the *Court* ever since; it stands as a memorial in my mind to Dame Frances's own encyclopaedic learning and to her generosity as a teacher. I owe my interest in the subject, and what skills I possess, to her and to the other members of the Warburg Institute. Indeed, without the kindness and encouragement of the then librarian, J.B. Trapp, I would have found it difficult to continue.

My other debts are also heavy: Eric Stanley read the whole edition twice and made very numerous, detailed suggestions. My husband, Denton Fox, tried, as far as proved consonant with matrimonial harmony, to teach me how to become a scholarly editor. George Rigg corrected my Latin. Roberta Frank read the whole edition, and Sheldon Zitner has contributed many helpful remarks and comments. The general editor of this series, Brian Merrilees, was interested and encouraging.

I have experienced much generosity and help from several libraries, especially from those who own copies of the poem. The John Rylands Library in Manchester, the Library of Columbia University in New York, and the Library of Trinity College, Cambridge, all provided me with copies of their witnesses. Mr Clifford Maggs of Maggs Bros was most generous. I have worked at the British Library and the Bodleian Library, at Merton College, Oxford, and Trinity College, Cambridge, and owe much to the kindness and efficiency of their librarians. The staff of the Pratt Library of Victoria College, in the University of Toronto, have eased my work at every turn.

Some of the work for this edition was completed during my tenure of a Social

Sciences and Humanities Research Council of Canada Leave Fellowship, and the book is being published with the aid of a grant from the same body.

All of the mistakes that survive are to be attributed to the ignorance, indolence, and sheer bloody-mindedness of the editor.

E. RUTH HARVEY
Victoria College
University of Toronto

Introduction

The *Court of Sapience* is an incomplete, anonymous, allegorical poem that enjoyed a certain popularity at the end of the fifteenth century. Its subject is wisdom, defined in the largest sense as 'the knowledge of things divine and human'; the poem is serious, instructive, and rather old-fashioned, the kind of work valued by Caxton and the audience that bought the books he printed. But thirty years after Caxton's edition the *Court* was still appreciated: Wynkyn de Worde thought it worth reprinting in 1510; Stephen Hawes tried to imitate its style in 1503–6, and his imitations, the *Example of Virtue* and the *Pastime of Pleasure*, enjoyed some success into the middle of the sixteenth century.[1] Since then the *Court* has fallen out of favour: there has been only one modern edition, that produced under difficult circumstances nearly fifty years ago by Dr Robert Spindler.[2] Another manuscript of the poem came to light after Spindler's edition had been published; but, although Dr Curt Bühler hoped to bring out a new edition,[3] no revised text has yet appeared. The neglect of the poem is surprising; not only is the work of interest as one of the earlier productions of Caxton's press and as a valuable witness to the taste of the early Tudor period, but it is also a work of considerable intrinsic merit. The *Court* contains good poetry. The first book is effective and appealing even to those who have no particular taste for didactic allegory, while the second book is, at the very least, undeniably instructive. The present edition is intended to supply another text of the poem, taking the new manuscript into account and correcting the transcription of the earlier manuscripts provided by Spindler.

THE WITNESSES OF THE *COURT OF SAPIENCE*

The *Court of Sapience* may be found in four manuscripts and two early printed editions. In all of these the text is incomplete. One of the manuscripts (British

Library ms Add 29729) is worthless as evidence for the establishing of a text since it is a careful copy of the first printed edition; it was made by John Stowe, who was interested in the poem.[4] A small fragment of the poem was printed by Stowe in his edition of Chaucer in 1561; this, too, is of little value, but it will be discussed below.

The manuscripts

British Library Harley 2251 (H)[5]
Folios 287v-93v contain *Court*, lines 71–516.
Harley 2251 is an incomplete volume of miscellaneous matter, most of it verses by Lydgate. It is written in a legible and distinctive hand, the work of a scribe whose productions have been traced by E.P. Hammond and A.I. Doyle. All of this copyist's known work falls within the reign of Edward IV (1460–83); in Harley 2251 this is substantiated by the presence of Lydgate's verses on the English kings with the added stanza on Edward IV. The scribe seems to have worked in close association with others: Harley 2251 is entirely in his hand, but Trinity College Cambridge ms R 3 21 (T; see below), contains one fascicle written by him bound up with others in different hands. Harley 2251 was copied in part from a manuscript written by John Shirley (d 1456; see DNB), which is now at Cambridge (Trinity College ms R 3 20), and in part from a lost manuscript also written by Shirley. The Harley scribe is known to be inaccurate; in Miss Hammond's words, 'this copyist is the type of workman who transfers his original line by line, glancing at his archetype no oftener; the type of workman to whom word-order is immaterial, and with whom the substitution of a synonym is constant ... From such a copyist we learn little or nothing as to the minutiae of a text' ('A Scribe of Chaucer' 29).

The *Court* occupies the last seven leaves of the Harley volume; it breaks off at the bottom of folio 293 at the end of a gathering. The opening words of the next line ('Triewth wold') are written as a catchword at the foot of the page. At the beginning, the whole of the prohemium is missing, and the initial capital A of line 71 is written very large in blue, as if to mark the opening of the poem. There is no title. The text is accompanied by three kinds of notes: 1 / Latin notes, sometimes quite long, written in the margins on either side of the verses; 2 / English (or occasionally Latin) summary notes, also written in the margin, which clarify the action; for the most part these say who is speaking – for example, 'Here spekith the Auctour' beside line 169; 3 / interlinear glosses, written over or just beside certain words in the poem. All these will be discussed below.

Trinity College Cambridge ms R 3 21 (T)[6]
Folios 51r-83r contain *Court*, lines 71–2079, omitting lines 324–9, 710–14,
771–7, 1022, 1067.
T is a large manuscript containing 320 folios. It was written in fascicles by
several different scribes; the second fascicle is in the hand of the scribe who
wrote Harley 2251 (H). The *Court* fills the third fascicle. T contains material
similar to that in the Harley manuscript and appears to belong to the same
period of time, the reign of Edward IV. Lydgate's verses on the English kings
(with the added stanza on Edward IV) are present; there is also a Yorkist
prophecy that 'oon Edward shuld conquere for harryes shuld reygne no mo'
(f 244r).

The *Court* begins at the top of folio 51. There is a long empty scroll sketched
above the title, which runs: 'Here begynneth a breue compilyd Tretyse callyd
by the Auctor therof, Curia Sapiencie.' The prohemium is missing. Beside the
first stanza (lines 71–8) is a small pen-and-ink drawing of the Trinity; the three
persons are represented in human form, each holding an emblem – a cross, an
orb, a church. The *Court* ends on folio 83r, which contains lines 2073–9;
beneath this stanza the scribe has written, 'Explicit processus de musica,' and
underneath this, 'Explicit hic tractatus qui vocatur Curia Sapiencie.' The rest of
the page and the next three pages are blank. If the blank leaves indicate that the
scribe suspected that there was more of the poem to come, the *explicit* would
seem to suggest that he gave up his expectation of finding it. The scribe was
careless, or his copy was bad: several lines are missed out in the course of the
poem, and the deficiency is concealed by running two stanzas into one or by
writing a short stanza; at one point (f. 62r) the fault is clearly in the exemplar,
for the scribe of T has written 'defectus hic' in the margin. He includes the same
Latin notes as in H, often writing them right across the page above the stanza
they refer to. He also has the summary notes and interlinear glosses and, in
addition, what may be called 'subheadings' – *incipits* and *explicits* of the
separate episodes of the poem, such as the supplications of the different
hierarchies or the treatises on the different arts. (The text of H ends before the
subheadings begin.)

Trinity ms R 3 21, like Harley 2251, belonged to John Stowe (d 1605), the
Elizabethan antiquary who collected manuscripts. He wrote the name 'John
Lydgate' at the beginning and end of the *Court* and carefully annotated the text
throughout, noting the omission of lines, evidently by means of a comparison
with the text printed by Caxton.

The text in the Trinity manuscript is the copy-text for Spindler's edition.

Columbia University Library, Plimpton ms 256 (P)[7]
Folios 1–34 contain *Court*, lines 57–2373; in its present state lines 1940–2009
are missing.

The Plimpton manuscript came to light after Spindler's edition had appeared. It
consists of thirty-four leaves containing the *Court*, bound together with
ninety-two leaves containing four prose devotional tracts: the *Twelve Profits of
Tribulation*; an English version of St Bonaventura's *Lignum vitae*; *The Treatise
of Love*; and the *Treatise of the Seven Points of True Love* (excerpted from
Suso's *Horologium sapientie*). The whole volume cannot be assigned a date
more precise than the last quarter of the fifteenth century.

The *Court* is written out clearly and regularly on ruled pages, five stanzas to a
page, with a line between each stanza. On pages with subheadings there are only
four stanzas if the subheading falls anywhere except at the top or bottom of the
page; this is to say that the scribe at times squeezes a subheading into a margin
at top left or bottom right, but he nowhere compresses a stanza or breaks one up
between pages. The leaves of the manuscript have been gathered in eights and
badly misbound, so that they now run in the sequence A^8 (-A1), D1, D2, D4, D5,
D7, D8, D3, C^8, B^8, E^4. A1 and D6 are missing. A1 was evidently lost very early,
for one of the former owners of the volume wrote 'Sum William Hodges' at the
top of the second leaf, and this signature has been assigned to a date near 1500.[8]
The second leaf is now very dirty. The fact that only eight stanzas (if Caxton's
text is to be trusted) are missing at the beginning of the poem suggests that the
first page of the manuscript was decorated with an illuminated initial or title,
similar to, but more elaborate than, the gold capitals that are distributed
through the second book of the poem to mark its main subdivisions.

The other leaf missing from the Plimpton manuscript turned up at Sotheby's
in 1974.[9] It has undergone more damage than its parent manuscript: the bottom
left-hand corner has been torn, affecting lines 1967–71 and 2006–7; and the
page has been cut down on the left-hand side and at the bottom, destroying lines
1972–4 and 2008–9 entirely and damaging 'incipit de geometria' in the margin.
The loss of the bottom edge of the page makes it impossible to tell whether or
not the scribe included the 'explicit de arsmetrica' after line 1974.[10] Although
this separate leaf has not yet rejoined the Plimpton manuscript, I have, for
simplicity's sake, designated it as P in the textual notes.

Unlike manuscripts T and H, P has no Latin notes, no summary notes, and no
interlinear glosses. It does have most of the subheadings found in T. P provides
variant readings for almost all the existing text and proves that the prohemium
given in Caxton's edition is part of the poem (it had been suggested that these
stanzas were contributed by Caxton himself).[11] Most important, the Plimpton
manuscript provides a unique copy of nine additional stanzas of the poem:

instead of concluding with Dame Faith, it goes on to describe Dame Hope and her attendants. While these new stanzas darken the problem of the transmission of the text, they do cast light on the structure of the work.[12] The explicit of Dame Hope is not followed by a general explicit of the whole poem; instead, on the verso of the last leaf of P, in the centre of an otherwise blank page there is an eight-line rhyming summary of the contents of the poem as it occurs in this manuscript (see below, page xvi).

In all three manuscripts punctuation is scanty and irregular. H has a period in the middle of almost every line, and P and T have periods at the end of some lines and stanzas, but in none of these manuscripts does the punctuation follow the sense. All three regularly capitalize the first word of a line but show no regularity in capitalizing other words.

The printed editions

Caxton's edition, *STC* 17015 (C)
Folio, 38 leaves, A-D⁸, E⁶, containing *Court*, lines 1–2310
There are three known copies of this edition of the *Court*; they are in the British Library, the library of St John's College, Oxford, and the John Rylands Library, Manchester.[13] I did not make use of the copy in St John's College. My edition of the poem is based on a xerox reproduction of the Rylands copy, the text of which is identical to that in the British Library. The leaf A1 is blank, and the poem begins without heading at the top of A2. Space has been left for a decorated initial. The poem is neatly printed with five stanzas to a page, except where there are subheadings, in which case there are only four stanzas.[14] There are no Latin notes, summary notes, or glosses, but most of the subheadings are given. The poem ends with Dame Faith, but there is no general explicit; instead, immediately following the 'explicit de fide,' there are four pages (E5, E6) of lists of things every Christian should know. This has no immediate connection with the poem as a whole, but it does provide a summary of matter pertaining to Dame Faith.

Caxton punctuated his text very lightly, using the period, solidus, and virgule (small slanting stroke). For example, the first five stanzas have no periods, four solidi (after 'howshold,' line 9; 'her,' line 12; and 'dresse' and 'forge,' line 35), and two virgules (after 'tyme,' line 11, and 'amende,' line 35). Capitalization is more regular: the first word in each line begins with a capital, and so do most of the proper names.

This edition may be dated by the type, classified by Blades as number 4, which Caxton used only between 1480 and 1483.[15] But although Blades assigns the

Court tentatively to 1481, his own conclusions about Caxton's punctuation would place it in 1483. He states that Caxton used the long and short comma (solidus and virgule) together only in that year: until 1482 the short comma appears alone, and after 1483 it entirely disappears.

Wynkyn de Worde's edition, STC 17016 (W)

Quarto, 42 leaves, A^8, B^4, C^8, D^4, E^8, F^4, G^6, containing *Court*, lines 1–2310, omitting lines 1436–63

The date of this edition, 1510, is given in the colophon. The only surviving copy is in the British Library. The first page is occupied by the title, *The Courte of Sapyence*, written in a scroll over a woodcut of Christ in majesty (Hodnett, no 538). This illustration has no particular connection with the *Court*; de Worde had used it before. I have checked every word of de Worde's edition against Caxton's and find myself in agreement with Spindler: it is of no textual interest; de Worde simply repeats Caxton's text, abridging it slightly by omitting the section on animals. He includes the lists of things every Christian should know at the end of the poem, corrects a few obvious misprints in Caxton, and adds a good many mistakes of his own.

The stanzas in Stowe's Chaucer (Ch)[16]

In 1561 John Stowe added a number of items to the works of Chaucer in the text that he had revised for printing. One of these additions was a *Ballade* in twelve stanzas. It is a complaint of a lover in disgrace with his mistress, of which the first four stanzas are, incongruously, taken from the *Court of Sapience* (lines 197–203, 218–24, 365–78) and adapted to their new situation by slight changes in wording. The words of Mercy and Peace to God fit the case rather awkwardly, and the transition to the secular argument in the fifth stanza is crudely done. Spindler places these four stanzas in the same textual tradition as TH, but they are in themselves worthless as textual evidence.

THE TEXT OF THE *COURT OF SAPIENCE*

A major difficulty facing a modern editor of the *Court of Sapience* is the question of how much of the material provided by the four major witnesses is authorial. No one of the sources H, T, P, or C contains all of the poem we know, and even in its fullest surviving form the work is still plainly incomplete. On the other hand, each witness adds something different to the narrative text, and each of these additions must be considered separately. It will be necessary to discuss in turn the verse narrative, the Latin notes, the summary notes and the glosses in TH, the subheadings, the rhyming epilogue in P, and the concluding lists in C.

Elements of the text

The verse narrative
Three of the four witnesses are acephalous. An explanation for the loss of the prohemium in TH is readily suggested by the example of P: both T and H go back to a common exemplar, which must have lost its first page. The ten stanzas of the prohemium fit comfortably on to one page in Caxton; it was probably only the decoration at the opening of the poem that saved the last two stanzas in P.

The case of the end of the poem is more problematic. The end of the text in H was left out when Harley 2251 was bound, but T finishes just before the end of Dame Music; C finishes after Dame Faith; and only P goes on to describe Dame Hope. It seems very likely that the poet fully intended to go on to the five other major virtues before waking his dreamer, but there is now no trace of any more of the poem. P is the only witness for the last nine stanzas, but there seems no reason to doubt their genuineness: they fit in perfectly well with the rest of the poem; Hope's attendants are the same as those in lines 1513–16; and there is no discernible difference in style. Perhaps the author wrote no more than we now possess, but it is unfortunate, and not reassuring, to have the witnesses stop at four different places.

The Latin notes
There seems to be no good reason why the Latin notes in TH should not be considered as authorial: they do not contradict the text, and they often supply an accurate indication of the source of the passages they accompany. A particularly good example of this is the Latin note on the third reason for the choice of the Son as a mediator: the note supplies a long quotation from *Legenda aurea* that logically precedes the reasoning given in lines 561–7. It is conceivable that an early reader of the poem became so interested that he looked up both the correct sources and suitable supporting material, but it does seem unlikely. On the other hand, reasons for omitting the notes are not hard to find: both Caxton and a neat writer such as the scribe of P might have thought that they would spoil the tidy regularity of the page; they would also have been difficult to set up in type. Caxton did not print marginal notes on this scale in any of the books he published at this period.

The summary notes
No conclusion can be reached about the summary notes. These brief statements in English serve, in the main, to identify the speaker of the adjoining lines of verse or to summarize the action taking place in the stanza. They could equally well be by the author of the poem or by an early reader of the manuscript from

which TH descend. If they are authorial, they may have been omitted in C and P for the same reasons suggested as causes for the omission of the Latin notes.

The interlinear glosses
The interlinear glosses occur in TH. They consist of words in Latin or English written over or beside certain words in the poem. Some add information; others seem pointless or mysterious, or wrong. One or two of them have moved in the course of transmission and are written over the wrong word. They suggest the work of a studious reader of the poem rather than the author, a reader who carefully worked over his copy, which then became the ancestor of TH.

The subheadings
The subheadings, or incipits and explicits, for the different sections of the poem occur in all three longer witnesses, C, P, and T (P does not have any in the first book). The use of these headings is logical and convenient in an encyclopaedic poem. There seems no reason to doubt their authenticity.

The rhymed epilogue in P
The last leaf of P contains eight lines of verse, in the rhyme scheme ababcdcd, that provide a brief summary of the contents of the *Court* (including Dame Hope). There seems to be no reason to regard this 'stanza' as the work of the author of the *Court*: it is execrable verse; it claims to conclude a poem that has plainly not concluded; and it is not written as part of the poem but spaced out by itself in the centre of the last page of the manuscript. It is probably the work of a scribe, but not the scribe who copied P, for at least two of the lines appear to have exchanged positions.[17]

The lists appended to C
The last two leaves of C are filled with short lists of miscellaneous religious material: the ten commandments, the seven sins, the works of mercy, and so on. These do not seem to have any particular connection with the *Court*, and there is no reason to believe that they were compiled by the same author. Dr. Bühler has suggested that Caxton used this commonplace material to fill up a couple of empty pages at the end of his book.[18] This may be true; but since the *Court* was printed in folio and ends very neatly at the foot of E4v, there need not have been any empty pages. Caxton may quite simply have felt that this was improving information pertaining to faith, which would bring the unfinished poem to a suitably moral end.

The relationships among the witnesses
Of the four witnesses, H and T have a common ancestor. A number of errors

shared by them distinguish their textual tradition from that of C and P (see, for example, the variant readings to lines 125 and 391). Neither H nor T is copied from the other (each contains omissions where the other has the full text), but both belong to a group of manuscripts associated with John Shirley.[19]

Beyond this, it is impossible to come to any decisive conclusions about the interrelationships of P, C, and TH. Neither P nor C is copied from the other: there are many cases where C has the correct word and P has a blank space, but P has the right version of C's jumbled lines 980 and 1352–4. There are about twenty-seven cases where P and C seem to concur in a wrong reading,[20] and it has been argued that the omission of the Latin notes in both of these texts is evidence for a common ancestor.[21] But none of the common errors is overwhelmingly convincing, and it does not seem impossible that the idea of leaving out such awkward appendages as the notes should have occurred independently. It complicates things considerably to discover that C has also thirty errors in common with T, and one or two of these seem fairly weighty (lines 677–8, 879–80).[22] There are only seventeen misreadings common to T and P, and all of them could be explained by coincidence.[23] C, therefore, seems to be connected with both P and T, but P and T seem to belong to different manuscript traditions. The only possible conclusion seems to be that there must once have been at least some more manuscripts than those we have now[24] and that the evidence is insufficient to construct a workable stemma.

None of the witnesses offers a particularly good text. T is exceedingly careless. The scribe omits a number of whole lines and repeats, omits, and alters words in a very arbitrary manner. Both P and C at least have the advantage that their pages are so designed that a missing line or irregular stanza would have been immediately noticeable. Caxton's copy (or its ancestor) must have been damaged at the edges because, on more than one occasion, someone has had to supply a new first or last line to a stanza (lines 980, 1352–4, 2114). All three main witnesses show remarkably little interest in preserving the poet's unusually regular metre; but, whereas C is anxious to keep the rhymes right (see, for example, C's version of lines 636–7), T is sometimes so abandoned as to ignore even the rhyme-scheme (rhyming 'went' with 'passe' in line 129, 'vary' with 'souerayne' in line 257).

The scribe of P followed his copy carefully, leaving a space in the line every time he found an illegible word. P's text tends to alter the order of words, to omit letters, and to insert additional short words (reading 'so parfite' in line 336, 'the vere' in line 543). Some of the more unusual words in the text gave him trouble: 'wyte,' line 67, is altered to 'witte'; 'adnichilate,' line 281, to 'adinclynate'; and 'asper,' line 422, to 'a spere of.'

Caxton's text (C) has a fairly large number of errors resulting from the similarity of the letters f and s or c and t in contemporary handwriting. He omits many short words but occasionally adds a phrase such as 'sauns doute' (line 251). His errors, though numerous, are most often of an easily corrigible kind: many are obvious misprints, and his substitutions of one word for another often advertise their presence by being hopelessly unmetrical. And C shows no embarrassment about printing nonsense, as long as it rhymes; this tendency is reassuring, for it suggests a minimum of editorial 'improvements' for the sake of the sense.[25]

Metre

The *Court* is written in rhyme royal, the stanza form established by Chaucer as the most suitable vehicle for serious poetry in English. Chaucer's imitators used this verse form extensively, but none of them shows anything approaching his skill. There is no general scholarly agreement on the rules of fifteenth-century metre; it seems apparent that many poets either did not want or were not able to work with the regular decasyllabic line. But when compared with Lydgate, Ashby, Hawes, and the author of the *Floure and the Leafe*, the author of the *Court* is remarkable for the metrical regularity of his verse. Although the three main witnesses of the poem all have a corrupt text, in all of them the overwhelming majority of lines is decasyllabic. The difficult question of emendation *metri causa* will be discussed below; here I wish to outline the metrical principles that may be discerned within the poem itself.

The only exception the poet seems to permit to the ten-syllable line (eleven syllables with a feminine rhyme) is the omission of the first syllable, thus producing a 'headless' line like Chaucer's 'Twenty bookes clad in blak or reed' (*General Prologue* 294), and there are only two clear examples of this in the *Court* (198, 489). There are two lines in the poem with only nine syllables in all three witnesses (503, 1443) that could be classified technically as examples of the Lydgatian type c or 'broken-backed' line; they might also be the result of scribal errors. There are an additional seventeen lines that are not decasyllabic in all three main witnesses but seem clearly to be the result of scribal errors.[26] There are a few more lines that do not seem to scan at the beginning or end of the poem, where there is only a single witness, and other lines in the poem seem comparatively rough or difficult (eg 1096, 1189, 1399, 1481, 1871), but these seem exceptional.

The following rules for pronunciation may be deduced:

1 Final -e is silent, but -(e)s of the plural and of the genitive singular is pronounced in all words, with the following exceptions:[27]

A In some polysyllabic words with a final unstressed syllable, expecially words ending in -r or -l, plural -(e)s is not syllabic: see 'pyllers' 939, 'pynacles' 940, 'colours' 1019, 'hunters' 1023, 'cradels' 1038, 'gardyns' 1176, 'appels' 1340, 'jardyns' 1341, 'garlandes' 1509, 'planettes' 1951.

B An -es ending in the first half of a line (third, fourth, or fifth, rarely sixth, syllable), especially one that comes before a pause, is often not syllabic. Compare the monosyllabic pronunciation of 'fooles' required by line 115 ('O foole of fooles, hast thou thy wyt assayde') with the disyllabic one in line 922 ('Soo done alday these wyse men fooles lere'), or 'teres' in line 193 ('Dystyllyng teres dysteyned al here chere') with line 212 ('My crystal eyen, see how theyr teres rayne'). Examples of a similar treatment of genitive -(e)s are rare, but compare line 563 ('And for mannes gylt gyltless suffre to dye') with line 608 ('Of mannes deth, that ryght in specyal').

2 Final -ed of the past participle is usually syllabic (see 'dysteyned' in line 193 above), but in some cases it is syncopated; see 'punysshed' in line 793, and compare line 891 for the unsyncopated form. In line 1718 'conteyned' must be pronounced, as it is elsewhere spelled, 'content' (1111), and 'illumyned' is regularly trisyllabic (see lines 1483, 1490, etc).

3 The third-person present singular ending of verbs in -eth is not always counted as syllabic although, since it once appears in a rhyme ('sayth' / 'fayth' 2276–8), it must be authorial on some occasions. This is to say that the poet may have come from a region where it was possible to use both -es and -eth, and all the witnesses have altered the -es ending to a consistent southern form in -eth.[28] Thus we have 'thynketh' (328, 2000) as a monosyllable, which points to an original 'thynkes,' but 'forthynketh' (732) is clearly trisyllabic. Thus 'lyeth' 202 etc, 'rydeth' 484, 'loveth' 830, 'sleeth' 987, 'dremeth' 1059, and 'trowith' 2359 are monosyllabic, but 'maketh' 44, 1630, 'sheweth' 1631, and 'groweth' 390 are disyllabic.

4 The metre also frequently reveals the northern tendency to elide medial -v- between vowels;[29] thus, for example, 'evyl,'[30] 'over,' 'never,' 'geven,' 'geveth' ('yeveth') are usually monosyllabic (exceptions occur in lines 104, 340, 433, 690, 934, 1530).

5 The poet rarely makes use of elision between words, but there are a few examples. Some are made obvious by Caxton's spelling – eg 'th'olyve' 1774, 'th'appostles' 1946, 2211, 'th'Archer' 2146, 't'apere' 914; others are 'the Egyptes' 2192, 'to offend' 530, 'to avoyde' 592; 'many a' is regularly disyllabic, and 'maner of' (1650) is possibly so; there is perhaps also an elision in 'unworthy is' (250).

There are a number of other words in the poem whose spelling tends to obscure the pronunciation that the metre requires; thus these words are regularly monosyllabic: 'heven,' 'eyen' (but see line 967), 'royalme,' 'swouned' ('swonyd'), 'thorugh' (but see line 717), 'Boece'; 'piteous,' 'soverayne,' 'hympne' are disyllabic; 'creature,' 'leopard,' 'aloes' are trisyllabic. 'Sapyence' is usually disyllabic, but can be trisyllabic on occasion.

Editorial principles

My edition is based on C as a copy-text. T has already been edited by Spindler, but both C and P are relatively inaccessible. Both are of approximately the same date; neither's text is appreciably better than the other, and they are of almost precisely the same length. I have chosen Caxton's text over P because it has fewer omissions; it has also the advantage that it must have been the version best known to readers at the end of the fifteenth century: even the comparatively small number of copies printed in an edition of that date would be larger than that of all the copies made by hand.[31] Wynkyn de Worde reprinted Caxton's text; whatever influence the *Court* continued to have in the sixteenth century, it would have been in this version. I have collated the witnesses C, Ch, H, P, and T, and I have corrected C in the light of their evidence, departing from the copy-text when it did not scan or make sense.

The dangers of correcting a text *metri causa* are evident, but for this poem a case can be made. It is evident that none of the witnesses cares very much about regularity of metre and hence is unlikely to have falsely 'corrected' an original; yet, in spite of their inaccuracies, the great bulk of the lines in the *Court* read as convincing decasyllabics. Lines that do not scan in one witness frequently scan perfectly well in another; lines that are unmetrical very often show other evidence of textual corruption, and comparison with the poet's sources often indicates that a difficult proper name or rare word has been incorrectly copied: an emendation that restores the original word from the source frequently also restores the metre. See, for example, line 1028, where C's 'abatystus' corresponds to the word 'abisate' in the source: 'abisate' is attested by T and makes the line metrical. Spindler tentatively classified a number of lines in the poem as possible 'licensed' irregularities on the Lydgatian pattern,[32] but new readings from P tend to restore many of these to regularity; in many cases the new readings seem completely convincing in sense as well as metre (see, for example, the textual notes to lines 80, 446, 1393, 1683, 2128). I am therefore persuaded that the author of the *Court* tried to achieve a consistently decasyllabic line, and I have emended C on this principle. Whenever another witness has a reading that scans I have accepted it, and whenever a line does not scan in any of the witnesses I have annotated it. All departures from the copy-text are recorded in the textual notes.

The question of lines that do not make sense is slightly different. I have corrected C when it is clearly wrong (either meaningless, or proved by the source to be incorrect) by following another, or both other, witnesses; but the relative independence of the three longer witnesses from each other means that when two of them agree against the third, the majority reading is most likely to be correct, although this principle must be modified in the light of the evidence from the incidence of common errors given above: the readings of PT are perhaps a shade more reliable than those of CP or CT. I have not, however, followed PT on the sixty-nine occasions where the C reading both scans and makes sense:[33] in such cases I have kept C's reading in the text and recorded that of PT in the apparatus; for, although I suspect that PT may be correct, the manuscript tradition is not so clear as to warrant the departure from a reasonable reading in any one witness. It also seemed important to stick as closely as possible to the version of the poem that enjoyed the most widespread audience.

In the choice of the existing elements in the *Court of Sapience* witnesses, I have included everything but some of the summary notes. The Latin notes from TH have been relegated to footnotes, and the glosses are included in an appendix. I follow Caxton in including the subheadings and have added to his text the nine extra stanzas on Dame Hope and the rhyming epilogue from P. The lists of things Christians should know have been retained, mainly because they would have been associated with the poem by Caxton's readers. The summary notes have been omitted for the most part because the great majority of them are of the type, 'Here spekith Trouth,' and their function can be served much more conveniently by modern inverted commas. Whenever a summary note appears to be in any way substantive, it has been included in a footnote. For the rest, this edition reproduces Caxton's edition. His spelling has been preserved, but u and v, i and j have been distinguished according to modern usage. Modern punctuation, capitalization, and word-division have been supplied; printer's contractions have been expanded, and obvious misprints, such as inverted letters, have been silently corrected. The punctuation of the first book is complicated by the speech-within-a-speech-within-a-speech construction; to avoid rows of inverted commas at the beginning of stanzas, I have used only one pair for each speech, without repeating them at the beginning of each stanza.

Authorship, place, and date
The author of the *Court of Sapience* is unknown. The poem has been regularly attributed to John Lydgate since the sixteenth century, probably on the authority of Stephen Hawes; but Spindler has proved, through an analysis of its language and metre, that the *Court* is not the work of Lydgate.[34] The process of dropping final -e has gone further than in any of Lydgate's works, and Lydgate's favourite patterns of versification are not present.[35] The poem itself does not have any of Lydgate's characteristic literary vices or virtues: the dramatic effectiveness and conciseness of the first book are as unlike Lydgate in one way as the unvaried patterning of the second book is in another.

Internal evidence of the author's identity is scanty and unreliable. The sources he used will be considered below, but it may be said here that they do not provide any clues to the problem of the poem's date. The direct authorial statements are brief. The poet claims that he writes at the command of a superior – 'I am constreyned for to wryte / By my soverayne' (lines 65–6); that he is young (or perhaps childish), ignorant (68), and 'conversaunt and borne in the partes / Where my natyf langage is most corrupt' (31–2). He admires Chaucer and Gower and their successors, but he admits that he can never attain their excellence and that his own book cannot please 'lordes whiche have delyte / In termes gay' (40–1). Most of this is probably only conventional modesty; little weight can be given to professions of youth and ignorance made at a time when it was not done to claim maturity and expertise. The 'soverayne' who commissioned the poem may have been the king, although at this date the word could be used to denote anyone of superior rank or status, and the poet may just be imitating Gower. The reference to 'lordes' may possibly imply some kind of courtly connection; more probably it simply means 'gentlemen.' The statement on his language is harder to assess. Spindler argues that the metrical evidence points to a dialect of the region of Chester,[36] which does not seem a prime candidate for an area where the language is 'with most sondry tonges myxt and rupte.' Perhaps the author intended only to account for the possibly unfashionable northernisms (such as 'chylder' and 'broder') in his poem. It does seem clear that all the extant witnesses have to some extent translated the poem from northern to southern English; see 117n, 896n, 979n, and the glossary.

The date of the *Court* is equally difficult to establish with any precision. The *terminus ad quem* is provided by Caxton's edition, which was printed between 1480 and 1483. The reference in the poem to the successors of Chaucer (d 1400) and Gower (d 1408) argues for a lapse of time since their death; and Spindler's linguistic arguments tend to point to a date later than Lydgate (d ca 1449). But Lydgate was a very old man at his death, and his linguistic habits would have been those of an earlier generation; 'later than Lydgate' need not necessarily mean after Lydgate's death. The main argument for a late date for the poem is adduced by Spindler. He pointed to lines 1447–9, which proved, to his mind, that the poem could have been written only for a Yorkist king; hence he established 1471, when Edward IV decisively secured the throne, as a *terminus a quo*. Lines 1447–9 occur in the list of animals and run as follows:

Jak-napys nyce made them al mynstralcye –
Now here, now there, in eche place was his fete,
Eche thyng object he gan to counterfete.

The key point here is the nickname 'Jack' used for a monkey. There is no recorded instance of this usage before 1522 in either OED or MED; there is, however, plenty of evidence that 'Jack Napes' was used as an insulting nickname for the powerful and hated William de la Pole, Duke of Suffolk, who was murdered in 1450.[37] Spindler argued that no writer could possibly have used the term Jack Napes without calling Suffolk to mind, and, since Suffolk was a Lancastrian favourite, no writer could have used this derisory nickname with impunity at a Lancastrian court; hence the *Court* must belong to a Yorkist circle and must therefore be dated after 1471. The argument requires either the name to have originated as a nickname for the Duke and then later to have been transferred to the animal, or the nickname to have become so firmly attached to Suffolk that for a period of twenty years it could not be used innocently of a monkey. But Suffolk's name was William, not John: it is more likely, as OED suggests, that 'Jack' was already a common name for a pet monkey and only achieved written prominence when it was attached to Suffolk as a byname (in reference to his badge, an ape's clog). If so, there would be no real reason why the name could not also continue to be used unsatirically, simply as a name for a monkey (they were not uncommon as pets: Henry VI had one). Even if the poet could be proved to have been working in circles where it was lacking in tact to use the term 'Jak-napys' immediately after Suffolk's death, it seems unlikely that the ban should have continued for twenty years. And even within those years there were intervals of Yorkist power. The ape in the *Court* occupies only three lines in a list of animals derived from a reputable encyclopaedia; the poem is wholly unsatirical, and over two thousand lines long. Spindler may be right in his belief that the *Court* is to be assigned to the reign of Edward IV, but the Jak-napys reference does not prove conclusively that it could not have been written earlier.

There are two other indications of the date of the *Court*, but neither of them is in any way conclusive. One is Miss Hammond's belief that the Harley manuscript derives from a known Shirley manuscript and a lost Shirley manuscript. Spindler argued that the *Court* could not have been in the lost Shirley manuscript because Shirley died in 1456, and Spindler was convinced that the *Court* was written in or after 1471.[38] But if there is no compelling reason to date the poem after 1471, more weight could be given to the supposition that, like the rest of Harley 2251, the *Court* existed in a copy made by Shirley and was therefore composed before 1456.

The second point concerns the single 'Wo worth' stanza (lines 463–9), which is common to the *Court* and to George Ashby's *Active Policy of a Prince*. Ashby (ca 1390–1475) was clerk of the signet to Henry VI and then to his queen, Margaret of Anjou; he wrote his *Active Policy* for their son, Prince Edward

(1453–71).[39] This poem consists of moral precepts on government written in rhyme royal; the most probable date for its composition is 1470, when things momentarily looked bright for the Lancastrian cause.[40] If it were possible to say which poet wrote the stanza and which borrowed it, the *Active Policy* would provide either a *terminus a quo* or a *terminus ad quem* for the *Court*; but the stanza is the kind of rhetorical expostulation that fits into a variety of contexts. In my view, it fits better into the *Court*: its context, Peace's speech, is a highly rhetorical lament, and the *Court* has several similar examples of anaphora and patterned lines.[41] Ashby shows no other examples of this kind of thing. If Ashby did indeed borrow this stanza from the *Court*, the *Court* must have been written in the reign of Henry VI, which incidentally allows more time for the diffusion and corruption of its text.

It has been suggested that Ashby was himself the author of the *Court*,[42] whom he resembles in his moralistic attitude and his habit of providing Latin notes to his poems. A comparison of their work does not support this: Ashby's verse is bumpy and undistinguished, and he is far more autobiographical than the author of the *Court*: his *Active Policy* is prefaced by eighteen stanzas on its author's qualifications, and *A Prisoner's Reflections* by seventeen. In each of these poems Ashby names himself in the verse and expresses great pride in his position and his illustrious employers. The *Court*, though a poem of much larger scope, has a more unassuming author. Nonetheless, the stanza in common to the two writers does perhaps support the claim of the author of the *Court* to have courtly connections.

Spindler's suggestion that the author of the *Court* was the author of the *Babees Book*, who might also have been the 'Master of the Henxmen' (well-born pages) of Edward IV, can be neither proved nor disproved.[43]

It does not seem possible at the present state of our knowledge to suggest an author for the *Court of Sapience* or to give it a date any more precise than the middle third of the fifteenth century.

THE PLAN AND SOURCES OF THE *COURT OF SAPIENCE*

The plot of the *Court* is exceedingly simple. The narrator, having decided to indulge in the amusements appropriate to youth, imagines himself to have entered upon a game of chess with the World and Dame Fortune, in which he is soundly defeated. Reason rebukes him for his folly; in distress he prays God to teach him the way to Dame Sapience and then falls asleep. At first he dreams that he is lost and bewildered in a strange place; he is hunted through a wilderness by wolves and suffers rough weather. At last he sees a light and a narrow, thorny path. After struggling along the path, he finds himself quite suddenly in a beautiful meadow beside a river. There he sees a lady walking with two companions, and he runs up to her. She tells him that her name is Sapience and her two companions are called Intelligence and Science; she exhorts him to leave the wilderness of the world and join them at her home, where she intends to rest after a great labour. The dreamer is delighted and offers to be her servant, but first he asks her to tell him more about the great labour she has just mentioned. Sapience then tells the story of the four daughters of God and how her counsel found a way for the redemption of mankind. This story occupies the whole of the first book.

In the second book, Sapience declares her intention of returning home and again invites the dreamer to accompany her. They set out, cross the River Quiet, and make their way to the castle of Sapience. On the way the narrator gives a series of catalogues of all the beauties he observes: the precious stones in the river, the fish, birds, beasts, flowers, and trees that exist there in a state of paradisal perfection and happiness. The castle itself has seven towers and three courts; the seven virtues live in the towers, and the three ladies, Science, Intelligence, and Sapience, each have one court. The seven virtues come down from the towers to greet Sapience at the gate, and Dame Philosophy, who lives in the castle keep, welcomes her with a kiss. Then Sapience and her companions make their way through the castle: first to Dame Science's court, then to Intelligence's, and last to the court of Sapience, where the dreamer meets Theology and the seven liberal arts. After this they start on the towers: first Faith's, then Hope's; the poem breaks off abruptly after the visit to the tower of Dame Hope.

The traditional figure of the 'house of Wisdom' (Prov 9:1)[44] is here carefully worked out as a medieval castle: the narrator sees the seven lofty towers from the outside, admires the outer walls and moat, and enters the main gate (lines 1471–1500, 1653–6). The gate leads straight into the outer courtyard where Science presides and Scripture teaches, and the great philosophers debate together in a special room or 'parlour' (1668–9). The second courtyard, where Intelligence has her domain, has more chambers, a hall, and a parlour full of theologians (1688–91, 1709–15). The third and most splendid courtyard, Sapience's own particular realm, contains a great hall, a chapel, and parlours for each of the seven arts. The dwellings of Faith and Hope are only briefly mentioned, but the description of the castle makes it evident that these virtues live in two of the seven towers (1499, 2206–7), five of which still remain to be explored by the narrator. The donjon or keep of a medieval castle was built within the innermost courtyard; hence the logic of the poet's architectural design suggests that the narrator would have gone on to meet the ladies Charity,

Prudence, Temperance, Fortitude, and Justice, and then perhaps have reached the heart of his vision by visiting the keep and embracing Philosophy herself, the true 'love of wisdom,' before waking from his dream.[45]

The poem we have is only a fragment, and this must be kept in mind in any discussion of its merits. Nonetheless, fragmentary as the *Court* is, the larger outlines of its scheme may be perceived. The poem explores the nature of wisdom, which is opposed to 'worldly occupation,' or the aimless busyness of earthly life. Wisdom was traditionally defined as 'the knowledge of things divine and human'; it could be distinguished from, but contained, science (knowledge of earthly things) and intelligence (knowledge of invisible things); it governed, or was supposed to govern, every aspect of man's life in the world.[46] The title, the *Court of Sapience*, expresses the same idea of wisdom.[47] The word 'court' has the primary meaning of 'courtyard' or 'enclosure,' but it may also be extended to signify the whole of a castle or manor-house built around a courtyard or courtyards (as in Hampton Court).[48] The 'court' of Sapience is thus not only her own courtyard, where the liberal arts live, but also the whole of the 'cumly castel' (line 1473) where she has sovereignty over all the inhabitants. The edifice is itself more of a peaceful 'mansyon' ('abiding-place' 905) than a defensive castle; it is perhaps not too fanciful to see in it as well some suggestion of a college building: the courtyards or quadrangles at Cambridge are still called 'courts.' But 'court' also means the household or retinue of a sovereign; in this sense, too, it is Sapience's household, not just her own courtyard, that is truly her 'court.' The different ladies who come to welcome her are different aspects of her nature and power, just as their chambers and parlours constitute different parts of her house.

All medieval ideas on wisdom were backward-looking; they could not be otherwise when the belief in the fall of man dominated all intellectual and moral endeavour. Original sin had cut man off from his creator, the divine wisdom; it had perverted the natural world and darkened human intelligence. Hence the three main sections into which the existing *Court* falls are connected by the allegorical journey 'home.' The dreamer learns, first of all, of the fall of man and his restoration by divine wisdom. Then, guided by Sapience, he sees nature in all the variety and beauty of its first creation: the birds, beasts, and fish in Sapience's park 'no raveyn had' where man's wilderness was full of beasts 'in devouring expert.' At last, in the Castle of Sapience, the dreamer learns the path of intellectual recovery: the seven arts 'styre folk to leve the world and drawe to heven.' Only the moral virtues remain to lead man back to his origin in God, the source of all wisdom, celestial, earthly, and human.

The execution of this design by the poet is uneven. Parts of the *Court* are laborious and cumbersome – the enormous gathering of undifferentiated allegorical ladies is particularly wearisome and unsuccessful – but the scheme of the poem is far from contemptible, and effective even in its present truncated condition. The separate elements placed within this scheme were derived from the received medieval field of knowledge; novelty, modernity, and originality had little to do with wisdom in the eyes of medieval writers. The *Court* is essentially encyclopaedic and has the encyclopaedia's virtues of clarity and conservatism. This does not mean that the author's handling of his material is either perfunctory or mechanical: he uses different sources for each part of his poem and usually carefully directs the reader to the work or works in question; but it is the substance, not the presentation of his matter that is his main concern. Probably for the same reason, the known sources are all books written a long time before the *Court*; they are established and venerable authorities who may be relied upon with confidence. The three main parts of the poem are unified by the figure of Sapience, who has a different connection with each kind of wisdom; or perhaps it would be better to say that Sapience, herself one and eternal, may only be seen by man against the backgrounds provided by revelation, nature, or knowledge. It is in the context of these different aspects of wisdom that the poet's six major sources will be described.

Wisdom and the four daughters of God
When Sapience tells the dreamer the story of her greatest triumph, she describes the reconciliation of the daughters of God, brought about by her counsel. This is a tale that occurs frequently in medieval writings; in English alone there are versions in *Piers Plowman*, Lydgate's *Life of Our Lady*, the Coventry plays, and the *Castle of Perseverance*; traces of the same story may be perceived in Milton's first plan for *Paradise Lost*.[49] In the *Court* it runs as follows: God, described as a powerful king, has four daughters, a son, and a servant. The servant Adam, though treated with great love and indulgence, breaks the commandment given by his lord and is thrown into prison to be tormented by four torturers. The king's daughter Mercy sees him there and begs for his forgiveness, but she is vigorously opposed by her sterner sisters Truth and Justice ('Ryght' or 'Ryghtwysenes'). The fourth sister, Peace, argues that they should all agree with Mercy, but Truth and Justice remain firmly opposed to any pardon. Mercy faints with grief, and Peace bids a long farewell to heaven before she departs into exile. Their brother, in great distress, seeks out Sapience to ask for advice; Sapience tells him that he must become man and die for man's sake in order to satisfy each of his four sisters. The angels add their supplications for man; the son becomes incarnate, ransoms man, restores Mercy to life, and satisfies the conditions of Truth and Justice. When they both say that they are well pleased, Peace reappears, and the sisters kiss one another.

The story has a long and interesting history, which is too complicated to discuss here in any detail.[50] It appears to have taken its origin from Psalms 85:10 (Vulgate 84:11): 'Mercy and truth have met each other: justice and peace have kissed.' A body of rabbinical traditions grew up around these words, but it was not until the twelfth century that St Bernard of Clairvaux blended them together to create a story that was the distant ancestor of the version in the *Court*.[51]

The story itself is a figurative rendering of a theological argument on the nature of Christ's atonement for man's sin.[52] Some of the early Latin fathers, particularly St Augustine, spoke of the fall of man as analogous to a servant changing loyalties: man chose the devil instead of God, and therefore divine justice required that God in some sense respect the devil's 'rights' over fallen man. But divine mercy prompted God to have pity on his creation. The redemption by Christ was then seen in two ways: either God recovered man by offering his son as a ransom for him, or he ensnared the devil into destroying the innocent Christ and thus made him forfeit by his abuse of power the rest of the human race. In this way God satisfied the requirements of both his justice and his mercy; the penalty for sin was paid, but man recovered his inheritance. Thirteenth-century theologians disliked this formulation of the doctrine of the atonement, insisting that the devil had no 'rights'; but by their time the imaginative possibilities of St Bernard's allegorical rendering had given the story a life of its own.[53] Like many others, the author of the *Court* used for his immediate sources two works derived from St Bernard; these were the *Meditationes* once ascribed to St Bonaventura and the short sermon entitled *Rex et famulus*.

Pseudo-Bonaventura, *Meditationes vitae Christi*[54]

The origins of the *Meditationes vitae Christi* have remained obscure. Until the eighteenth century the work was attributed to St Bonaventura, the great Franciscan theologian and devotional writer (d 1274), but his authorship has been disputed ever since then. It is now believed that the true author was another Franciscan, who worked in Tuscany in the latter half of the thirteenth century.[55] The author of the *Court* shared the medieval view that the *Meditationes* was the work of St Bonaventura (line 607n).

The author of the *Meditationes* retells the story of the Gospels, urging his readers to try to imagine the scenes as if they were present. His first chapter concerns the council in heaven, which took place before the Annunciation. First the angels plead with God to restore man; then Mercy and Peace try to persuade God to show pity. God summons the other sisters, Truth and Justice; Mercy and Truth argue; the dispute is given to the Son to settle, and Peace reproaches her sisters for quarrelling. The Son writes down his judgment: if death can be made into a good thing, the penalty will be paid, satisfying Justice and Truth, but it will not be cruel, and so Mercy will not suffer. Both Mercy and Truth look for someone who will undertake to make death good, but it is only when they return to the council after a hopeless search that Peace names the Son as the only possible victim. God assents, and Gabriel takes his message to Mary.

The *Meditationes* was an enormously successful work: more than 217 manuscripts are known to exist,[56] and an English translation was made as early as 1410 (although the author of the *Court* did not use it). The version of the story of the daughters of God in the *Meditationes* is taken directly from St Bernard, but some details are altered; the outline is compressed and the wording simplified. The author of the *Court* used the *Meditationes* for the episode of the angels' supplication, and he was influenced by the wording of the sisters' speeches,[57] but for the main outline of the narrative he followed the version in *Rex et famulus*.

Rex et famulus[58]
One of the most influential versions of the story of the daughters of God is the brief, undated, anonymous sermon entitled *Rex et famulus*. Its author is unknown. It is printed among the works of Bede, but that attribution is certainly a mistake. The author of the *Court* seems to attribute *Rex et famulus*, or something very like it, to Robert Grosseteste, bishop of Lincoln, 'Lincolniensis' (d 1253),[59] but there is no reason to regard so late a testimony as authoritative.

Rex et famulus takes as its text Psalms 85:10 (Vulg 84:11) and repeats the narrative part of St Bernard's sermon in a much briefer form. The King has four daughters, a son, and a servant. The servant fails in loyalty by breaking an easy commandment and aggravates his offence by blaming his master; he is delivered to the torturers.[60] Mercy is overwhelmed with pity for him and pleads with her father for his forgiveness. Truth and Justice make their opposing pleas in the same form as that used by Mercy[61]; Peace flees away without speaking. The 'most wise son' ('filius sapientissimus') offers to settle the quarrel; he takes Mercy to earth, enters the prison, overcomes death, and returns to heaven with the servant. All the sisters are satisfied, and Peace returns.

The author of the *Court* used this version for the outline of his story; but he developed the speeches of the sisters, added the figure of Sapience[62] and the deadly swoon of Mercy, and did not send Mercy to earth with the son.

The theological boldness of the story, which made it unacceptable to the great scholastic theologians, is increased rather than played down by the poet of the

Court. His poem is about wisdom, the aspect of God that creates, redeems, and instructs and which, from the earliest times, was identified with the Son, the second person of the Trinity.[63] In this part of his poem the author departs from his sources in substituting Sapience's advice for the son's own initiative: Sapience is, in one sense, the second person of the Trinity; in another sense she is that which links the Son with the created universe (Sapience's park) and the truth contained within all human sciences (the inhabitants of her castle). The different episodes of the poem point to the one central figure of Sapience, the allegorical representative of a single absolute quality, which man can perceive only through images and analogies. Thus the poet's emphasis on Sapience in the story of the daughters of God enables him to exalt the divine wisdom while developing the 'conflict' between God's mercy and justice; he avoids the heresy of postulating disturbance in the bliss of heaven even while describing the quarrel; the 'wisdom' of God subsumes and contains his 'justice' and 'mercy.' Since the story recounts a mystery, the redemption of man by the incarnation of the Son, its proper medium is allegory, for allegory essentially clarifies and explains the abstract in terms of the sensory, without equating the two. By making the story more allegorical (by means of the figure of Sapience), the poet can also make it more concrete and dramatic.

In the *Court* the conflict in heaven is realized more vividly, both as a family quarrel and as a legal dilemma, than in the sources. The servant, man, stands in a feudal relationship to his lord, whose 'promesse and statute' (line 323) he deliberately breaks. His crime renders him a 'proude traytour' (229), guilty of lèse-majesté under medieval law:

The crime of lese-majesty takes many forms, one of which is where one rashly compasses the king's death, or does something or arranges for something to be done to the betrayal of the lord king ... or gives aid or counsel or assent to those making such arrangements, even though what he has in mind is not carried into effect.[64]

Hence man's punishment by four torturers is properly the severe penalty prescribed by medieval justice (for justice, like wisdom, was seen as universal, in origin all one):

If he is convicted he shall suffer the extreme penalty with torture, the loss of all his goods, and the perpetual disherison of his heirs ... Let the accused be arrested at once and consigned to gaol, nor is he to be released by pledges or by bail without special instructions from the lord King ...[65]

Hence Mercy's pleas for forgiveness are both an expression of her own pitiful nature ('Have thow mercy, or deth myn herte wyl wound' 203) and a formal appeal for 'special instructions' – an appeal, however, that rests on an acceptance of the servant's guilt: appropriately, her words echo the phrases of the Mass for the Dead.

Where the author of *Rex et famulus* emphasizes the deadlock in heaven by having the first three sisters make highly symmetrical pleas, the poet of the *Court* carefully characterizes them by their different styles. Truth rebuffs Mercy's emotionalism by being cold and logical; she inquires dispassionately into the case and rests her argument on a point of theology, the 'purveyaunce and prescyence' (lines 271–2) of their father. Justice ('Ryght'), 'ferful to behold,' is above all judicial; she rehearses the whole case against man and gives her verdict 'as ryght asketh' (295–328). The last sister, Peace, is virtually a new creation. Her first speech is an attempt to reason her more intransigent sisters into a reconciliation; it combines an emotional, rhetorical plea for mercy with legal maxims and logical reasoning, an appeal to all the sisters at once (338–92). With Mercy's deadly faint and the exile of Peace (for which there was only a hint in the sources)[66] the poet brings the tale to a new climax: Peace's long farewell to heaven (425–97) is at the same time a lament for exiled man and a ruined world; it inaugurates while it describes the 'time of deviation' between creation and redemption. The tragedy of man's fall is shown to have been both a universal and a personal disaster, a tragedy in heaven as well as on earth. Strictly speaking, such a statement is heretical[67]; only allegory could present so bold and sympathetic a concept.

The dilemma is solved by Sapience, who interprets the servant's crime as a challenge to the wisdom of God. Only the Son, who supremely represents that wisdom, can reconcile Mercy, Truth, and Justice and restore Peace. The figure of the chivalric challenge, introduced by Sapience, is taken up by the angels in their pleas for man. The poet here deserts *Rex et famulus* for the *Meditationes*; his interest in the suffering and sympathy of heaven for man finds fresh expression in the supplication of the angels, and his characteristic skill enables him to develop the single speech of his source into three suitably differentiated prayers. The great counsellors and judges of the first hierarchy plead that God should vindicate his honour by rescuing his own image, man, from the insult of captivity; the second hierarchy, the order of angelic knighthood, begs God to 'take man by conquest' and overcome the 'proude prince of derkenes'; the messengers of the hierarchy of archangels report that 'debate' is everywhere while heaven's enemies are victorious. The son solves the legal 'cause' by triumphantly responding to the challenge. He becomes Mercy's champion and undertakes to 'doo feete in armes' for her sake, as a knight for his lady. The 'ryght of redempcyon' (line 826) gives the son legal 'tytle' to the servant: he has both bought him with his own suffering and won him in 'batayle' against the enemy. Justice is satisfied, Truth confirmed; Mercy is restored and her realm enlarged, and Peace returns with the end of 'debate.' Sapience's great labour ends with the reconciliation of fallen man with God; and the highest manifestation of divine wisdom has been explained to the dreamer and the audience.

Wisdom and the natural world

The main source for the central section of the *Court* – the description of the scenery and wildlife on the way to Sapience's castle – is the medieval encyclopaedia of Bartholomaeus Anglicus.

Bartholomaeus Anglicus, *De proprietatibus rerum*[68]

Bartholomaeus is a relatively obscure figure: he was an English Franciscan friar from the University of Oxford who worked at Paris and Magdeburg in the earlier part of the thirteenth century. His encyclopaedia of natural history (in the medieval sense of the term) was very widely read; by 1500 it had been printed in French, Spanish, Dutch, and English translations, as well as in at least twelve editions of the original Latin. Although the English translation had been made very early (by John Trevisa in 1398), the author of the *Court* did not make use of it.

The nineteen books of *De proprietatibus rerum* contain descriptions of 'natural things' drawn from a very wide variety of authors, classical, Arabian, and medieval. Book I deals with God, the highest nature, book II with angels, and book III with man. After this Bartholomaeus moves on to consider the four elements that make up the world and the creatures that inhabit each of them. Here the author of the *Court* found his material on precious stones (XVI), fish (XIII xxvi), water and rivers (XIII), flowers and trees (XVII), birds (XII), and animals (XVIII). Bartholomaeus arranged his chapters alphabetically by subject, and the *Court* retains traces of this order, especially in the catalogue of precious stones.

One other feature of *De proprietatibus rerum* proved useful to the author of the *Court* for the third part of his poem. Frequently there was attached to the text of Bartholomaeus' encyclopaedia a list of the authors on whose work his compilation was directly or indirectly based. The poet of the *Court* made use of this list twice: once to provide the names of a group of natural philosophers to accompany Dame Science (lines 1674–90) and once to supply Dame Logic with a court of philosophers (lines 1881–9). Some other 'authorities' cited in the text of the *Court* were similarly borrowed from Bartholomaeus and cannot be used as evidence of the poet's learning.

For this edition of the *Court*, I have given references to the most readily available edition of *De proprietatibus rerum*, that published in Frankfurt in

1601 and reprinted photographically in 1964. But this is a very late edition in which the medieval Latin spelling has often been corrected or 'classicized': thus, for example, medieval 'ypotamus' (XIII xxvi) appears as 'hippopotamus,' and 'noset' (XVI lxxi) as 'batrachius.' Spellings in the *Court* are naturally much nearer to the medieval Latin spelling, which may be found in Trevisa's translation or in some of the earlier printed editions of Bartholomaeus.

Modern readers find the orderly array of medieval natural history that constitutes the middle section of the *Court* tedious.[69] It allows no scope to the poet's gifts for dialogue, discreet characterization, and emotional expressiveness; but, for this aspect of wisdom, his aims are more likely to have been order and propriety. It was an accepted medieval belief that the study of the natural world and its properties was virtuous because 'by the werkys is the werkeman knowen'[70]: all creation proclaimed its maker by its order, variety, and beauty. Indeed, an even more widespread theory held that the created world provided the only way for man to understand God and 'invisible things,' and a verse from St Paul was often quoted to prove it: 'for the invisible things of him from the creation of the world are clearly seen, being understood by the things which are made' (Rom 1:20).[71] Bartholomaeus expresses this view in his preface to *De proprietatibus rerum*:

Saynt Denys, that grete philosopher and solempne clerke, in his boke namyd *Of the Hevenly Jerarchies of Aungelles*, testyfieth and wytnesseth the same, sayenge in this manere, 'Whatsoever ony man wyll conjecte, feyne, ymagyne, suppose, or saye, it is a thynge impossible that the lyghte of the hevenly dyvyne clarete, coverte and closid in the Deyte or in the Godhede, sholde shyne uppon us, yf it were not bi the dyversitees of holy covertures. Also it is not possyble that oure wytte or entendement myghte ascende unto the contemplacyon of the hevenly jerarchyes immaterielles yf our wytte be not ledde by some materyell thynge as a man is ledde by the honde, soo by thyse fourmes visible our wytte maye be led to the consyderacyon of the gretnesse or magnytude of the moost excellent bewteuous clarete dyvyne and invysyble.[72]

The 'holy covertures' of creation both conceal and reveal the divine wisdom: they make plain, in the only way man can understand, the invisible glory of the creator. God made the world so 'that suche thinge shold yssue that myght vnderstande and knowe the noblesse of his power and of his sapyence,'[73] just as a poet makes an allegory, to lead the contemplative mind onward. Hence the interest in the *Court* (and in Bartholomaeus) in the 'properties of things': the hidden powers of the precious stones and herbs are tokens of the power and wisdom of their maker.

Learning and the seven liberal arts

The seven liberal arts of medieval educational theory have their origin in the seven main branches of knowledge in the late classical system of education.[74] The first three, grammar, logic, and rhetoric, interlock to form the *trivium*, 'the place where three ways meet'; the student who had mastered them was held to have acquired a complete skill in words, both written and spoken. This came to mean a mastery of the Latin language and literature and training in all the arts of discourse: preaching, argument, debate, and the techniques of logic. The remaining arts, arithmetic, geometry, music, and astronomy, dealt with the abstractions of quantity and magnitude. Arithmetic taught the properties of number; geometry was concerned with spatial measurement; music was seen as the science of numerical relations, and astronomy as the study of moving magnitudes. These four arts united in the 'four-way place' or crossroad of the *quadrivium*. The origins of all the seven arts may be traced back to classical Greece: they were called 'liberal' because they were the knowledge befitting a free man, not that of a slave or of one who had to earn his living. Arithmetic and music were not seen as the skills of the merchant or musician; they were essentially abstract sciences. Nor was the number of the liberal arts fixed at seven in the classical period: gymnastics, medicine, and architecture (the latter two in their theoretical aspects) were sometimes included as proper subjects for study.

The seven liberal arts came to the Christian Middle Ages chiefly through the writings of Martianus Capella (fl 410–29), Cassiodorus (ca 490–583), and Isidore of Seville. The latter two writers were deliberately baptizing a pagan system for Christian purposes; Cassiodorus in particular pointed out the usefulness of the various arts to the Christian faith: music, for example, would help men to sing psalms, and arithmetic and astronomy would enable scholars to work out the date of Easter. Cassiodorus was also partly responsible for the tradition that the number of the liberal arts was significant: he held the seven studies to be mysteriously interlinked and to provide in themselves the whole sum of human philosophy, the 'seven pillars' hewn out by the wisdom of God in Proverbs 9:1.[75] Isidore of Seville provided the more complex hierarchies of subjects given in the *Court*, lines 1555–1652, but the importance of the seven major arts, which are each given a whole section of the poem, reflects the older notion of the comprehensiveness of their doctrine. Cassiodorus, however, is probably only an indirect source; the poet made direct use of Isidore.

Isidore of Seville, *Etymologiae*[76]

St Isidore (ca 560–636) was Archbishop of Seville when Spain was under the rule of the Visigothic kings. He was actively concerned with the cultivation of a well-educated clergy; the *Etymologiae*, his best-known work, is a compilation of late classical learning, preserved and transmitted with the idea of making it useful to Christians. In it the etymology or 'true meaning' of a word is seen as an essential clue to its nature: Isidore deals with the arts and sciences of his day by analyzing the meaning of the terminology they employ. (His etymologies are now thought to be largely fanciful.) He begins with the seven liberal arts, giving all the derivations of words connected with them; he names the inventor of each, the subdivisions of the subject, and the standard authorities that may be consulted by the student. In some cases he gives quite a detailed account of the subject matter of the art. After the arts, he deals with medicine and law, God and the angels, the church and non-Christians, language, man, beasts, the elements, the earth, cities, fruits, and various arts and crafts. Because the work was not arranged alphabetically, it was used as an encyclopaedia rather than a dictionary; but it lay behind the large medieval dictionaries and was frequently used as an authority in works on many subjects. The *Etymologiae* was not displaced by later textbooks: copies of it are frequently listed among the few books used in fifteenth-century English schools.[77]

The author of the *Court* used Isidore frequently. He mentions him by name in lines 1094, 1195, 1256, and 2190, and in the Latin note to line 99; lines 1555–1652 are translated almost directly from the *Etymologiae*, and Isidore is a pervasive influence throughout the whole section on the quadrivium.

Although Isidore's work remained fundamental throughout the Middle Ages, the separate disciplines of the liberal arts gradually developed, and new texts were discovered and written. The study of the trivium produced a large number of new textbooks, particularly on grammar and logic. The author of the *Court* knew a good deal about logic, but his knowledge cannot be traced to any single book; for grammar and rhetoric, however, his indebtedness to a famous thirteenth-century work is both deep and explicit.

Joannes Balbus, *Catholicon*[78]

The *Catholicon* was the largest and best of medieval Latin dictionaries. It was compiled by the Dominican friar Giovanni Balbi of Genoa (Joannes Balbus Januensis, often called 'Januens'), who completed his work in 1286. Although the great bulk of the *Catholicon* is a fully alphabetized dictionary, the author regarded his work as a Latin grammar: the first fifth of the book is made up of four short grammatical *tractatus*, and the dictionary constitutes the fifth tractatus on *prosodia*. Each word is given its correct spelling, accent, derivation, and meaning, together with notes on its declension or conjugation. Balbus often includes a quotation exemplifying usage and sometimes adds a considerable essay on a point of theology, morals, or natural history touched on by the word in question. He made extensive use of earlier dictionaries, especially those of Papias of Lombardy (ca 1053) and Uguccio of Pisa (d 1210), as well as Isidore's

Etymologiae. The *Catholicon* was enormously successful: it survives in 117 manuscripts; it was one of the first books to be printed (Mainz 1460), and it was reprinted at least twenty-four times before the contempt of the humanists forced it out of use in the next century. It was frequently used in English schools and universities.[79]

The *Catholicon* was used a good deal by the author of the *Court*, who quotes from it in his notes to lines 146 and 673 and introduces 'the Januens ... in grete estate' into his text in lines 1832 and 1916. Most of his account of grammar and rhetoric seems to derive from the *Catholicon*. In addition, he made less obvious use of information given in the *Catholicon* in his passages on cosmic disorder (lines 474–92) and the size of the world (lines 1996–2009). Other instances of possible indebtedness are recorded in the notes.

The presence of the seven arts in Sapience's own court, equipped with their pagan inventors and exponents, points to their complete absorption into the Christian world. It did not matter, in the medieval view, that the arts were a legacy of paganism: rather, they represented man's own proper 'natural' achievement. The wisdom embodied in the liberal arts was man's original perception of the workings of the divine wisdom: the arts themselves were part of man's own endowment by his creator. It was said that Adam possessed a perfect knowledge of the seven liberal arts in Paradise but that this had been obliterated by sin.[80] Over the centuries, by exerting natural reason, man gradually rediscovered his lost arts and, in doing so, approached, in the way appropriate to him, his own source of true wisdom.

Hence the seven arts in Sapience's court are a part of the same wisdom that redeemed man and created the natural world; the arts by their own nature 'styre folk to leve the world and drawe to heven' (line 2205). To recover wisdom is to recover goodness; the seven arts lead naturally to the seven virtues. The virtues themselves are a blend of the four pagan cardinal virtues and the three Christian theological virtues. Prudence, Justice, Fortitude, and Temperance belonged to the ancient world of natural qualities; Faith, Hope, and Charity depend on revelation, on the restoration planned by Sapience for man. The arts and virtues together complete the design of the workings of wisdom in human history.

Other sources
One other source known to have been used by the poet remains to be considered: the *Golden Legend* of Jacobus de Voragine.

Jacobus de Voragine, *Legenda aurea*[81]
The *Legenda aurea* is a large collection of lives of the saints, originally produced by Jacobus de Voragine (d 1298). Besides saints' lives, the *Legenda aurea* also

contains a good deal of Biblical history, notes about feasts of the church, and other miscellaneous information. It was very widely read, and many different texts survive since countries adapted it to their use by adding their own national saints. It is best known in England in the translation that was made by Caxton and printed in 1483. Unfortunately for our purposes, Caxton abridged the text; citations from the *Court* are to parts of the text omitted in the English version.

The author of the *Court* did not make extensive use of the *Legenda aurea*, but he must have known it very well since his citations are from two relatively obscure passages. One comes from the long discourse of St Silvester to the Jews: Silvester's response to the sixth Jew is used in the poem as the third reason for the incarnation (lines 561–7); the other is a note on the orders of the angels, taken from Voragine's chapter on the feast of St Michael the archangel.

Besides the six works named above, the author of the *Court* mentions a number of other authors and texts. Some of these he must have learned about at second hand: it is very unlikely that he read Democritus, Varro, or Plato, but he would have known about them from the references in Bartholomaeus and Isidore. The names that are not to be found in his major sources are more interesting. The author of the *Court* knew, at least by name, the English theologians Robert Holcot (d 1349) and William of Nottingham (d 1251), and he used the work of John Ridevall (fl 1331–40). He mentions as authorities in grammar John Garland (early thirteenth century) and Thomas Hanney (fl 1313); and lists, on rhetoric, Geoffrey of Vinsauf (fl ca 1210), Peter of Blois (fl 1190), Richard de Pophys (late thirteenth century), and the *Letters of Pharaoh* of John of Limoges (early thirteenth century). His list of logical treatises cannot be identified with any certainty, but he knew enough about geometry to have heard of Theodosius of Bithynia and Euclid. In music he quotes a leading authority on mensural music, Jean de Muris (fl 1321–81), as well as the work of the older John of Affligem (ca. 1100–21). In fact music appears to be his most up-to-date subject: his use of the word 'crochet' is among the earliest recorded in English, and the note itself is not recognized by Jean de Muris.[82] None of this is, unfortunately, of any help in dating the *Court* more precisely, but it does seem to make evident that the poet had had a university education of a rather old-fashioned kind. The university syllabus had been based on the idea of the seven liberal arts that led up to theology (although in practice logic predominated and the quadrivium was neglected); probably either Oxford or Cambridge in the fifteenth century would have provided the kind of education the poet reveals.

Other references in the *Court* suggest that the author was a cleric. Besides knowing of such theologians as Holcot and Nottingham, he is able to introduce apposite phrases from the mass into his poem; he refers to the Athanasian Creed, and he shows a good deal of familiarity with the Bible. If he had pursued a university career, it is very likely that he would have been in orders; at that date there was still small scope for the university-educated layman. In addition, there are aspects of the first book that suggest some kind of legal background for the poet: he occasionally cites legal maxims; twice he gives a reference to the body of Civil Law, and once he quotes a principle from Canon Law. This is not enough to prove anything conclusively, but it is suggestive. Whoever wrote the *Court* was interested in the legal 'dilemma' in heaven and at least took the trouble to look up the various laws and principles on which the problem turned.

The author of the *Court* put all this learning into a poem written in formal rhyme royal, in the vernacular, prefaced by a tribute to Chaucer and Gower. It is a poem that is essentially backward-looking, uninfluenced by and unconcerned with any humanistic stirrings that may have been taking place either at Oxford or at court, under the influence of the uncle of Henry VI, Duke Humfrey of Gloucester. But the *Court* is not to be despised for its conservatism: against the humanistic fragmentation of history and learning, it represents the impressive medieval attempt to unify human history and experience. The author's anonymity is oddly fitting: he writes not as a scholar, cleric, or individual, but simply as a scribe, the human 'refrendary' of universal wisdom.

NOTES

1 Hawes, *Pastime of Pleasure* line 1357, includes the *Court* among the works of Lydgate. Whitney Wells, 'Stephen Hawes and the *Court of Sapience*' RES VI (1930) 284–94, demonstrates Hawes' indebtedness to the *Court*; Spindler lists the words and phrases common to the *Court* and the *Pastime* in his introduction to the *Court*, pp 120–3. The *Example of Virtue* was written in 1503–4, and printed in 1509, 1520, 1530; the *Pastime* was written in 1505–6 and printed in 1509, 1517, 1554, 1555.

2 *The Court of Sapience* ed Robert Spindler (Leipzig 1927; reprinted 1967); reviewed by W. van der Gaaf *English Studies* x (1928) 18–22. Spindler did not transcribe the manuscripts himself; he inherited the transcriptions and notes made by Joseph Jäger, who had been killed in the First World War. There are several errors and obscurities in Spindler's text that do not exist in the manuscripts and early editions.

3 For the Plimpton manuscript, see below, pp xii–xiii. Curt F. Bühler 'Notes on the Plimpton Manuscript of the *Court of Sapience*' MLN LIX (1944) 5–9

4 Spindler 22–4. Besides copying out the Caxton edition, Stowe also 'corrected' the text of the poem in the Trinity manuscript, which was then in his possession (see below, p xi). He also owned the Harley manuscript of the poem.

5 See the *Catalogue of the Harleian Manuscripts in the British Museum* (London 1808) ii 578–82. My account of this manuscript is indebted to E.P. Hammond, 'Two British Museum Manuscripts (Harley 2251 and Adds 34360) A contribution

to the Bibliography of John Lydgate' *Anglia* XXVIII (1905) 1–28, corrected by the later article, 'A Scribe of Chaucer' *Modern Philology* XXVII (1930) 27–33; and A.I. Doyle, 'An unrecognised piece of Piers the Ploughman's Creed and other works by its scribe' *Speculum* XXXIV (1959) 428–36. I am indebted to Richard F. Green for drawing my attention to these works.

6 See M.R. James *The Western Manuscripts in the Library of Trinity College Cambridge* ii (Cambridge 1901) 83–95; also the articles in note 5 above. Hammond and Doyle believe both T and H to have come from the same scriptorium or copying-shop; Hammond thinks Trinity R 3 19 (see note 16 below) has connections with the same group.

7 This manuscript was originally in the library of the Earl of Carlisle; it was sold at Sotheby's in April 1927 and passed into the possession of Mr George A. Plimpton, who bequeathed it to Columbia University. The nine stanzas on Hope and the rhyming summary of the poem were first published by Karl Brunner, 'Bisher unbekannte Schluszstrophen des *Court of Sapience*' *Anglia* LXII (1938) 258–62. I am most grateful to Columbia University Library for their kindness in supplying me with a microfilm of the whole manuscript and of the unpublished thesis of Grace M. Schubert, '*The Court of Sapience*: a collation of the Plimpton Manuscript with introduction and notes' MA Columbia 1937.

8 Seymour de Ricci *Census of Medieval and Renaissance Manuscripts in the United States and Canada* (1935–7; reprinted 1961) ii 1799; Schubert iii

9 Sotheby & Co *Catalogue of Western Manuscripts and Miniatures* 9 December 1974, lot 25. The leaf was sold to Maggs Bros. I am most grateful to Mr Clifford Maggs for allowing me to examine the leaf and for giving me a xerox copy. This leaf must be the Castle Howard fragment listed in the Brown-Robbins *Index*, although the line numbers given there are not correct.

10 A couple of hooks of ascending letters are just visible.

11 Bühler 'Notes on the Plimpton Manuscript' 6. Joseph Ames suggested that the whole poem was written by Caxton; his view was convincingly refuted by William Blades, *The Life and Typography of William Caxton* (London 1861–3) ii 114–6. See also Spindler 99–105.

12 The poem has been criticized as if it were complete by Curt F. Bühler, *The Sources of the Court of Sapience* (Leipzig 1932) 9 (based on Spindler's text); and by Karl Brunner, 'Bisher unbekannte Schluszstrophen' 258 (commenting on the poem as we now have it). See below, pp xxv–xxvi.

13 There are, in addition, two torn leaves (B3 and B6) in the British Library (shelf mark IB 55056), and two (E1 and E3) in the Bodleian (Douce fragments); these contain no variants from the other copies.

I am most grateful to the librarian of the John Rylands Library for providing me with a xerox reproduction of the Rylands copy of the *Court*.

14 There are two exceptions: 'Incipit processus de tercia curia' on f D3v and the explicit

on B7v seem to have been omitted by accident and then squeezed in later between two stanzas.

15 Blades *Life and Typography* ii, pp xxxv, xxxvii, 114–7

16 *The workes of Geffrey Chaucer* 1561 (*STC* 5075) f cccxliii (Ppp vv). Stowe took the *Ballade* from Trinity College Cambridge ms R 3 19, a manuscript he also owned and which Hammond assigns to the same group as H and T. The date of R 3 19 is uncertain: it contains Ashby's *Prisoner's Reflections* (written in 1463), but it may be as late as the early sixteenth century; see Spindler 24–6.

17 Brunner 'Bisher unbekannte Schluszstrophen' 262

18 Bühler 'Notes on the Plimpton Manuscript' 8–9. Without the religious material there would have been only two folio sheets in the last gathering, but Caxton did at times produce two-sheet gatherings – eg in *Godfrey of Boulogne* in 1481; see William Blades *The Biography and Typography of William Caxton* (London 1877) 249. Caxton may have been printing the *Court* from a manuscript in which the poem was followed by such lists: there are several similar lists in T.

19 See above, notes 5 and 6.

20 See textual notes to lines 128, 304, 357, 442, 450, 466, 571, 603, 631, 761, 779, 812, 907, 979?, 1342, 1364, 1451, 1528, 1567, 1649, 1767, 1796, 1867, 1868, 1930, 2001, 2045, 2051.

21 Schubert, introduction x-xi

22 See textual notes to lines 80, 211, 311, 342, 446, 450, 460, 506, 527, 677–8, 851, 879–80, 1012, 1014, 1045, 1068, 1106, 1175, 1180, 1216, 1275, 1359, 1393, 1557, 1564, 1569, 1586, 1683, 1876, 2017.

23 See textual notes to lines 106, 372, 476, 584, 1190, 1601, 1945. The other cases are: 268 'permitte'; 552 *om.* 'that'; 560 *om.* 'thus'; 833 'neuer'; 1120 'for his'; 1518 'pite and'; 1714 *om.* 'that'; 1800 'on'; 1910 'declare'; 1979 'his.'

24 The 'Woo worth' stanza that is common to the *Court* and to George Ashby's *Active Policy* (see below, pp xxiii–xxiv) has, in Ashby's poem, textual features that link it to both the CP text (reading 'that Iugement' in line 691 [*Court* 466]) and to the TH text (reading 'that right' in line 694 [*Court* 469]). Hammond, 'A Scribe of Chaucer' (see note 5 above), has demonstrated that the scribe of H used more than one manuscript when making a copy of Chaucer; it would seem necessary to postulate a similar practice in the manuscript tradition of the *Court* to account for the evidence that survives.

25 See, for example, Caxton's version of lines 361, 636–7, 1352–4.

26 Lines 538, 592, 638, 949, 991, 997, 1017, 1215, 1223, 1295, 1406, 1458, 1539, 1653, 1774, 1794, 1802

27 This rule obtains with great consistency: even monosyllables ending in a vowel, such as 'tree,' become disyllabic in the plural, unless they fall under exception B below. See lines 1326, 1360, and compare line 1379; see also the notes to lines 1375, 1797, 1939.

28 The isogloss line for this dialectal distinction runs from the Wash to the River Dee: the -es ending is standard to the north, -eth to the south. This metrical usage therefore tends to confirm Spindler's conclusion that the poet's dialect was that of the region of Chester. See map 2 in the *Plan and Bibliography* volume of *MED*, p 8.

29 See *OED*, V: 'Elision of v when not initial has taken place extensively in dialects, especially those of the North and Scotland.'

30 'Evyl,' though not etymologically related to the word 'ill,' had become synonymous with it by the twelfth century. Hence 'evil' was frequently written when it was intended that 'ill' should be pronounced; see *OED, ill; Court* 403, 1495, 1596, etc.

31 H.S. Bennett, *English Books and Readers 1475–1557* (Cambridge 1952) 224, estimates the output of Continental printers to have been 400–500 copies per edition, but he thinks that Caxton may have printed rather fewer.

32 See note 35 below.

33 Seven of these readings are small points of word order, and two are cases where C has a plural for PT's singular. Thirty-eight of the remainder are very trivial differences, which barely affect the meaning at all. The twenty-two places where C's reading makes a difference are lines 122, 167, 216, 310, 726, 745, 751, 785, 932, 952, 1121, 1211, 1291, 1424, 1443, 1555, 1656, 1809, 1987, 2024, 2043, 2057–8.

34 Spindler 46–105

35 Spindler's examples from the *Court* of lines of the kind of Lydgate's type C or D may be greatly reduced by accepting new readings from P. For example, the eighteen type C or 'broken-backed' lines (lacking the unstressed syllable at the caesura) include eight (80, 311, 446, 1014, 1393, 1683, 2128, 2141) that become regular with readings supplied by P and two (763, 1730) that are regular in CP. Line 2047 is not irregular, and 592, 1096, and 1189 are only doubtfully so; line 1443 is regular in TP. There is only one witness (C) for 19 and 2303, and both may be easily emended. Only line 503 is clearly abnormal in all three major witnesses. Similarly, of the thirteen type D or 'headless' lines (lacking an unstressed syllable at the beginning), only 198 and 489 are irregular in all witnesses. For the frequency of these types of line in Lydgate, see Derek Pearsall *John Lydgate* (London 1970) 60–3.

36 Spindler 73–9

37 Spindler 80–3. See also *OED, jackanapes.* For Suffolk, see the article by C.L. Kingsford *DNB* Pole, William de la. A satirical poem, 'For Jake Napes Sowle, Placebo and Dirige,' is printed in *Political, Religious and Love Poems* EETS OS 15 (1866) 6–11.

38 Spindler 14–15. For Hammond, see above, notes 5 and 6.

39 *George Ashby's Poems* ed Mary Bateson (1899) introduction; *Active Policy* lines 688–94. See also the article by Sidney Lee *DNB* Ashby.

40 Since in *Active Policy* (line 65) Ashby says he is nearly eighty, the latest possible date in the lifetime of the prince would be the most plausible for the composition of the poem. For the career of Prince Edward see the article by James Gairdner *DNB*

Edward, Prince of Wales. The prince had been in exile from the Yorkist victory at Towton in 1461 until 1470; he was killed after the battle of Tewkesbury in May 1471.

41 See, for example, *Court* 372–8, 428–96.

42 Bühler *Sources of the Court of Sapience* 17

43 Spindler 105–14. *The Babees Book* has been edited by F.J. Furnivall, *Manners and Meals in Olden Time* EETS OS 32 (1836) 1–9.

44 British Library ms Arundel 83 (fourteenth century) f 5r contains a diagram of a tower of wisdom. It differs from the castle of Sapience in that it is built entirely of virtues, not arts, but the fundamental idea is very similar. There is another one in Bodleian Library ms Laud Misc 156 f 65r. See also M.W. Evans *Medieval Drawings* (Feltham, Middx 1969) plate 74.

45 *Court* 10–11 might suggest a much greater extension of the poem, perhaps an account of Sapience's activity in human history similar to Wisd 10–19.

46 See *Court* 146–58n. Note that wisdom in that quotation contains law, for both the lawsuit in heaven and human law reflect the same eternal wisdom.

47 The title may well be the author's. T begins, 'Here begynneth a breve compilyd Tretyse callyd by the Auctor therof Curia sapiencie,' and the title is found in the Latin explicit to book I in both T and C. P shortens the explicit, leaving out the title.

48 See *OED*, court. Hampton Court is of course later than the *Court of Sapience*, but it shows the culmination of the tendency of fifteenth-century 'great houses' to combine aspects of fortified castles (moat, gatehouse, crenellations, etc) with much greater elaboration and comfort in the private apartments and with multiple courtyards. Fifteenth-century college buildings, such as Queens' College, Cambridge, were in fact constructed on an adapted model of the normal plan of a great house; see Geoffrey Webb *Architecture in Britain: the Middle Ages* (Harmondsworth 1956) 166–7. South Wingfield Manor and Haddon Hall are fifteenth-century examples of great houses with courtyards, great halls, and other features found in the *Court*; see Nicolaus Pevsner *The Buildings of England: Derbyshire* (London 1953) 141–8, 217–8.

49 W. Langland *Piers the Plowman* B text xviii 112–424; John Lydgate *The Life of Our Lady* ii 1–350, ed J.A. Lauritis and others (Pittsburgh 1961) 310–35; *Ludus Coventriae* ed K.S. Block, EETS ES 120 (1922 [for 1927]) 97–103; *The Castle of Perseverance* lines 3129–649, in *The Macro Plays* ed M. Eccles EETS OS 262 (1969) 95–111. Characters called Justice and Mercy appear in three of Milton's early plans for *Paradise Lost*; in draft ii, Justice, Mercy, and Wisdom were to debate 'what should become of man if he fall.' See John Milton *Poems* ed Alastair Fowler and John Carey (1968) 419–21.

50 The most convenient short account is in Kari Sajavaara, *The Middle English Translations of Robert Grosseteste's Chateau d'Amour* (Helsinki 1967) 54–90.

Sajavaara corrects and supersedes earlier studies on the subject. Hope Traver, 'The Four Daughters of God: a Mirror of Changing Doctrine' *PMLA* XL (1925) 44–92, contains information on the early evolution of the story.

51 St Bernard *Sermo in Annuntiatione Dominica*, in *Sancti Bernardi Opera* v *Sermones* ii, ed J. Leclercq and H. Rochais (Rome 1968) 13–29. It is also printed in PL 183, cols 383–90.

52 See J. Rivière *Le Dogme de la Rédemption au début du Moyen Age* (Paris 1934) appendice II. The theme is pervasive in St Augustine; two important passages are *De Trinitate* XIII xii–xv and *De libero arbitrio* III x.

53 Some of the many versions of the story are described by Hope Traver, *The Four Daughters of God* (Bryn Mawr 1907), and by Bühler, *Sources of the Court of Sapience* 18–31; but both of these authors are in error about the sources of the *Court* because they did not know the *Rex et famulus* version of the story (see note 58 below). A recently published Latin play written by an Englishman ca 1460 contains a long scene of the debate between the daughters, based on St Bernard's account; see Thomas Chaundler *Liber Apologeticus de Omni Statu Humanae Naturae* ed Doris Enright-Clark Shoukri (London and New York 1974).

54 I have given references to the Latin text in A.C. Peltier (ed) *Opera Omnia S. Bonaventurae* (Paris 1864–71) xii 509–630; but in addition I consulted some of the early printed editions, where the text differs considerably; see, for example, *Vita Christi secundum Bonaventuram* (Paris sd) in the British Library (IA 40872). The English translation by Nicholas Love has been edited by Lawrence F. Powell (*The Mirrour of the Blessed Lyf of Jesu Christ* [Oxford 1908]). In my account of the work I have also used *Meditations on the Life of Christ: an Illustrated Manuscript of the Fourteenth Century* trans and ed Isa Ragusa and Rosalie Green (Princeton 1961).

55 Ragusa and Green xxi–xxii

56 Ragusa and Green xxiin. This figure includes all versions of the text.

57 See *Court* 274n.

58 Published by Sister Mary Immaculate [Creek], 'The Four Daughters of God in the *Gesta Romanorum* and the *Court of Sapience*' *PMLA* LVII (1942) 951–65; the text is also printed among the works of Bede, *Homiliae subdititiae* civ PL 94, cols 505–7.

59 See *Court* 792-8n.

60 The presence of the four torturers distinguishes *Rex et famulus* and works descending from it from other versions of the story that derive more directly from St Bernard.

61 The speeches are all in the pattern of Misericordia's words:

Numquid ego sum filia tua Misericordia et non tu diceris misericors? Si misericors fueris, famuli tui miserearis, et si famuli tui non miserearis, misericors non eris. Si misericors non fueris, me Misericordiam filiam non habebis.

Am I not thy daughter Mercy, and art thou not called Merciful? If thou art merciful, have mercy on thy servant; if thou hast not mercy on thy servant, thou wilt not be merciful. If thou are not merciful, thou wilt not have me, Mercy, for a daughter.

62 In St Bernard's version of the story the judge is King Solomon, a traditional type of wisdom. In both pseudo-Bonaventura and *Rex et famulus* the judge is the Son, whose chief attribute is wisdom (see *Court* 533–95 and notes). One phrase in pseudo-Bonaventura may have suggested the figure of Sapience as judge to the author of the *Court*: after the Son's judgment, 'they were all astonished at the word of wisdom' ('obstupuerunt omnes in verbo sapientiae'). The figure of Sapience also appears in the story in Deguileville's *Pelerinage Jesuchrist* and in French versions deriving from it (see Traver *The Four Daughters of God* 74–95), but there is no other reason to assume that the author of the *Court* borrowed, or needed to borrow it from there.

63 See *Court* 533–5n. The wisdom literature of the Bible provides some important parallels with Sapience; see Prov 1–9; Wisd 6–9; Ecclus 1, 4:12–22, 6:18–37, 14:22–15:19, 24, 25:1–16. John 1:1–14 uses the Old Testament vocabulary of wisdom to describe Christ; see C.H. Dodd *The Interpretation of the Fourth Gospel* (1953; reprinted 1970) 273–8.

64 Henry de Bracton (d 1268) *De legibus et consuetudinibus Angliae* ed G.E. Woodbine, trans S.E. Thorne (Cambridge, Mass 1968) ii 334 'De crimine laesae majestatis'

65 Bracton ii 335–6. Bracton explains at the beginning of his book that kings should imitate God, whose vicars they are on earth, by employing justice, not strength, for God himself redeemed man by mercy and justice, not power.

66 Peace does not flee in Bernard or pseudo-Bonaventura; *Rex et famulus* says only 'Pax fugit in regionem longinquam' ('Peace fled to a distant place').

67 It is axiomatic that with God there can be no grief or sorrow: 'tristitia et dolor ex ipsa sui ratione in Deo esse non possunt' (Aquinas *Summa contra Gentiles* I lxxxix, in *Opera Omnia* ed S.E. Fretté, xii [Paris 1874] 93); see also St Anselm *Proslogion* viii 'How God is merciful and impassible,' in *Anselm of Canterbury* ed and trans J. Hopkins and H. Richardson, i (Toronto and New York 1974) 77; and the *Glossa Ordinaria* on Gen 6:5. An early heresy, propounded by Praxeas, was called the Passionist or Patripassian heresy because it implied that the Father suffered with the Son in the redemption of man. It arose in fact out of the controversy over the identity or distinction of the persons of the Trinity, but Tertullian in his refutation argued vigorously that the Father is incapable of suffering. See Tertullian *Adversus Praxean* trans Holmes, in *The Writings of Tertullian* ii (Edinburgh 1870) 401–3; J.F. Bethune-Baker *An Introduction to the Early History of Christian Doctrine* (London 1903) 103–4; J.N.D. Kelly *Early Christian Doctrines* 5th ed (London 1977) 121.

68 The most accessible edition is Bartholomaeus Anglicus, *De rerum proprietatibus*

(Frankfurt 1601), reprinted photographically by Minerva (Frankfurt 1964). I also consulted the edition by Fridericus Peypus (Nuremberg 1519), Trevisa's English version published by Wynkyn de Worde (Westminster 1495), and the modern edition of Trevisa by M.C. Seymour and others, 2 vols (Oxford 1975).

69 C.S. Lewis, *The Allegory of Love* (London 1936) 263–4, declares himself 'half pleased and half tired' by this part of the poem, which he says is 'prosaic' only 'in some incorrigibly scientific passages.' Bühler, *Sources of the Court of Sapience* 43, says, 'This part of the poem, we may gather, was not particularly interesting to the poet, for ... he falls into a purely mechanistic verse and a pedantic array of the names of the various natural phenomena.'

70 The French encyclopaedia *Image du Monde* (1245), which was translated and published by Caxton in 1480, contains this statement in a chapter explaining how knowledge began to be recovered after the fall; see *Caxton's Mirror of the World* ed O.H. Prior (London 1913; reprinted 1966) 22.

71 Bartholomaeus includes this verse in the preface to *De proprietatibus rerum*; it also lies behind the argument of Vincent of Beauvais, *Speculum quadruplex* (Douai 1624) generalis prologus vi.

72 Trans Trevisa, Wynkyn de Worde f A2r. The version in the Seymour edition is quite different.

73 *Mirrour of the World* 12

74 See E.R. Curtius *European Literature and the Latin Middle Ages* (1948) trans W. Trask (New York 1953) 36–42; Paul Abelson *The Seven Liberal Arts* (New York 1906; reprinted 1965) 1–10.

75 Cassiodorus *Institutiones* ed R.A.B. Mynors (Oxford 1937) 89

76 Ed W.M. Lindsay (Oxford 1911; reprinted 1962)

77 See Nicholas Orme *English Schools in the Middle Ages* (London 1973) 92, 125–6.

78 I used the text of the *Catholicon* printed by Adolf Rusch (Strasbourg 1475?) in the British Library (IC 660). More conveniently available now is the photographic reprint of the Mainz 1460 edition put out by Gregg International Publishers. For Balbus, see the article by A. Pratesi in *Dizionario Biografico degli Italiani* v 369–70. Information about the *Catholicon* is given in Aristide Marigo, *I Codici Manoscritti delle 'Derivationes' di Uguccione Pisano* (Rome 1936).

79 Orme 92–3, 125–6

80 Thomas Aquinas *Summa theologiae* I xciv 4; *Mirrour of the World* 153: 'Adam knewe alle the seuen scyences lyberall entyerly, without faylling in a worde, as he that the creatour made and fourmed with his propre handes.' The idea pervades medieval educational writings; a good example of a detailed exposition may be found in Hugh of St Victor, *Didascalicon* trans Jerome Taylor (New York 1961).

81 Jacobus a Voragine *Legenda aurea* ed Th Graesse, 3rd ed (1890; reprinted Osnabrück 1969)

82 See *MED*, crochet. The earliest citation of the word in this sense is 1440.

THE COURT OF SAPIENCE

The Courte of Sapyence

1

The laberous and the most merveylous werkes
Of Sapience, syn firste regned nature,
My purpos is to tell as writen clerkes;
And specyally her moost notable cure
In my fyrst book I wyl preche and depure;   5
It is so plesaunt unto eche persone
That it a book shal occupye alone.

2

Sone after this I shal Wysedom descryve,
Her blessyd howshold, and her wonnyng place;
And than retourne unto her actes blyve   10
As she them wrought by tyme, processe, and space.
Al this mater she taught me of her grace –
I spak with her, as ye may here and rede,
For in my dreme I mette her in a mede.

3

O Clyo, lady moost facundyous,   15
O ravysshyng delyte of eloquence!
O gylted goddes, gay and gloryous,
Enspyred with the percyng influence
Of delycate and hevenly complacence!
Within my mouth late dystylle of thy showres,   20
And forge my tonge to glad myn audytours.

4

Myn ignoraunce, whome clowded hath eclippes,
With thy pure bemes illumyne al aboute;
Thy blessyd breth lete refleyr in my lyppes,
And with the dewe of heven thou them degoute,   25
So that my mouthe maye blowe and encense oute
The redolent dulcour aromatyke
Of thy depured lusty rethoryck!

5

I knowe myself moost naked in al artes,
My comune vulgare eke moost interupte,   30
And I conversaunte and borne in the partes
Where my natyf langage is moost corrupt,
And with most sondry tonges myxt and rupte,
O lady myn, wherfor I the byseche
My muse amende, dresse, forge, mynysse, and eche!   35

6

For to al makers here I me excuse
That I ne can delycately endyte;
Rude is the speche of force whiche I must use:
Suche infortune my natyf byrth may wyte.
But, O ye lordes whiche have your delyte   40
In termes gay, and ben moost eloquent,
This book to yow no plesaunce may present;

7

But netheles, as tasted bytternesse
Al swete thyng maketh be more precious,
So shal my book extende the godelynesse   45
Of other auctours whiche ben gloryous,
And make theyr wrytyng more delycyous;
I symple shal extolle theyr soveraynte,
And my rudenes shal shewe theyr subtylte.

8

O Gower, Chaucers, erthely goddes two,   50
Ofthyrst of eloquent delycacye,
With al youre successoures fewe or moo,
Fragraunt in speche, experte in poetrye,

You, ne yet theym, in no poynt I envye;
Exyled as fer I am from youre glorye   55
As nyght from day, or deth from vyctorye;

9
I you honoure, blysse, love, and gloryfye!
And to whos presence my book shal atteyne,
His hastyf dome I pray hym modefye,
And not detraye, ne have it in dysdayne,   60
For I purpoos no makyng to dystayne.
Meke herte, good tonge, and spyryte pacyent –
Who hath these thre, my book I hym present,

10
And as hym lyst lete hym detray or adde.
For syth I am constreyned for to wryte   65
By my soverayne, and have a mater glad,
And cannot please, paynte, enourne, ne endyte,
Late ignoraunce and chyldhode have the wyte.
I aske no more but God, of his mercy,
My book conserve from sklaunder and envy!   70

Explicit Prohemium.

11
All besy swymmyng in the stormy flode
Of fruteles worldly medytacyon,
To purpoos late, nothyng semed so good
As to lete youthe have domynacyon,
And for to put in sequestracyon   75
Eche other thyng that hym shold cause unrest;
And thus to bed I went with thought my gest.

12
The chesplayer, or he a man have drawen,
Hath only thought to make good purveaunce
For kyng and quene, aulfyn, knyght, roke and pawne;   80
Echone of these he hath in remembraunce.
So eche estate and worldly governaunce
In one eschekker in my mynd I sawe,
But I ne wyst what draught was best to drawe.

13
Fyrst, my desyre was to have drawen my kyng,   85
At hertes lust, in sure prosperyte;
But in the chesse I had espyed a thyng:
The kyng to purpoos may not passe his see,
To make hym way, or some pawne drawen bee;
Than bothe to guyde the kyng and pawnes eke   90
And al other, my wyttes were to seke.

14
I thought how by moral phylosophye
The chesse was founde, and set in dyversite
Of draught for a myrrour of polocye;
The whiche vertu departed is in thre: 95
Fyrst must man conne hymself reule in degre,
Efte his houshold, and than in unyverse,
Cyte and reygne; these ben the thre dyverse.

15
Arestotyl, in his *Poletyke Book*,
The fyrst of these seyth hyght 'monestyca';   100
The second parte, whoso hath lust to loke,
Of polycy hyght 'yconomica';
The thyrd partye is cleped 'poletyca';
But of al these syn I had never scole
To playe at chesse I thought me but a foole.   105

16
For in this bord eschekker of my mynd
As I forth put a man, or drawe a draught,
Forth come the World, with Dame Fortune unkynde,
And sayd, 'Eschek!' and so strongly they faught
Ayenst me that al my men were caught   110
With theyr eschekkes – so touche they eche astate
That, or I wyst, sodenly I was mate.

17
Than come Reason, and thus to me she sayde,
'With moble Fortune and fals Worldlynesse,
O foole of fooles, hast thou thy wyt assayde   115

With any man to countre them at chesse?
Thou mayst not fynd a poynt of sykernesse,
For in theyr draught al deceyte is include.
Goo forth,' quod she, 'a foole I the conclude!'

18

Than was I woo, and prayd to God abone   120
To teche me weye unto Dame Sapyence,
That she myght lerne me som discrecyone;
For wele I knowe my propre neglygence,
Myn ignoraunce, myn insuffycience,
Fer from al help; for whiche I gan to wepe,   125
Whyles at the last I felle upon a slepe.

19

Thus brought on slepe, my spiryt forth gan passe,
And brought I was methought in place desert,
In wyldernes, but I nyst where I was –
In moche derkenes, in caves, in moche coverte,   130
With wylde beestes in devouryng expert,
Now woode, now water, now hylle, now valeye,
Now wynde, now rayne – iwys, I knewe no weye.

20

The wylde wolves after me sewen fast,
I wold flee theym, but wele flee I ne myght,   135
And of a way I was ware at the last,
Thorny and streyte, encomerous to the syght;
Thyder I went, I was ware of a lyght,
But forth I throng with thornes al to-rent,
And thanked God of lyght whiche he had sent.   140

21

Oute from a mede moost hevenly unto loke,
Aboute whiche ran a lusty ryver swete,
A lady cam, and two with her she toke.
I ran to her, and lowely gan her grete;
The watres name asked I, she sayde, 'Quyete.   145
And sone,' she sayd, 'my name is Sapyence,
Intellygence this hyght, and this Scyence.

22

Unto al vertues we ben ladyes thre,
Bothe in offyce and degree dyfferent.
It is my parte to knowe dyvynyte;   150
My suster here hath knowlege dylygent
Of creatures in heven and erthe content;
And Dame Scyence of thynges temporal
Hath knoulege pure; thus maist thou know us al.

23

Of us al thre I am the moost soverayne;   155
And yf the lyst me descryve and dyffyne –
I am the trewe propre knowlege certayne
Of erthely thyng, and eke of thyng dyvyne.
Ay fresshe and grene and lusty is herte myne;
Though I seme yong, ful old my yeres bene,   160
For sapyence in old folk is ay sene.

24

The desert place of fere thurgh which thou come
Is dredeful worldly occupacyon.
Sone, leve that place and duelle with me at home;
Thou shalt have wytt, lust, delectacyon,   165
Grace, helpe, lyf, hele, eterne salvacyon.
Now wyl I rest that travayled have al daye,
For my labour is brought al unto playe.'

25

Glad was I tho, and on kne felle adoune,
Held up myn handes, and sayd I wold ful fayn   170
Her servaunt be, with alle subjectyon;
'But, lady myn, maystres and hole soverayne,'
Quod I, 'telle me your labour and your payne
That ye so long have had.' 'I wyl,' sayd she,
'Yeve audyence, the gladder shalt thou be.   175

26

A doughtful prynce, most myghty and most digne,
Moost excellent, and moost vyctoryous,
Havyng a sonne and four doughters benyngne

And a servaunt, whiche with affectuous
Love and desyre he cherysshed in his hows,   180
A maundement yafe his servaunt in certayn,
The whiche he brake, and deth shold be his payn.

27
Foure tormentours the kyng cleped to hym;
Bad one hym put in bitter pryson soure,
Another shold quyck flee hym, lyth and lym,   185
The third kil hym, the fourth shold him devoure.
The four doughters herd telle of this rumoure
(Whos names ben Mercy, Trouthe, Ryght, and Pease),
But Mercy thought hyr faders yre to cease.

28
She loked doune into the pryson depe,   190
Her loved servaunt sawe she syttyng there,
For whome hyr hert gan bothe to blede and wepe;
Dystyllyng teres dysteyned al here chere.
She gan unlace her tressyd sonnysshe here,
Nakyd her brest, and for compassyon   195
Byfore here fader on knees fel adoun.

29
"O mercyful, and O most mercyable
Kyng of kynges, and Fader of pyte,
Whos myghty mercy is inmensurable,
O Prynce eterne, O benyngne Lord," quod she,   200
"To whome mercy is yeven of properte,
Of thy servaunt that lyeth in pryson bound
Have thow mercy, or deth myn herte wyl wound.

30
I am soverayne above thy werkes al,
I am the pure avaunt of thy godhede,   205
I am thy child, thy gemme celestyal,
The mynyster of al thy godlyhede,
The sustenaunce that al mankynde doth fede,
I am the tresour of thy deyte,
O Prynce of pees, my bone now graunt thou me!   210

31

See how I sytte dyssheveld on my knee,
My crystal eyen, see how theyr teres rayne,
My rosy lyppes, see how they perced be,
The bemed chere eke of my chekes tweyne
See how the tery ryver doth dysteyne;   215
My swannysshe throte with syghes in distraynte,
My breste forbete – see, fader, al is faynte!

32

And yf thow wolt graunt me yon prysonere,
And gyfe me leve to lose hym oute of payne,
Al this dystresse, and al myn hevy chere   220
To al gladnes thou myght restore agayne.
Thy high vengeaunce why shold thou not restrayne
And shewe mercy, syn he is penytent?"
With that cam Trouth, and asked what it ment.

33

To Trouthe than spack hyr fader reverent   225
And sayd, "A servaunt whiche I loved best
On payne of deth I yave a commandement,
Whiche for to kepe in hym was al my trest;
But he it brake, and as proude traytour kest
Me to supplaunt; and I made my behest   230
For his trespaas he shold dye at the lest.

34

My doughter Mercy prayth with voys pyteous
I wold foryeve, and on hym have pyte;
For, syth my mercy is moost copyous,
I must it shewe, thus argueth she to me."   235
"Nay, nay," quod Trouth, "fader, it may not be;
Thow must of force observe thyne owne statute,
And thy promesse fulfylle for any sute.

35

Thynk that I am thy doughter Veryte,
That of al trouthe doothe execucyon,   240
Withouten whome thyne eterne deyte

Were vycyate with imperfectyon;
Thy wyl is lawe, thy promesse is reason,
And syth thy wyl and thy promesse also
Was he shold dye, thow mayst not goo therfro.   245

36
Fro thy godhede put oute al varyaunce,
Stable thy sentence, and thy just jugement;
Lete execute in dede the same penaunce
That was for brekynge of thy commaundement."
Than sayd Mercy, "Unworthy is that assent,   250
For every resonable creature
Withoute mercy may not lyve ne endure.

37
Knowe ye not wele that I am sempyterne,"
Quod Mercy tho, "How may ye me refrayne?
I am lady above the heven superne,   255
Though ye in erthe be pryncesse and soverayne.
My myghty grace is never voyde ne vayne:
Ergo I must yone servaunt penytent
Save fro the deth. Assoylle this argument!"

38
"Ryght sensyble and preygnaunt for youre parte   260
Is that strong argument," quod Veryte,
"But to dyspute, Mercy, is not myn arte:
Nor hole ne herne, the playne longeth to me;
And permanent I am as wele as ye;
And syn of force my fader must be trewe,   265
From his byhest how may ye hym remewe?

39
And yf ye thynk he breke not his byhest
For to permute with mercy his vengeaunce –
For one is God – than wold ye, at the lest,
In his godhede include bothe ignoraunce   270
And hastynesse, and exyle purveaunce
And prescyence; and aske eke myght I sone
Why hyght he that, that better were undone?"

40

Than sayd Mercy, "Wherto was Mercy wrought
But yf Mercy had execucyon?   275
Wherto on me was al my faders thought,
And al his joye in my creacyon?
Was I not made for restauracyon
Of hevenly blysse, and for necessyte
That bothe angel and man must have of me?   280

41

And yf so were I were adnychylate
The hevenly court may not restored be;
My faders royalme were vayne and vacuate,
A power howshold it were withouten me.
Why shold I not than have a soveraynte   285
And complement of my petycyon?"
Than answerd Trouth, "For ye aske no reason!

42

Though ye al day argue for youre purpoos,
Trouthe shal delyver at her owne volunte:
My lyberte in no poynt wyl I loos!   290
I am my faders chyld as wele as ye,
And Ryghtwysenes I wote wil holde with me."
And with that word, Trouthe for hir suster went,
Dame Ryghtwysenes, whiche was anon present.

43

On godely wyse, but ferful to behold   295
Come Ryghtwysenes, al bemed ful of lyght;
For she ne spareth for hote ne for cold,
For hyghe, for lowe, for to fulfylle al ryght.
"My sustres stryve," quod she, "with voyce on hyght;
I wyl dyscusse, and theyr contencyon,   300
As ryght asketh, brynge to conclusyon.

44

To his servaunt I thynk what trust and grace
My fader had, and eke what charyte;
And how in erthe for hym he made a place

Of lust, delyte, and of al lyberte;   305
Eche erthely thyng eke to his soveraynte
He bad enclyne, and be obedyent,
Whyles he truly fulfylled his commandement.

45
What thyng in erthe he couthe or myght devyse
For hertes rest and lyves sustenaunce   310
On hym gan laugh in al the godely wyse,
And at his lust made hym obeysaunce.
Exyled from hym was all unhappy chaunce,
Adversyte myght never his steppes sewe
To his mayster whyles he was servaunt trewe.   315

46
And yf so were he brake his commandement,
My fader made a constytucyon
That prysoned and al quyck flene and rent,
Dede and devoured, shold be punycyon
For his trespaas and his transgressyon;   320
That both pure love and fere this just precept
Shold hym excyte that it were trewely kept.

47
Notwithstandyng the promesse and statute,
The trust, the love, the bounte and kyndenesse,
Yone freel servaunt, subjecte to servytute,   325
Gan to conspyre with al ungentylnesse,
And of the just mandement made ful transgresse;
Wherfor of ryght me thynketh he must be dede."
"Late be," quod Pees, "that is a cruel rede."

48
And with that word, Pees come into the place, 330
Whoos persone was patron of portature;
Her rosy lyppes, with chere ful of grace,
Offred kyssyng unto eche creature;
Phebus hymself with al his bemed cure
May not be lyke the lyght of her vysage,   335
So pure perfyte was that hevenly ymage.

49

And on this wyse she gan her tonge affyle,
And sayd, "O Trouth, O Ryght, what may this mene?
Is it youre purpoos Pees for to exyle,
And to make Mercy nevermore be sene?   340
And to ordeyne deth for to regne as quene?
This were no more but to depryve expresse
My faders royalme of his soverayne rychesse.

50

Syth every royalme that hath dyvysyon
Within hymself must nedes be desolate,   345
And we ben four for one conclusyon –
For to sustene the reame and his estate –
Among us foure why shold thenne be debate?
And syth that lawe wyl rather lessyn peyne
Than it extende, lete Pees and Mercy reygne.   350

51

My faders royalme debate suffreth no whyle,
It is of rest and of tranquylyte;
Bycause of whiche he wryteth in his style,
'The Prynce of pees, the Auctor of pyte,
Kyng of mercy, and Lord of al bounte';   355
Thus nede of force must Pees regne and prevayle,
Stryf and debate perysshe and al aquayle.

52

The chyef avaunt and commendacyon
Of this hyghe royalme is for it is of pees;
Than wherto make ye disputacyon   360
Contrarious? Leve youre debate and cese!
With stryf I wyl not duelle, withouten lees,
And yf debate me from this royame dyssever
The lond of pees destroyed is forever!

53

But syth soo is ther is a trespaas done,   365
Unto Mercy lete yeld the trespasour.
Hit is her offyce to redresse it soone,

For trespaas is to Mercy a meryour,
And ryght as swete hath his apryce by soure,
Soo by trespaas Mercy hath al her myght;   370
Withoute trespas Mercy hath lak of lyght.

54
What shold physyk, but yf that sykenes were?
What nedyth salve, but yf there were a sore?
What nedeth drynk where thyrst hath no powere?
What shold Mercy, but trespaas goo byfore?   375
But trespaas be, Mercy were lytel store;
Withoute trespaas, none execucyon
May Mercy have, ne yet perfectyon.

55
But suster Trouth, ye may regne as pryncesse
Withoute falshede, and have youre soveraynte   380
Withoute injure, and so may Ryghtwysenes;
Eke withoute werre I, Pees, may alweye be;
But Mercy kyndely hath no properte
Without trespas, of whiche she hath her myght,
Ryght as the sonne the mone yeveth al hyr lyght.   385

56
Therfor I rede, as for conclusyon,
That we obeye Mercy with one acord;
And that we leve al oure dyscencyon,
For lytel thynge, as clerkes bere record,
With pees groweth, and grete thynge with discord   390
Wyteth awey – therfor lete pacyfye
Our lust to one, and falle we to Mercy."

57
"Late be," quod Trouthe, "to yow I nyl assent."
"No more wyl I, ywys," quod Ryghtwysenes.
And with that word, Trouthe to her fader went   395
And thus she sayd, "O Ground of sothfastnes,
O permanent, O veray Trouthe endeles,
Hold thy byhest, and support Veryte,
For Ryghtwysenes acordeth unto me."

58

These wordes said, Ryghtwysenes knelyd doun   400
And sayd, "Fader, syth it is myn offyce
To yeve condygne remuneracyoun
To evyl and good, to eche vertu and vyce,
And not to spare for prayer ne for pryce,
And if I shal thy godhede gloryfye,   405
That Trouthe asketh, I must nede justyfye.

59

The forsayd caas recordyng in my mynd –
How soone thy servaunt lust the to offend,
And how he was fals, cruell, and unkynd –
To thy byhest I must of ryght attend,   410
And nede of force to jugement condescend;
Wherfor I yeve sentence dyffynytyve:
In forme forsayd that peyne to deth hym dryve."

60

Of this processe to have the trewe entent,
I wol thou wyte,' quod Sapyence to me,   415
'This myghty kyng is God omnypotent
In one godhede regnaunt, and persones thre,
His sone is Cryst, his doughters in degre
Ben vertues four annext to his godhede,
His servaunt is old Adam, as I rede.   420

61

Retourne we now to oure mater ageyne:
Al thorugh darted with asper maladye
Mercy felle doune – she myght no lenger feyne –
As in a swonyd, or in a lytergye;
Peas, seyng that, stood in on extasye,   425
And at the last, with pyteous voyce and wylde
She sayd, "Alas! Peas is for ay exyld!

62

O mercy, God, see my suster Mercy
Lieth in a swouned, deyng for lak of brethe,
For Trouthe untrewe and Right unrightwisly   430

Ayenst us hath yeven sentence of dethe;
I wyl not rest, but goo thorugh holt and heth,
Exyled awey, retourne wol I never;
Farewele, fader, farewele thy reame forever!

63
Farewele, Mercy! Farewele thy pyteous grace –   435
So weleawey that vengeaunce shal prevayle!
Farewele the bemed lyght of hevens place –
Unto mankynd thou mayst no more avayle,
The pure derkenes of helle the doth assaylle;
O lyght in vayn, the clyppes hath the incluse,   440
Man was thy lord, now man is thy refuse.

64
O Seraphyn, yeve up thyn armonye,
O Cherubyn, thy glory do away,
O ye Trones lete be al your melodye,
Your jerarchye dysteyned is for ay!   445
Your maystres Mercy see in what array
She lyeth in swoune, and y-lorne with debate!
Farewele, farewele, pouer houshold desolate.

65
O soverayne myghty Domynacyons,
O ye Vertues, and O ye Potestates,   450
O Pryncypates, with al your hevenly sownes,
Archangel, Angel – O thryes thre estates!
Your spouse Dame Pees overset is with debates;
Now may ye wepe, and, jerarchyes thre,
Your ordres nyne may not restored be!   455

66
Farewel ye alle; Dame Mercy lyeth in swoune
For Sothfastnes accused hath mankynd,
And Ryghtwysenes, that shold do al reson,
Hath dampned hym as cruel and unkynd;
Mercy and Pees for hym no grace may fynd,   460
Notwithstondyng jugement may have no sute
Bycause of pees but it be execute.

67

Woo worth debate that never may have pees!
Woo worth penaunce that asketh no pyte!
Woo worth vengeaunce that mercy may not cees!   465
Wo worth jugement that hath none equyte!
Wo worth that trouth that hath no charyte!
Woo worth that juge that may no gilty save!
And wo worth ryght that may no favour have!

68

Farewel Saturne, Jove, Mars, and Phebus bright,   470
Farewel Venus, and farewel Mercurye!
Farewel, thou shynyng lady of the nyght,
I was your guyde, but now awey goo I.
O cruel Mars, thy tempestouse fury
Now mayst thou shewe, and Jupyter, thyn ire,   475
Now mayst thou rayne with dartes ful of fyre.

69

I was the reyne that held yow al togyder,
I brydled yow and set yow in acord;
But now I goo, ywys and I not whyder,
Wherfor of force ye must falle to dyscord.   480
O thou soverayne of al bataylle the lord,
Now mayst thou send Comete thy messager
To sygnefye that batayle negheth nere.

70

Whan Flora rydeth, and cold awey is gone,
With Jupyter than mayst thou mete att luste,   485
And june in somme sygne of the Aquylone,
Engendre fyre and make herbes combuste,
Enfecte the eyer, and so togyder juste
One with other, hote, cold, moyst and drye,
Contraryous stryf for the vyctorye.   490

71

Now may ye fyght and make both wynd and reyn,
And erratyk ay in your courses be;
For Pees is gone, that youre ire dyd refreyn,

And stabled you in al tranquylyte.
Farewel ye al, with al your brode contre;   495
Farewel, fader, thy reame may never encrees!"
And, with that word, evanysshed Dame Pees.

72
The faders blysse, the soverayne joy and chyef
Of al the heven, the broder to Mercy,
This woful caas seeyng, and this meschyef,   500
For me ywys dyd send ful hastely;
"O Sapyence," he sayd ful pytously,
"With somme counceyl help now in this nede;
With reuth perced myn herte begynneth to blede.

73
For Pees is gone, and Mercy lyeth in swoune   505
Without comfort, so weleawey the whyle!
Eke desolate is thys hevenly regyon
But Mercy reygne, and Pees com from exyle.
O Sapyence, help now to reconcyle
My suster Pees, and Mercy to comfort,   510
And to this fyne with counceyl me support!"

74
"O mayster myn, O soverayne myghty lord,
Hard is this caas," quod I, "withouten lees:
Hygh is that help that may bryng to acord
Mercy and Trouthe, Dame Ryghtwysenes and Pees;   515
Mercy wold save her man, and vengeaunce sees,
Trouth wyl not so, ne yett Dame Ryghtwysenes,
And for this stryf Pees is to wyldernes.

75
Echone of them wil no wey be remeved
From her entent. Hit is incomerous   520
Them to acord – how shold it be contreved,
Syn twoo for two stond ay contraryous?
This solen caas is wonder studyous;
For this acord whoso that shal fulfylle
Must nede of force performe their aller wylle."   525

76
"But, Sapyence, who may best plese them al
And gyve echone hir ful desyre expresse?
I mene the wretche that lyeth in pryson thral
Mercy to have, and his gylt to redresse,
And not to offend Dame Trouthe and Ryghtwisenes,   530
And revoke Pees – who shal this doo?" quod he,
"In one godhede syn we be persones thre.

77
My Fader is ay ful of lastynge myght,
And al wysedom appropred is to me,
Of al godenes the blessyd hevenly lyght   535
The Holy Ghoost hath to his propyrte;
Thus myght, wysedom, and goodenes that ben thre
Ay of one wyl may this accord make.
But of us thre who shal the treuse take?"

78
My wyttes hole I gadred unto me,   540
And fynally as for conclusyon,
"O mayster myn," I sayd, "it lyeth in the
Of this acord the execucyon,
And on thre wyse I prove it by reason;
Wherfor of force for to make this accord   545
Dyspose thyself; be both subjecte and lord.

79
Thy Fader is so ferful, wel thou wost,
That Pees and Mercy dar not compromyt
In hym as juge; and eke the Hooly Goost,
In whome al grace, godenes, and reuth is knyt,   550
Dame Trouthe and Ryght for juge wyl not admyt,
For wel they wote that he is Mercyes frend;
Wherfor thyself of this must make an end.

80
Yone wretche desyred not thy Faders myght,
Ne yet the goodenesse of the Hooly Ghoost,   555
For thy wysedom he cast with the to fyght

And smote thy sheld amyd the hevenly hoost;
For whiche thyself must answer, wel thou wost,
Not thy Fader, ne yet the thyrd persone –
The help of this thus lyeth in the alone.   560

81
These sustres four who that shal pacyfye
Must be the sone of man, and take mankynd,
And for mannes gylt gyltles suffre to dye,
And raunson man; than thynk I in my mynd,
Syth but one Sone the Trynyte may find,   565
Whiche Sone thou art, that by necessyte
This solempne acte lyeth fynally in the." '

82
Than sayd myself, 'O lady Sapyence,
O good beldame, or ye forther procede,
Vouchesauf to telle your noble reverence   570
Why myght, wysedom, and godenes, as ye rede,
To thre persones whiche are in one godhede
Appropred ben? Are they not peregal?
And coeterne, and consubstancyal?'

83
'Yis, sonne, ywys,' quod Sapyence to me,   575
'They ben al thre in godenesse, wyt, and myght
Egal and lyke, of one substaunce they be,
But yet ywys thou clepyst them aryght
Whan that thou sayest the Fader ful of myght,
The Sone of wyt, the Spyryte of goodenesse;   580
This wyl a cause that is in kynd expresse:

84
A fader is, thou wost, a name of age,
Of impotence, and of debylyte;
A sone a name is of youthe and courage,
Of inscyence and instabylyte;   585
A spyryte is a name of cruelte,
Of hyght and pryde; this mayst thou propre fynd
And eke comune, yf thou wolt see in kynd.

85

Wherfor the Fader in the Trynyte
We clepe "myghty," the Sonne, "ful of all wyt,"   590
The "good" Spyryte; this is of propyrte
To avoyde the vyce that in kynd is knyt;
But of them al, sone myn, I wyl thou wyt
In myght, with grace, more excellent is none:
Echone hath al, and al thre is but one.   595

86

Retourne we now, sonne myn, to oure matere.
My soverayne lord, the broder of Mercy,
Sayd, "Sapyence, I see it now so clere
That this accord in me is fynally.
But hard it is to take mankynd and dye.   600
Nevertheles, Mercy to recomforte
And save mankynd, suche deth nere but disporte."

87

With ful effecte he conclude in his herte
Of al mankynd to make redempcyon –
Yeve deth for lyf, yeve joye for peynes smerte,   605
Leve soveraynte, and make subjectyon;
The angels eke had suche compassyon
Of mannes deth, that ryght in specyal
To help mankynd they cast among them al.

88

Unto counceyl the holy spyrytes went,   610
The jerarchyes with theyr hevenly collage,
To pray for man it was theyr hole entent,
That he myght come to his old herytage
Oute from the carybde, and the smoky cage
Of servytude, the whiche hym had incluse   615
Four thousand yere; he myght it not refuse.

89

The jerarchye next to the Trynyte,
With hevenly voys pytous and delycate,
Kneled adoune and sayd, "O God, we be,

As thou wel wost, to the inmedyate;   620
As assessours we ben to thyn estate,
Cubyculers also of thy godhede,
To our prayer, O myghty God, take hede!

90
The to byhold is our soverayne solace,
Our lyf, our lust, and oure ay lastyng blysse;   625
The hyghe glory that shyneth in thy face
The wyt of kynd may not conceyve, ywys,
And syth that man soo lyke unto the is,
And fourmed was unto thyne owne lykenesse,
Oute of thy blysse why lyeth he in derkenesse?   630

91
What honour is, or yet what worthynesse
To thy godhede to suffre thyn ymage
Devoured be, and drenched in derkenesse,
For whome thou made lyght to be herytage?
And syth our blysse is hole in thy vysage,   635
O welawey! why shold the shap of it,
The to dysteyne, alwey in derkenesse sit?

92
Wherfor we pray, O prynce ful of grace,
Thou have pyté of man thy creature;
His bondes strong vouchesauf ones to unlase;   640
Lete not thy shap so long derkenes endure;
Yeve somme reward unto thyn owne honoure –
For now is tyme of Mercy and of Pees,
And tyme is come that al vengeaunce shold cees!"

Explicit supplicacio prime jerarchie.

Incipit invocacio secunde jerarchie.

93
Than kneled doune the seconde jerarchye   645
And humbly sayd, "O soverayne lord of al,
We be y-made thy myghte to magnyfye,

And to observe thy lawe imperyal,
As worthy lordes that in general
With besy cure supporten thyn empyre,   650
And with knyghthode obeyen thy desyre.

94
Hens from us al the proude prince of derkenes
As captyve took lordes of eche estate;
Than man was made, thurgh thy hevenly godenes,
For to restore this kyngdom desolate.   655
But weleawey! wherto was man create?
Syth that the lyon of al cruelte
In his derk lake of hym hath soveraynte.

95
Our worthy lordshyppes, and oure maners old,
O myghty God! how long voyd shal they be?   660
Thyn heyres eke how long shal deth withhold?
Syth thou art lyf, why hath deth soveraynte?
If thou be kyng, to thyn honour thou see!
Soo bynd the fend, and take man by conquest
Unto thy blysse, and set thy regne in rest.   665

96
Four thousand yere and more is suffysaunt
For to punysshe old Adam for a tast;
And welawey! helle is exuberaunt
With his ofsprynges, and our reame stondeth wast;
Now rewe on man, though that al mercy hast,   670
For now is tyme of Mercy and of Pees,
And tyme is come that al vengeaunce shold sees!"

Explicit supplicacio secunde jerarchie.

Incipit supplicacio tercie jerarchie.

97
The archangels than with theyr jerarchye
Kneled adoune, and sayd with voyce benyngne,
"O God, thou wost we be alwey redy   675
To thy godhede to yeve lovyng condygne,

To what provynce the lust us to assygne
Withyn thy reame, as trewe and dylygent
Offycyals we doo thy commaundement.

98
Thy messagyers, we be redy alway,   680
And in thy reame to what place we be sent
We cannot fynd but Pees is gone away,
And Mercy lyeth with wepyng al beshent,
For Trouthe and Ryght to her wyl not assent
To save mankynd – our reame which shold restore –   685
Whereso we goo, debate is us byfore.

99
Our enemyes eke of us have vyctorye
Whyle thy chylder contynue in dyscord,
And, but mankynd be brought unto thy glorye,
Thou mayst never them four bryng to accord.   690
On thyn old mercy, O good God, record,
And syth eche thynge to the possyble is,
Pease thy chylder, and bryng mankynd to blisse.

100
The faders herte by kynd shold be pyteous
Of his childer, and wayle for theyr absence;   695
Wherfor we pray, O Prynce vyctoryous,
Send for Dame Pees, bryng her to thy presence,
And to mankynd graunt a playne indulgence;
For now is tyme of Mercy and of Pees,
And tyme is come that al vengeaunce shold cees!"   700

Explicit supplicacio tercie jerarchie.

101
That excellent prynce of al worthynesse,
That myghty lord, that fader gracious,
That rote of ryght, that welle of godelynesse,
That noble kyng, that mayster gloryous,
That soverayne syre, and moost vyctoryous,   705
Byheld his royalme al wasted with ruyne,
And in hymself to pyté gan enclyne.

102

He herd also how pytously compleyned
His hevenly court of his regne desolate,
And how Mercy with teres was dysteyned,   710
And Pees his chyld exyled for debate,
And how mankynd was so incarcerate
That by no wey he myght his realme restore;
Than gan his herte for pyté wax al sore.

103

Unto Mercy he gan his hede to held –   715
Which was in poynt thurgh weping for to spille –
Than thorugh darted his herte gan to yeld,
And droppes smale of pyté to dystylle;
His blyssed sonne than knewe hys faders wille,
Felt iren hote, and thought tyme for to smyte;   720
And up he rose with al lust and delyte.

104

He kneled doune and sayd, "Fader of myght,
I am thy sonne in whome al wysedome is,
And wel I wote thou faryst not aryght,
For chylder thyn ben at debate, ywys.   725
Yeve me this cause, O soverayne Lord of blys,
I shal reward echone with theyr entent,
And man ageyne to thy blysse represent."

105

"Swete, swettest sonne," quod that good fader tho,
"Of thy behest I am entyerly glad;   730
Doo what the lyst to brynge man oute of woo.
But it forthynketh me that I man made,
I mene the godhede, that suche gladnesse hade
For to make man, in the must take mankynd,
And penaunce bere his bandes to unbynd."   735

106

"With humble hert, fader, to doo thy wylle,
With love and lust, with sad and hole desyre,
I am redy; and what thou wolt I wylle;

Thy pure plesaunce I may not but desyre.
I wyl pursewe the ryght of thyn empyre."   740
Quod that good sonne, with spyryte dylygent,
And up he rose, and to his suster went.

107
He took her up and godely gan her kysse,
Embraced her unto his herte and sayd,
"O swete Mercy, O pryncesse of al blysse,   745
O suster myn, O godly yongly mayde,
With salt teres why be ye thus arrayde?
I am that wyght that shal youre sorowe cees,
And save mankynd, and bryng ageyn Dame Pees.

108
Cast up youre eyen, behold, I am your brother,   750
Your lyf, your lust, your love, your champyon,
And for your sake myself shal and none other
Become a man, and suffre passyon
To help mankynd, and with double renoun
Bryng hym to yow, and save hym whiche was thral,   755
That mortal is, I shal make inmortal.

109
Thus shal I doo your herte to recomforte,
Your soveraynte eke for to magnyfye;
Ful manfully I shal my payne comporte,
And thynk on yow as on myn owne lady,   760
Doo feete in armes, and obteyne vyctory;
Yeve Trouth and Ryght theyr owne desire at fulle,
And every gylt you at lust to adnulle."

110
Revygure gan that goodely lady tho,
The brothers speche was salve to al her sore;   765
She thanked hym as cure of al her woo,
She kissed him swete, she loved him more and more.
"O prynce," she seyde, "whiche shal my ryght restore,
What may I do your thank for to deserve,
That redy ben for me to lyve and sterve?   770

111

O swete, moost swete brother and al my knyght,
O veray cause of al myn hertes rest,
To yeve reward where shal I gader myght
To your kyndenesse? I not how I may best
Thank yow for this – but, O prynce worthyest,   775
Me as your owne commaund ay as ye lyst!"
Thus al was wel, and eyther other kyst.

112

The Trynyte to counceyl went anon,
Conclude in hast a messager shold goo
Unto the mayde, the doughter of Syon,   780
To salewe her, and for to say her to
The Sonne of God, to bryng man oute of wo,
Moder and mayde, she shold bere and conceyve;
Whiche message done, she goodely gan receyve.

113

She thanked God with herte, lust, and desyre,   785
And in eche poynt submytte her to his wylle;
The Holy Ghoost was redy to enspyre –
His swete breth her brest with blysse gan fille;
The Sonne of God ful prevely and stylle
Within her wombe took incarnacyon,   790
And borne he was for mannes salvacyon.

114

He knewe the cause of his four sustres stryf,
And how by sentence man shold punysshed be:
Fyrst in the pryson of this present lyf,
Rent with unhele, flayn with adversyte,   795
Dye at the last, and with al cruelte
Suffre wormes devoure hym in his grave;
Hard was this payn, and eche man shold it have.

115

This to redresse, hymself in pryson was,
Flayne with scorges, and rente upon a rode,   800
Suffred the deth, and caused no trespaas,

A monyment his corps fomyng of blode
Devoured, than he rose to life and yode
Hymself to helle, and losed man anone,
Had hym to blysse unto his fadres trone.   805

116
He took with hym to blysse, and made her quene,
His swete moder, the blessyd mayd Marye,
To pray for man, and mankynd to sustene;
And unto her commended Dame Mercy,
Whiche for her child she took ful thankfully,   810
And sayd she wold for man be advocate
If Trouthe and Ryght eft wold wyth man debate.

117
And unto Mercy goodely thus he sayd,
"O bele suster, to yow now have I brought
With double honour man, for whome ye prayd,   815
And youre desyre in eche thyng have I wrought;
So ryghtwysely and trewely have I bought
Hym with my blode that Trouth and Ryght certayn
Have al theyr lust, and no cause to compleyne.

118
If man unkynd resorte unto his gylt   820
Ageyne the kyndenes whiche that I have done,
And Trouthe and Ryght wol deme hym to be spylt,
Yet your desyre ye shal obteyne ryght sone,
For my moder shal come and aske a bone,
And say, 'Swete sonne, thynke on thy passyon,   825
And save the ryght of thy redempcyon.

119
Thynk how of man I cam, and am thy moder,
And thou my lord, my maker, and my child,
Eke thou art man, and man is thy ful broder,
And hym best loveth Mercy thy suster myld: 830
If man therfor offend with werkes wyld
Thynk thou hym bought, and be no lenger wroth –
That ones was lyef, lete nevermore be loth.

120

For man to dye, and efte hym for to lose
Inconsonaunt it were to al reson: 835
What wight in erthe or heven yet wold suppose
That so solempne and hye redempcyon,
As is thy deth, shold in conclusyon
Be vayne and voyde? Suche raunson precyous
Must in effect be alwey fructuous.   840

121

Double tytle thou hast of propyrte
In every man, for thou his maker is,
His savyoure, and al good hath of the;
If he dysplese, offend and doo amys,
Or wold forsake thy lordshyp or thy blysse,   845
Yet is he thyn; thou made hym; thou hym bought;
Hym to forsake, thy tytle wyl it nought.

122

The more, ywys, that thou hast done for man,
The more fervent on hym shold be thy thought.
Thy chyef avaunt is how thou gat and wan   850
Hym with batayle, and from his foes hym brought;
Eke love is more swete that it dere is bought;
Al these in one, yf thow in mynde revolve,
Thy love from man nothing shal mow dissolve.

123

Yet to mercy more strong the to excyte,   855
O blessyd sonne, see how I syt on kne,
Byhold these brestes smal with al delyte
That yafe the sukke the mylke of chastyte,
Byhold the wombe of whiche thou born wold be,
Byhold the hondes that on my lap the layd,   860
Byhold thy spouse, thy moder, and thy mayd!

124

And for al this, have mercy, sonne, of man,
For next thyself, I derest have hym bought;
For wel thou wost the swerd of sorowe ran

Out thurgh myn hert, when thou on rode was brought,   865
And I the sawe with woundes al besought;
Syth thus in payne I had my part with the,
Part of my wyl for man, sonne, graunt thou me!'

125
Thus shal my moder say yf man offende,
O suster myn, youre lust for to sustene;   870
Eke I myself, his trespaas to amende,
My woundes wyde shal hold both newe and grene,
Dystyllyng bloode ful fresshe they shal be sene;
If with mankynd my fader wyl debate
When he them seeth, he mowe no lenger hate.   875

126
Therfor be glad, O suster myn Mercy,
Have here your man, do with hym what ye lyst."
She kneled doune, took hym ful thankfully,
Enbraced hym, and ofter syth hym kyst
Than tonge can telle – unneth her spyrit wyst,   880
For pure gladnes, in what place to abyde;
Her perfyte blysse perced the heven wyde!

127
Forth than he went unto Dame Veryte
And sayd, "Suster, be ye not yet content?"
"Yis, broder myn," quod she, "in al degre,   885
For trewe it is that man was neclygent,
More than I aske eke is his punysshement."
Than went he forthe unto Dame Ryghtwysenesse,
Asked the same, whiche answerd thus I gesse,

128
"O swete broder, man is for his trespaas   890
More punysshed than I myself desyre;
I am content debate awey shal passe."
And with that word, Pees, fervent as the fyre,
Was present tho, for staunched was al ire;
Mercy and Trouthe mette at theyr owne lyst,   895
And Ryght and Pees togyder hertely kyst.'

129
To whiche kyssyng, O myghty Prynce of pees,
Thou bryng us alle as thou starf on a rode,
And graunt me grace, or I of makyng cees,
To thy plesaunce somme mater that is good   900
For to compyle, to help me from the flode
Of fruteles worldly medytacyon,
And fynd a wey to my salvacyon.

Explicit liber primus de curia sapiencie qualiter misericordia et veritas
obviaverunt sibi, justicia et pax osculate sunt.

Incipit prohemium secundi libri.

130
Forth to procede in mater of my booke,
And to dyscryve the solempne mancyon   905
of Sapyence, moost hevenly unto loke,
Whos feete ben sette in al perfectyon,
And to avoyde the obloqucyon
Of fals tonges, and thank for to deserve,
Thou graunt me grace, O good goddesse Mynerve!   910

131
My style thou dresse, my langage thou depure,
My wytte inforce, thou mynystre matere!
For, syth I am moost symple creature,
I nyl usurpe in thy palays t'apere
But thou me guyde to shewe in what manere   915
I shal pronounce thynges whiche thou dost me see;
Thy refrendary only wyl I be.

132
The pure knowlege and veray sentement
Of thy wysedom was never my dower,
But as the sonne, in lyght moost excellent,   920
With his bemes the mone illumyneth clere,
Soo done alday these wyse men fooles lere;
Wherfor thy wysedom, as thou lust me teche,
O lady myn, in my book wyl I preche.

Explicit prohemium.

Incipit liber secundus.

133
Whan Sapyence her besy cure had told,   925
Whiche is rehercyd in the forsayd booke,
Unto her home she sayd retorne she wold;
Intellygence and Scyence with her she tooke,
And on myself ful goodely gan she loke,
And said, 'Beel sone, yf thou wilt wend with me,   930
Come on in hast, ryght welcome mote thou be!'

134
Forth went we thens unto a ryvers syde
Whoos name is Quyete, ful of al swetenesse;
Oute over whiche, with arches hyghe and wyde,
A brydge was sett, ful of al lustynesse;   935
The marble stone the solempne worthynesse
Of geometry shewyd on suche a wyse
Soo good a werk that no wyght couthe devyse.

135
The pyllers strong enarched with effect,
With pynacles and towres ful of blysse,   940
And, alured clene, yave suche a digne prospect
That suche a brydge was never seen, ywys;
And on a towre this scrypture wryten is:
'Who dredeth God, come in, and ryght welcome!
For drede of God is way of al wysedome.'   945

136
I entred on the brydge with Sapyence;
She led me over unto the ryvers syde,
'Come in,' she sayd, 'put the forth in presence,
For suche a syght, thurgh al the world wyde
Thou never sawe so ful of lust and pryde,   950
So gloryous, as here is for the nones.'
As gravel is, so were the precyous stones:

137
The alabastyr, the electorye,
The aurypygment, and the argeryte;
The asteron, ful of hevenly glorye;   955

The adamante eke, and the asteryte;
The amatyst, and eke the amatyte –
Whiche bryght stone withstondeth the myght of fire –
Soo good a syght no spyryte myght desyre.

138
The alabastre whyte yeveth vyctorye;   960
And ire swageth the shynyng argeryte;
And love refourmeth the sayd electorye;
The adamant eke; but the asteryte
Hath in hymself a sterre ful of delyte;
The aurypygment hote is in effect;   965
The amatyst yeveth ryght good intellect;

139
The pale byrel, that heleth eyen sore,
And helpeth love, and stauncheth enmyte;
The selydon, that wit lost can restore,
And medycyn is to old infyrmyte;   970
The carbuncle, that hath his soveraynte
When derkenes is; the precyous crisolyte,
Whiche fendes fleen and holden in despyte;

140
The calcydone, whiche hard is in to grave;
The crysopasse, most shynyng on the nyght;   975
The crystal clere, that seke men oft doth save;
The corall rede, whiche flux stauncheth aryght;
The ceranne stone in thonder which hath myght;
The calcophan, that voyces sore doth clence;
The cabiate, that techeth elloquence;   980

141
The dyadek, that doth spyrytes to preche;
The dyonys, whiche hateth drunkenes;
The good eschyte, that is the womans leche
In byrthe of chyld, and cause of theyr gladnesse;
The emachyte, that stauncheth bloode expresse;   985
The elytrope, whiche is the sonnes foo,
And venym sleeth, with many vertues moo;

142

The stone enydros, moost wondre in kynd,
That ay dystylleth droppes to the syght,
And never moyst ne les men shal it fynd –   990
'The wepyng stone' a clerk seyth it hyght;
The epystyte, whiche is a stone ful bryght,
Frendful to corn; and excolycerose,
In colours fele, as clerkes don depose.

143

Ther was also the gentyl gagates,   995
Good for women that long in childbed pyne,
Whiche, yf a mayd drynk, it shal hyr plees,
And in her body hold it wele and fyne –
Were she corrupt, she shold anone uryne;
The galachyte, for mylk moost proufytable,   1000
Ther was also, in vertu commendable;

144

Geratycen, whiche is a noble stone,
Blak in colour, but vertuous in myght,
And maketh men beloved where they gone
If they hym bere, and telleth them aryght   1005
What other thynke; the jaspre grene of syght,
Holsome ayenst the feverous accesse,
There sawe I lye, ful of al lustynesse.

145

The good jacynct, that is ryght comfortable,
And in pestylence a noble medycyne;   1010
The adachyte, that hath, withouten fable,
Within hymself another stone full fyne
That sweteth water wonder to dyvyne;
The jerachyte, whiche yf a man do bere,
There may no flees with bytynge do hym dere.   1015

146

There was the good irys of Arabye,
Holsome for women in theyr chyldbed;
The stone jena, that techeth prophecye;

The sad camen, with dyvers colours lede,
The idropsy whiche heleth, as I rede   1020
In bookes old; and eke lygurius,
That colour lost restoreth unto us;

147
A noble stone, that is for hunters good,
Lipparia whiche is cleped aryght –
For beestes wyld, be they never so woode,   1025
To his presence he bryngeth thorugh his syght;
The alabandyne, that to bloode yeveth myght;
The abisate, whiche thurgh hete wyl remayn
Seven dayes in hete, as noble clerkes sayn;

148
The margaryte, whiche is both bryght and whyte,   1030
Eke medycynable and comfortatyf;
The magnes sad, that yeveth grace and delyte,
And soveraynly hath vertu attractyf;
The mellanyte, whoos juce is exceptyf,
Swete as hony, in colour whyte and grene;   1035
The good myryte, whiche hath an odoure clene;

149
The stone memphyte; and eke the melochyte,
That chyldern yong whan they in cradels bene
Kepyth of kynd from noy and al dyspyte;
The stone nitrum, that helpeth to wasshe clene;   1040
The medus eke, good for blyndenes of eyen;
The stone noset, whiche in the tood men fynd,
And nyghe venym he waxeth hote of kynd;

150
The onychyne, that is a stone of Inde;
The onyx eke, in whiche as a myrrour   1045
His owne ymage a man may see and fynd;
Optallyus, of many straunge colour,
That is to theves good patron and socour;
The oryte eke, that saveth from beestes wyld,
And suffreth not women to be with child;   1050

151
The paryus; and eke the prassyus,
Grene of colour, and good for feble syght;
The pyrryte stone, anone whiche brenneth us
Within our hond yf we hym presse aryght;
The stone ponyte, whiche hath a wondre myght,   1055
Good for women, and of hymself alone
He bryngeth forth ryght swyth another stone;

152
The stone quyrryne, that doth the sleper say
Whatso he dremeth; and eke the quandras good,
That can encrese brestes with mylk alway;   1060
The good ruby, that stauncheth alwey bloode;
The reben eke, the whiche of beestes woode
The strong bytyng heleth for evermore,
And noble medycyne is for woundes sore;

153
The good saphyre, most noble and moost digne   1065
Of al stones, and moost preservatyf,
Causer of pees, and to sore eyen benyngne,
Of hete unkyndely is moost repressyf,
It maketh glad, it is comfortatyf,
It stauncheth blode and swete, and chastyte   1070
He loveth best, and doth the venym flee;

154
The grene smaragde, that is ryght medicynable
Ayenst tempest, sykenes, and fantasye;
The sardonyx, that is ryght commendable,
Frend to mekenes, and hateth lecherye;   1075
The sardius, that maketh men hardy;
The sonnes gemme, ful of bemes bryght;
The serenyte, that in love hath his myght;

155
Topacius, goode for men lunatyke,
And stauncheth ire, and swageth hevynesse,   1080
It holsome is eke to men frenetyke;

The good turkoys, that engendreth gladnesse,
Good for the syght; the zemeth, that sykenesse
Heleth dyvers; the zyngynt, whiche of kynd
Refreyneth blode, and holdeth man in his mynd;   1085

156
Al other stones whiche ben precyous
There myght men see, ful of al pure delyte –
But I of force must be compendyous,
Therfor of them I wyl no ferther wryte.
Of theyr vertues I touche here but a lyte;   1090
Theyr propertees whoso lust to have told
I counceyl them, go loke in bookes old:

157
As in a book cleped *Lapydarye*,
In Isodore, or Dyascorydese,
By phylosophres, as by Platearye,   1095
Or Barthylmewe – loke who may the please,
Natures and kynd there mayst thou see at ease,
Suche thynges as longeth not to my matere;
Another feld I have in hast to ere.

158
And yf the seme that here be stones straunge   1100
And thou in Englysshe can them better name,
Doo as the lyst theyr names for to chaunge,
So my langage and my book thou not blame,
For I suppose ther be fewe wordes lame,
For by the Latyn for the more suerte   1105
I name theym al, and for more comunte.

Explicit descripcio lapidum in littore rivi consistencium.

Incipit descripcio rivi.

159
Than al my lust was goodely to byhold
That good water, that noble element,
That ryver swete in his kynd moyst and cold,

That is the holsome perfecte nutryment   1110
To every thyng that is in erthe content:
To corne, herbe, tree, plant, and eche thyng lyvyng
It geveth his drynk, and clenseth al foule thyng.

160
The erthe he maketh to be plentyuous,
He tempreth welle also the heven abonne,   1115
And with his subtyle vapour curyous
He geveth the ayer incorperacyon,
And densyth hym, and, as of hyghe renoun,
Into the hyght to stye is his solace,
For to chalenge heven for wonnyng place;   1120

161
From whens he fallith, distillyng shoures swete,
Replenysshyng, percyng, and conjunctyf
Unto the erthe, but to the hevens hete
His moyst vapor is moost temporatyf;
His droppes swete eke ben moost nutrytyf   1125
And cause of lyf to eche thyng anymate –
Withouten hym, al thyng were vycyate.

162
For thorugh the erth he goth with his moisture
And perceth hym thurgh his diffusyon;
The partes of the erthe eke thorugh his cure   1130
Ben stabled sad, and taken unyon,
Elles for grete hete and hyghe entencyon
Of soverayne drought, ryght by necessyte,
Unto powder they shold dyssolved be.

163
He is to fysshe holsome and profytable   1135
As ayr to beest, and cause of al theyr blysse;
His propertees, that ben moost commendable,
Dame Scyence there declareth wel, ywys;
And as a glas so speculer he is
Of thyng object the shap to represent.   1140
Of hym hath nede al thyng in erth content!

164

He wyl ay meve without rest or constaunce
Whyles that his party superfycyal
Be adequate by ryght and lyke dystaunce
Oute from the erthe, ryght from the myd of al;   1145
And of the sonnes lyght celestyal
Into the heven he maketh reflectyon –
The natures four he passeth in renoun!

165

Of water thus to speke in general,
Ther may none fynd a goodely properte   1150
But in hymself this ryver hath them al;
In Paradys he had his soveraynte
Bothe oute and in to renne with lyberte;
From sulphur veynes and from metal ure
He can absteyne, and be ay swete and pure.   1155

166

Basilius in his *Exameron*
Descryveth water and his properte,
Whoso hath lust, he may loke hym upon;
But I myself wol flee prolyxyte,
And of my ryver speke as lyketh me: 1160
What shold I say? Hym to here and behold,
Al erthly joye passeth a thousand fold.

167

His hevenly sownes, his grones delycate,
His swete murmour, his subtyl cours and stylle,
His fresshe colour whiche no storme may abate,   1165
His sapour swete havyng refleyr at wylle
Myght say ascaunce, 'On this wyse be I wyl,
For to excyte oute from the hevens place
Nature to come to see of my solace.'

168

O Physon, Tygrys, Gyon, Eufrates,   1170
O Doryx eke, the floodys of Paradys!
O Jordan, Cobar, and thou Edapces,

Danybyus and Pharphar at devyse,
Abana eke, as wryten clerkes wyse –
Whiche of Damask with his moysty passage   1175
The gardyns grene fulfylleth with herbage –

169
O Tybre, Rodan, Yber, Leyre, and Sayne,
Geron, and Ryne, with many watry drope,
And O ye solempne floodys and soverayne
Of Asia, Affryke, and of Europe!   1180
Among yow al is not a goodely sope
Lyke to this ryver in comparyson;
The occyan doth hym subjectyon!

170
O ye floodes, and O ye other al
That have your cours out thorugh the erthes space,   1185
Ye ar not lyke in no poyntes specyal
To this ryver in bounte nor in grace!
And whoso lust floodes to knowe and trace,
In Barthylmewe, in his fyften book,
Among his provynce may he goo and loke.   1190

171
Holy Scripture eke maketh mencyon
In Genesis, and other places moo,
Of flodys fele, and theyr condycyon,
And phylosophers tellen them also
As Isidore, but al this lete I goo;   1195
Of this ryver, and his enornement gay –
I mene of fysshe – now somwhat wol I say.

Explicit descripio rivium.

Incipit descripcio piscium.

172
This lusty fysshe within this ryver swete
There swymmyng oores, whiche we fynnes clepe,
They put in use to lere to swymme and flete;   1200

Now at the ground, and now above they lepe,
Now dysceverd, and now upon an hepe,
Nou here, nou there, now endelong, nou overthwert –
The syghte of them myght hele eche wounded hert.

173
Somme had a lust to sewe the sonnes lyght,   1205
Somme to the pryvate umbre gan to attend,
And gadred in theyr bodyes to the syght,
Shote oute on lengthe, theyr courage to extend;
Theyr parfyte blysse nature myght not amend!
Of net, ne hooke, ne deceyte were they aferd –   1210
What shold I say? They had a joye in erde.

174
The whale, the dolphyn, and escaryus,
The carabo, and eke effimeron,
The cakodryl, and uranoscopus,
The see-swyn, and eke fascolyon,   1215
The myllago that fleith the water on,
The hamio that dredeth ay the hooke,
With many moo, whoso hath lust to loke.

175
The myllamur, castor, ypotamus,
Auronnea, phager, serra also,   1220
The conger eke, the fysshe whiche hyght corus,
The pyke, the luce, the samon see I tho,
The swerd-fyssh, with many other moo,
The roche, the tenche, the lamperey, and the ele,
The flouk, the playse, the flounder good to fele,   1225

176
The crabbe, the lobster, and the craveys eke,
The welk, the oystur, and the muscul good,
The trowte, the perche – ther was no fyssh to seke
That in the see, in ryver, or in flode,
In ponde, stewe, dyke, that ever swam or yode,   1230
Whoso hym sought, anone ther may hym see,
In lust, in blysse, and al prosperyte.

177
And yf so were he had of kynd a vyce
In ony poynt, or were malycyous,
Fro he were brought in that ryver of pryce   1235
And tastid of that water gloryous,
He shold anone be good and vertuous;
Shortely to say, to eche fysshe, grete and smal,
It is preservatyf and medycynal.

178
Theyr names al I nede not to reherce,   1240
For every fysshe that goodely is in kynd
In this ryver hadde lust for to converce;
Who lust hym seke, anone ther may hym fynd.
It is the pure holsome ryver and kynde,
And of eche nature and complexyoun   1245
To every fysshe it is refectyoun.

179
Whosoo lust knowe dyversyte of fissh
And how they varrye in theyr mansyon,
How they them fede, and whiche is good in disshe,
Of theyr wysedom and generacyon,   1250
Of theyr vertue and operacyon,
Of what shap eke, what substance, and what kind
That they are of, thou may in bookes fynd:

180
By Arystotyl in his *Book of Beestes*,
By Jorath eke, Ysydore, Plenius,   1255
By Avycen, by Barthylmewys gestys,
By Constantyn, and by Basylyus,
By Ambrose eke, that suche mater to us
Declareth wele in his *Exameron* –
Whoso hath lust, goo loke these clerkes on.   1260

181
For I wyl not make declaracyon
Of suche maters that ben collatural,
It were, ywys, to long disgressyon

Nature of fysshe to telle and name them al;
It must suffyse my scripture general, 1265
For now I wol my penne with wrytyng fede,
And somwhat telle of that moost hevenly mede.

Explicit descripcio piscium.

Incipit descripcio prati.

182
The soverayne honour of the erthes space,
The swete moder, the fresshe moneth of Maye,
To Flora sent, and prayd her of her grace 1270
That she wold come with her enormentes gaye
For to reveste, depaynt and to arraye
This blessyd mede with parfyte dyversyte
Of colours fressh, ful of solempnyte.

183
She come ryght glad, enourned it in hast 1275
With herbe, floure, tree, and al fruyte precyous;
Her thryfty cure in no poynt wold she wast,
For eche good thyng was there most plentyuous –
O Paradys with thy syght gloryous
Thou art not now but as an ymage feyned! 1280
This parfyte mede al thy blysse hath dysteyned.

184
The rose, the lylé, and the vyolet,
Refleryng, shynyng, and payntyng the ground,
Rody and bryght, with hevenly colour set,
In blode and mylk and asure gan habunde; 1285
The rede, the whyte, the blewe wich there was fond
Gan represent in colours and delyte
The ruby, the saphyr, the margaryte.

185
The purpyl two ar godely staunchyng blode,
The two laughyng ben precious medycynable, 1290
The hevenly two ayenst payne be goode;
And to the nose the fyrst is delectable,

And to the syght the second amyable,
The thyrd in tast ryght goodely is bysene –
The rose, the lyllé, the vyolet I mene.   1295

186
The fayr jacynct, the laughyng premerose,
The dayse, the good gylofur floure,
With al other herbes, withouten glose,
That gendren flour or sede of fresshe colour:
Agnus castus the worthy peramour   1300
Of chastite, the good saffron also,
The tyme, the mynte, the rewe, with many moo;

187
The rosemary, the sawge, the savery eke,
Arystologye also, long and round;
The annys good, the bete, goode for the seke;   1305
The dyten eke, that is good for a wound;
The selydon ryght goodely on the ground;
The century, and eke the fumytere;
The malve, the dok, the dragaunce, and the brere;

188
The marygold, cleped the ilytrope;   1310
The bure, the fenel, and the percele;
The letuse swete, with many melky drope;
The coryandre, that hound doth to flee;
The plantane eke, the mandrage ther I see,
With al other that groweth on the ground: 1315
Eche goodely herbe hath lust there to habound.

189
Theyr names al it nedeth not to wryte,
Ne theyr vertues – my labour only is
For to descryve what lust and what delyte,
What plesance, comforte, honour, and what blysse,   1320
Unto this mede they mynystred, ywys;
The syght of them, and of their yongly floures
Was verray salve and hele to al langours.

Explicit descripcio florum et herbarum.

Incipit descripcio arborum.

190
A hevenly wood was on that other syde
And closed in with that ryver aboute,   1325
Planted at lust with trees ful of pryde;
The blossmy bowes unto the erthe gan loute,
The cedre tre, presumptuus and stoute,
Havyng dysdayne in erthe only to abyde
Among the sterres his hede began to hyde.   1330

191
He and the palme, and eke the good cypresse
Gan ryse, burgyn, and refleyre with delyte;
The bowes brought forthe frute of al gentylnesse,
And gaf umbre unto that solempne syght;
With double blysse eche tree was insygnyte: 1335
With frute to man, with umbre to the ground,
Thus honger there ne hete myght not habound.

192
The peretre, the olyve, the appyltree
Wexe grete and grene, and eke moost plentyuous
In peres, in bowes, in appels of bounte;   1340
The almond tree with jardyns fructuous,
Dystyllyng gumme from his bole precyous;
The fyrre, in hyght unto the cyder lyke;
The amonum; the rede aromatyke;

193
The aloes; the gentyl canne and good,   1345
Whoos marugh and juse is made in sucre swete;
The balsamum dystyllyng in a flode
His gentyl baume made thurgh the ground to flete;
The cynamom, with fresshe oder replete;
The good spyknarde; mastyk, the gum rosyn;   1350
Olybanum, the precious thure and fyn;

194
With grapes, hony, with thure, and herbes digne,
Thys wood wax moyst, gan flow, refleyre, and sprede;
The first two bene in sapoure right benygne,

The other ben in myght strong as I rede; 1355
The fyrst in tast the tother done excede,
The second ben help for the strong accesse;
They staunchyn thyrst, they helpen in sykenesse.

195
Thyk, fayr and grene in bowe, bark and in leves,
The cedre was soverayn of trees al; 1360
The top, the bole, the rote among the greves
Herberd, norysshed, and swete in strondes smal
The byrd, the bee, the water specyal:
The byrd in bowes, the bee bred in the bole,
And in the rote the welle dystylled hole. 1365

196
The bowes above brought forth bothe byrdes and fruyte,
The bole, the bark, offred hony and waxe,
The rote benethe, the moyst and cold refuyte
Of al the erth made to habounde and waxe;
The hony swete felle doune in droppes laxe, 1370
And, with the bawme and juse of floures glade,
In the water electuarye they made.

197
The sturdy oke, the asshe, the plum tree,
With acornes, chattes, and with the damecyne;
Al other trees with theyr frutes in degre: 1375
The rampe, the more, the laurer, and the pyne,
The cherubynte, swetyng the swete rasyne;
The byrche, the box, the alme, the sycomore,
The fyge, the vyne – of trees I speke no more,

198
For every tree and fruyte in especyal, 1380
And every spyce, as mace, gynger, and clowe,
Peper, and greynes, with other spyces al
That ever on tree or busshe or herbe gan growe,
There was at lust; and Zepherus gan blowe
Oute thorugh the mede, and casia to refleyr; 1385
Theyr perfyte blysse illumyned al the eyer.

Explicit descripcio arborum.

Incipit descripcio avium.

199
The besy byrdes in theyr melodye
Theyr hevenly voys gan to entone anone;
Theyr aungelyk ravysshyng armonye
Out thorugh the heven unto the hyest trone   1390
Gan perse, and passe the nyne ordres echone;
'O Cherubyn,' they sayd, 'come here to us,
Lere with what tune thou shold synge thy *Sanctus*!'

200
The throstel-cok upon the cedre grene,
The nyghtyngale upon the blosome thorn,   1395
The noble swan with whyte fethers and clene,
The gentyl larke fleyng among the corne,
Ne cesed not to syng from even to morne
With al other foules of pure plesaunce –
Theyr voys gan daunte unto the concordaunce.   1400

201
Eche other foule in kynd there had his blysse,
His lust, his comforte, and his sustenaunce;
They had no nede raveyn to use, ywys,
Eche thyng obeyed to theyr hertes plesaunce:
Debate ne strif, dyscord, ne yet dystaunce   1405
Among them myght not engendred be,
Echone other supported in degre.

202
The proud pecok his tayl began to whele,
On which the sparkyng sonne so puerly brent
That to the syght he semed, every dele,   1410
An archaungel doune from the heven sent:
Al hevenly colours in hym were content;
His tayl, the floures, the byrdes eke, ywys,
The eye, the nose, the ere fed with al blys.

203
The egle fresshe, soverayne of fowles al,   1415
The good gooshauk, the fresshe faucon of pryse,

With al other that to dysport royal
Dysposed ben, ther regned at devyse;
The gentyl dowve innocent of al vyce,
The turtyl trewe, the fenyx syngulere –   1420
In lust, in blysse, togeders al they were.

204
The holsom pertryche, and the pellycane,
The sparowes eke, the plover, and the pye,
The popyngay, the roke, the henne, the crane –
Theyr names al here for to specyfye   1425
It nedeth not, for every foule shortely
That is in kynd, and hath in vertu myght,
In al comfort rejoysed there his flyght.

205
They flee at lust, there is nought them to lette,
They bylde in blysse, they have al lyberte,   1430
They nede not drede for gyler ne for nette,
Flee where they wol, they ben in al suerte;
The wynd, the rayne, ne none adversyte
May them dystourbe, al joye is them among;
The heven above delyted in theyr songe.   1435

Explicit descripcio avium.

Incipit descripcio animalium.

206
The noble lyon, and the leonesse,
The unycorn, the olyfaunt also,
The leopard, the wolf, the bere expresse
Withouten ire in rest and pees gan goo;
The herte, the hynd, the buk, and eke the doo,   1440
The bole, the oxe, and cowe and eke her caulf
No raveyn dredde: pees was on every half.

207
The herte, the hynde, and the gentyl doo,
Proude and myghty, and lepyng lustely,
In hede and brest, on foote eke to and fro,   1445

Japed, paced, and started meryly;
Jak-napys nyce made them al mynstralcye –
Now here, now there, in eche place was his fete,
Eche thyng object he gan to counterfete.

208
The brocke, the pantere, and the dromydare,   1450
The asse, the camyl, the lynx ful of syght,
The bore, the swyne, the whesel, and the hare,
The foxe, the tyger of most spedy myght,
The hound, the whelpe, the ermyn bryght and whyght,
The squerel eke, the myse, the cat, the ramme,   1455
The ghoot, the kyd, the hors, the shepe, the lamme –

209
Al other beestes, shortely for to wryte,
That ben in kynd, that mede gan sustene
In pees and rest, in comforte and delyte,
Eche best and byrd, fysshe, floure, and herbes grene   1460
To stert, to synge, swymme, laugh and refleyre clene
In wood, in nest, in water, and the mede;
Theyr parfyte blysse unto the heven gan sprede.

210
The waters sowne, the lusty fysshe and feyre,
The good ceason, the yongly sonne and bryght,   1465
The mede, the herbes, the floures and theyr refleyre,
The blosmy bowes, the fowles fresshe of flyght,
The tendre wynd, with his brethe and his myght
Enspyryng thorugh the blossomes at devys,
Depaynted new an hevenly paradys.   1470

Explicit descripcio animalium.

Incipit descripcio castri mansionis Sapiencie.

211
Whan I had sene that solempne soverayne syght,
Dame Sapyence led me a lyte besyde
Unto a cumly castel shynyng bryght,

Ful of al solace, delyte, lust, and pryde;
In whoos circuite with vawtes large and wyde   1475
Of parfyte blysse y-set were towres seven,
The hyght of whiche astyed up to heven.

212
The dyke of hyt, y-fourmed with delyte,
Fulfylled was with water of Quyete;
The marbyl stone the alabaster whyte   1480
By geometry so frendely gan mete
That suche a wall in hede, body, and fete,
With precyous stones illumyned at devyse,
Was never seen; hit passed Paradyse!

213
Upon a roche it was grounded and set,   1485
And every buttras ful of ymagery;
Eche pynacle, kirnell, towre and towret
With gold and perle and stones curyously
Depaynted was, and poudred lustely;
And on the yate, illumyned with al blysse,   1490
With gold lettres thys wryten was, ywys:

214
'This is the weye to vertu and to grace,
To connyng, knowlege, wyt, and al wysedome;
This is the wey unto that hevenly place
Ther storme ne stryfe, syn, vyce, ne evil may come;   1495
This is the wey to that solempne kyngedome
Where rest, pees, blysse and comforte seceth never;
Come in who wyl, and ryght welcome forever!'

215
Seven ladyes bryght doune from the toures seven
Came to the yate, with many ladyes moo,   1500
Servauntes to them whoos names wol I nevene:
Feyth, Hope, tofore with Charyte did goo,
Prudence the wyse, Dame Fortytude also,
With Temporaunce and Ryghtwysenes, ywys,
Met Sapyence, and hertely gan hyr kys.   1505

216
With Feyth was Clennes and Vyrgynyte,
Dame Contynence, and Dame Devocyon,
Dame Lowlynes, the maide eke Chastyte –
On whoos hede was thre garlandes of renoun:
One for vyrgyns and theyr relygyon,   1510
One for spoused peple that lyven clene,
The thyrd for wedowes, yf they pure contene.

217
With Hope was Gladnes and Contrycyon,
Dame Discyplyne, and eke Dame Pacyence,
Confessyon, and Contemplacyon,   1515
The blessyd lady eke Dame Penytence;
With Charyte was Grace and Indulgence,
Pees and Acord, Pyte, Compassyon,
And Dame Mercy, emperesse of al renoun.

218
With Dame Prudence was Counceyl and Reson,   1520
The Drede of God, and Tractabylyte,
Dame Dylygence and Dame Dyscrescyon,
Dame Provydence, causer of al bounte;
With Temporaunce was Dame Benygnyte,
Moralyte, Maner, and Tolleraunce,   1525
Dame Sobrenes, and propre Suffysaunce.

219
With Fortytude was Dame Perseveraunce,
Rest and Quyete, Sylence, Stabylyte –
Ay of one strengthe withouten varyaunce,
And never proude for no prosperyte,   1530
Nother yet grutchyng for adversyte;
With Ryghtwysenes was Lawe and Correctyon,
Trouthe, Ryght, and Dome, and Execucyon.

220
Than come a lady, Dame Theologye,
With ladyes seven her sewyng in a route;   1535
Dame Sapyence they salewyd ful humbly,

Kyst her with blysse, and lowely gan to lowte,
Echone other enbraced al aboute,
Glad of that metyng ful of grace;
What shold I say? It was an hevenly place!   1540

221
There was Gramer, ground of scyences al;
And Dyaletyk, ful of pure knowyng;
Dame Rethoryk, scyence imperyal;
Dame Arsmetryk, wise in proporcyonyng;
Geometry, that mesureth every thyng;   1545
The lady Musyke, and Astronomye;
These ladyes seven sewed Theologye.

222
Than from the dongeon grete within the place
(A solempne towre whiche styed up to heven),
Philosophie, the lady ful of grace,   1550
With ladyes come, as after I shal neven;
To Sapyence the way she took ful even
And sayd, 'Welcome, suster and soverayne!'
They kyssed swete, of other bothe were fayne.

223
Philosophye is, who lust to dyffyne,   1555
Knowlege of erthely and eke hevenly thyng,
Y-ioyned with the sad study and fyne
Of governaunce honest, and good lyvyng;
It is also the probable connyng
Of worldly thyng and goodely thyng, ywys,   1560
As in as moche to man possyble is.

224
She is cleped also the arte of artes,
And eke of deth the medytacyon;
Hyr beyng eke y-set is in two partes:
In pure scyence and oppynacyon;   1565
Scyence thynge techeth by certayne reason,
Oppynacyon is in uncertaynte
When thyng by reson may not proved be;

225

As yf the sonne be more in quantyte
Than is the erthe, how moche eke is the heven,   1570
Of what mater, and yf he stable be
Or yet moble – thys cannot scyence neven;
If that the mone be massy, holowe or even –
This knowe we not by propre pure reason,
But this we have by oppynacyon.   1575

226

This soverayne lady, Dame Phylosophye,
Within herself al artes doth contene –
Nature and kynd, vertu and polycye,
How they y-taught, eke execute, shold bene
In her wysedom she hath groundely and clene;   1580
Wherfor to her annexed ben sustres thre,
Whiche ladyes ben of al soverayne bounte.

227

The fyrst suster is cleped Natural,
Whome folk of Grece clepyn Dame Phisyca;
The second hyght the good pryncesse Moral,   1585
Whome they of Grece eke clepe Dame Ethyca;
They clepe also the thyrd Dame Logyca,
Whome oure clerkes clepyn Racyonal;
Phylosophye hath these in especyal.

228

The fyrst doth teche the cause of every thyng,   1590
His propre kynd, his kyndely properte;
And in the second is thrifte of lyvyng,
Knowlege of vertues and of honeste;
When kynd and vertues may than knowen be,
The thyrd suster cometh with her resoun,   1595
Of evyl and good makyng dyscrecyoun.

229

Millesius, one of the sages sevene,
In Grece fyrst drewe, as in the craft of kynde,
By his reason the causes of the hevene,

and of eche thyng the nature gan he fynde; 1600
Than come Plato, a worthy clerke of kynde,
For natural art sought oute geomatrye,
Arsmetryk, musyk, and astronomye.

230
Dame Ethyca, pryncesse of polycye,
Good Socrates fyrst founde for governaunce, 1605
To knowe vertu, and conne lyve honestly;
And four ladyes he sought, ful of plesaunce,
To serve Dame Ethyke with obeysaunce:
Whoos names ben Prudence and Ryghtwysenes,
Dame Fortitude and Temporaunce, I gesse. 1610

231
Than fond Plato the lady Racyonal,
Whiche, whan that kynd and vertu knowen bene,
Techeth eche man by reson specyal
To understonde the subtyl strengthe and clene
Of kynd and vertu, what they wold and mene; 1615
Than sought he oute Dame Dyaletyca,
To serven her with Dame Rethorica.

232
In these thre sustres grounded may we fynd
Dyvynyte, yf we loke wele, ywys,
For eche dyvyne other speketh of kynd 1620
As in the noble book of Genesis,
Or of maners, as in Proverbiis,
Or of logyk, for whome dyvynes al
The Cantycles taken in specyal.

233
Some sayne that Philosophicall Resoun 1625
Hath ladyes twoo subject in specyal:
The fyrst hyght Inspectyve, whoos eye aboun
Dyscerneth thyng whiche is celestyal;
The second lady hyght Dame Actual,
That of eche thyng maketh discrecyoun 1630
As it sheweth in operacyon.

234
Dame Inspectyve hath servyng ladyes thre:
Dame Natural, and eke Dame Doctrynal,
The thyrd in heven hath syght and soveraynte,
Wherfor she hyght the pryncesse Dyvynal; 1635
The fyrst techeth the kynd of thynges al,
By craft the second geteth intellect,
The thyrd invysyble thynges hath respect.

235
Dame Doctrynal hath servauntes four, ywys:
The good Arsmetryk, and Dame Geometrye, 1640
Dame Musyk eke, the lady ful of blysse,
The fourth pryncesse hyght Dame Astronomye;
Of these four ladyes must I specyally
Herafterward in my treatys endyte,
Of them no more wherfor now wyl I wryte. 1645

236
Dame Actual hath other ladyes thre –
As Dame Moral, and Dame Dispensatyve,
Dame Cyvyle hyght the thyrd ful of bounte;
The fyrst dysposeth to eche man on lyve
Maner of lyvyng; the second is actyve, 1650
Which can her houshold rewle withoute doutaunce;
The thyrd all cytees hath in governaunce.

Incipit processus de prima curia.

237
We entred in this yate ful of blysse
Unto the fyrst court, ful of hevenly lyght,
Whiche Dame Scyence had in kepyng, ywys, 1655
With hows and ward, loyal, lusty, and bryght,
Ellumyned fresshe and peynted to the syght
With propre kynd of eche thyng temporal:
Man, beest, herbe, tree, ther maist thou know them al.

238
Scripture there taught hou man shold governe him, 1660
And what he is in body and in bloode,
Of what mater in lythe or yet in lym,

Why this is evyl, and why that thyng is good,
Why this is tame, and why that beest is wood,
Al polycy in erthe, and al knowlege   1665
Dame Scyence ther had in that herbergage.

239
There was al natural philosophye,
And in a goodly parlour see I syt
The philosopher with his companye
Tretyng of kynd, and what longeth to it;   1670
There was clerk note, there was konnyng and wyt,
They poynt, they wryte, they dyspute, they depure,
They determyne eche thyng that hath nature.

240
Arystotyl, Averous, Avycenne,
Good Algazel, Galyene, Appollynus,   1675
Pyctagoras, and Plato with his penne,
Macrobius, Cato, Boecius,
Rasus, Isake, Calyxte, Orbasius,
Salustius, Theophyl, Ypocras –
With many mo whoos names I lete pas.   1680

241
These had delyte to serven Dame Scyence,
And to have knowlege in phylosophye;
They worshypped her, they dyd hir reverence,
Theyr hole desyre was to her soveraynly;
They wake, they work, they study besyly,   1685
Whyles that they ben with Dame Scyence expert;
Theym to byholde myght ravysshe every hert!

Explicit processus de prima curia.

Incipit processus de secunda curia.

242
Unto the second court than in we yode,
The cure of whiche had Dame Intellygence,
With halle, chambres, with toures hye and good,   1690
Ful of al lust, and hevenly complacence;

There was depeynted with al reverence
The heven, his blysse, and who duelleth in it,
The jerarchyes in nyne ordres y-knyt.

243
Of what degre was every jerarchye,   1695
Of what offyce, and of what observaunce,
And why the fyrst eke hyght 'ypyphanye',
There was depaynted with al pure plesaunce;
Of Lucyfer and his unhappy chaunce,
And of the spyrytes whiche that with hym felle,   1700
There myght men see, and of the payne of helle.

244
Oure wyttes fyve when they begyn to fayle,
As in eche invysyble creature,
Intellygence must yeve us than counsayle –
By her we have parfyte knowlege and pure;   1705
When eye, nose, ere, mouthe, hand eke is unsure,
And we by them may gete no pure scyence,
Than must us renne unto Intellygence.

245
There was Denyse, Bernard, Bede, Barthilmew,
The good cardynal the swete Bonaventure –   1710
With eyne enspyred, whiche had sene and knew
The pryvy counceyl of the fyrst nature –
And many moo, within a parlour pure,
Of clerkes whiche that were contemplatyve,
There see I sytte, hevenly thyng to descryve.   1715

246
Theyr names al I may not now reherce –
The multitude of them so passyng bene
They may not al be conteyned in a verce –
But to byhold how fresshe, lusty, and grene
Was theyr desyre to loke on bookes clene,   1720
And hevenly thyng with eye mental to see,
Al erthly joye it passeth in degre!

Explicit processus de secunda curia.

Incipit processus de tercia curia.

247
Wyth joy and blysse and delectacyon
Dame Sapyence, that good godly goddesse,
Unto her ward, soverayne of al renoun,   1725
Than led us forth unto a halle expresse,
Whoos blysse, beauté, luste, and parfyte noblesse
Al erthly place passeth a thousand fold;
The joy of it with tonge may not be told!

248
Hit was an heven only to loke it on,   1730
Soo ravyssyng it was, and elegaunt;
O Pryamus, and thyn halle Ilyon
With al his propre beauté pure plesaunte,
For to be lyke it is not suffysaunt
Unto this halle, whiche made was by nature,   1735
As for a maystry chyef in portrature.

249
It hanged was with aras-werk in gold,
Ful of stories of wysedom and of wyt:
The Parables moost godely to byhold,
Ecclesiastes eke than folowed hit,   1740
The boke of Sapyence ful wel y-wryte,
The good book eke Ecclesiasticus
Al wysedom there declare gan and dyscusse.

250
And on the dayse Mynerve (that hyght Pallas)
The goddesse of wysedom ful of all lyght   1745
On hevenly wyse portreyed and peynted was:
A lady fayr, enarmed fresshe and bryghte,
Whoos hede was with the reynbowe bound and dyghte,
A crest above, her ryght honde had a spere,
The other syde a sheld of crystal clere;   1750

251
Her hede was ferful and eke monstruous
For dyvers serpentes henge her hede aboute;
Bryght eyen she had, and clothyng precyous

Of colours thre, delycyous and stoute;
An olyve tree with braunches on a route, 1755
On whiche a nyght-crowe lustely was set
Stode her besyde; it myght not be made bet.

252
And what it ment, there told Dame Sapyence,
'This is the goddesse of al wyt soverayne
Depeynted thus with lust and reverence, 1760
Y-gete she was of Jupyteres brayne;
To moral sence it is as moche to sayne
That al wysedom commeth from God above,
Whoome poetes clepen "Jubyter" and "Jove."

253
Eke wysedom hath armour of al vertu, 1765
The bryght reynbowe of love and frendlyheede,
The crest honour, the ferful hede to shewe
With serpentes dyvers is the parfyte drede
Of God, of deth, and of the hyghe falshede
Of his enmye the fende, ful of despyte – 1770
Every wyse man that serpent must hym byte!

254
She hath the ryght spere of correctyon,
The sheld of fortytude and pacyence,
Th'olyve of pees, the nyght-crowe abonne
Whiche is the byrd of mekenes and sylence; 1775
She hath the eyen of reson and prudence;
Her clothyng eke, that is of colours thre,
Betokenyth feyth, hope, and charyte.'

255
Wysedom or prudence whoso lust descryve,
Or her array, parfyte and lustely, 1780
I counceyl hym that he goo loke belyve
Fulgencius, in his *Methologye*:
Fyrst in 'Satourn,' and hym than counceyl I,
Goo loke in 'Juno,' 'Neptune,' and 'Pluto,'
There shal he see whiche thyng I lete overgoo. 1785

256

Was never place in erthe so gloryous
As is the worthy halle of Sapyence,
With hows of offyce, moost delycyous,
Inhabyte ful with folk of reverence;
And in a chapel ful of complacence,   1790
Within a shryne, lusty to al devyse,
Set with al blysse was Salamon the wyse.

257

Theologye a Byble took anone
And torned to many a story fyn;
The gospellers – Mark, Mathew, Luke and John –   1795
The doctours four, as Gregor and Austyn,
Jerome, Ambrose, expert in thynges dyvyne,
Unto her cam, aboute her al they syt;
There myght men lere of wysedom and of wyt.

258

There studyed Holcote upon Sapyence,   1800
And Notyngham upon the gospellers,
The good clerk the Mayster of Sentence,
Seynt Thomas eke, worshyp unto al freres,
The Mayster of the Storyes with his feres,
And many one moo, good clerk and dyvyne,   1805
Than for to telle my wyttes can dyffyne.

Incipit brevis tractatus de grammatica.

259

With Gramer were foure ladyes wel besene,
Of whiche the fyrst hyght Dame Ortographye;
Within a parlour, lusty, fresshe and grene,
There was eke gentyl Ethymologye,   1810
Dyasyntastica, and Prosodye;
These sustres four, dyfferent in offyce,
Served Gramer as lady ful of pryce.

260

The first taught lettres and how men shold write;
The second taught the partes of reson –   1815
To telle eche word truly is her delyte,

And which is nowne, which verbe, and which pronowne;
The thyrd dyd teche parfyte constructyon;
The last eche word yave his tyme and accent;
And in these foure al gramer is content.   1820

261
These four served that scyence litteral
In wrytyng, pronouncyng, and construyng
Of lettre, syllable, word, reson – with al
She hath her pryncypal consyderyng;
She is the ground, the yate, the entryng   1825
To al the noble artes lyberal:
By her frendshyp they be made specyal.

262
There was Moyses, Cadmus, and Carmenta,
Ebrard, Ferryn, Johan Gerlond and Donate,
Prescyane, Petyr, Thomas de Hennaya,   1830
Lambart Papy – they wryte erly and late –
The Januens was there in grete estate,
And Arystotyl, for theyr bookes wyse:
Catholycon, and Paryarmonyse.

263
Hugucyon, with many auctors moo,   1835
Wrytyng ther was, and lokyng on Gramer,
Whoos names al shortely I lete overgoo;
They may not doo but prolong my matere.
Many a babe of soverayne hevenly chere
Desyrous al in connyng to habounde   1840
Aboute Dame Gramer satte to have theyr grounde.

Explicit brevis descripcio gramatice et ejus parcium.

Incipit brevis tractatus de dialetica.

264
Within another parlour, ful of blysse,
With many clerk and scoler of yong age
Dame Dyaletica was set, ywys;

She red them al; Latyn was theyr langage.   1845
They al of her asked none other wage
But that they myght dyscerne and eke depure
Trouth from falshede – that was theyr aller cure.

265
Her parlour fresshe, her clothyng proude and stout,
Of *dyffert*, *scire*, and of *incipit*   1850
With sophysmes full depeynted was aboute,
And other maters, as of *desinit*.
The *Comune Treatys* taught she them therwith:
Whiche, whatkyns, what is proposicion,
What thyng he is, and his dyvysyon;   1855

266
Whiche is subject, couple, and predicate,
And how he is reson indycatyf,
And when he hath unyversal estate,
Partyculer, or is affyrmatyf,
Indefinite, singler, or negatyf;   1860
Whiche subalterne, whiche contradictyon,
Whiche is contrarye, taught she by resoun.

267
Equypollens, and eke conversyon,
Sylogysmus, maner of arguyng,
And for to make an oblygacyon   1865
She taught hem there with lust and al lykyng;
Fast they dysputen in theyr comonyng,
With sophyms strong straunge maters they discusse,
And fast they crye oft, '*Tu es asinus!*'

268
The *Unyversels*, and the *Natures Good*,   1870
The *Predycamentes*, the *Topykes* also,
The *Pryncipals*, the *Elynks* – as they stood
She red them al, with many tretes moo;
She taught them way to procede and to goo,
And to atteyne to al phylosophye.   1875
Her to byhold, it was blysse hevenly!

269
The phylosophres whiche reherced bene
With Dame Scyence in her fyrst court of al
With this lady eke goodely were bysene,
And had concours to her in especyal: 1880
Alfred, Haly, Jorath, and Juvenal,
Eraclius, Affricane, Demostene,
Mercurius, and noble Damascene,

270
Gyles, and Euclide, Rufus and Cythero,
Democritus, and Physyologus,   1885
Syr Theoprasse, Tytus and Cipio,
William Conches, Zeno, Johannycus,
Syr Tholome, Varro, and Plinius,
Salustyane, Permenides also,
And many on, whoos names I lete goo.   1890

Explicit brevis tractatus de dyaletica.

Incipit brevis tractatus de rethorica.

271
Dame Rethoryke, modre of eloquence,
Moost elegaunt, moost pure and gloryous,
With lust, delyte, blysse, honour and reverence,
Within her parlour, fresshe and precyous,
Was set as quene; whoos speche delycyous   1895
Her audytours gan to al joye converte –
Eche word of hyr myght ravysshe every herte!

272
And many clerk had lust her for to here,
Her speche to theym was parfyte sustenaunce;
Eche word of her depured was so clere   1900
And illumyned with so parfyte plesaunce
That heven it was to here her beauperlaunce;
Her termes gay of facund soverayne
Cacephaton in no poynt myght dystayn.

273
She taught them all the craft of endytyng: 1905
Whiche vyces ben that shold avoyded be,
Whiche ben the colours gay of that connyng,
Theyr dyfference, and eke theyr properte,
Eche thyng endyte how it shold poynted be –
'Dystynctyon' she gan clare and dyscusse   1910
Whiche is coma, colym, periodus.

274
But whoso thynke my wrytyng dul and blont
And wold conceyve the colours purperate
Of rethoryke, goo he to *Tria sunt*,
And to Galfryde the poete laureate,   1915
To Januens a clerk of grete astate –
Within the fourth parte of his gramer book
Of this mater there groundely may he loke.

275
In Tullius also, moost eloquent,
The chosen spouse unto this lady free,   1920
This gylted craft of glorye is content;
Gay thinges y-made eke yf the lust to see
Goo loke the *Code* also, the *Dygestes* thre,
The bookes of lawe and eke of physyk goode;
Of ornate speche there spryngeth up the floode.   1925

276
In prose and metre of al kynd, ywys,
This lady blyssed had lust for to playe;
With her was Blesens, Richard de Pophis,
Farrose pystyls, clere, lusty, fresshe, and gay;
With metres were poetes in good array: 1930
Ovyde, Omer, Vyrgyl, Lucan, Orace,
Alane, Bernard, Prudencius, and Stace.

Explicit processus de rethorica.

Incipit de arsmetrica.

277
Arsmetryke than amyd the ladyes al
As pryncesse goodely had her mansyon;
Echone of her had nede in specyal,   1935
Bycause of whiche she was of grete renoun;
And al her craft by numeracyon
Was for to sette eche thyng in his ordre,
Withouten her ben the sex artes unsure.

278
She told us there how both the erthe and heven   1940
Had theyr makyng and theyr parfectyon
In dayes syxe and eke in nyghtes sevene,
How thre persones and one God aboune
The trynyte conteyneth with renoun,
How Moyses, Ely, and how Cryst hymselve   1945
Fast fourty dayes, and of the apostles twelve.

279
In hooly wryte moche thyng y-nombred is,
Of whiche by her we have cognycyon;
And in this world eche creature, ywys,
Is made by numeral proporcyon: 1950
Four elementes, the seven planettes abone –
These be dystynct in trewe nombre certayne;
Withouten her al craftes be but veyne.

280
It is wryten that God al thyng hath made
In weyght, in nombre, and eke in mesure,   1955
Of arsmetryk wherfor he shold be glad
Of ony thyng whiche lyst have knowlege pure;
When oure, weke, moneth, or yere there is unsure,
Theyr currycles, theyr tymes, and theyr space
By this lady to trew knowlege we trace.   1960

281
She taught nombre, whiche is odd and which even,
Devyded hym with subdyvysyon,

Ten fygures eke of augrym gan she nevene
And calendres for numeracyon;
She told the craft of computacyon   1965
To adde, dymynew, and to multyplye;
Eche thyng to count she taught us craftely.

282
She taught us eke what thyng that nombre was:
'A multytude of unytees,' she sayd;
And with her set the old Pyctagoras,   1970
Nychomacus, of whome moche good is sayd,
Apuleius and Boece, ryght wele arrayd –
These were the fyrst in Latyn and in Grewe
That in the crafte of nombre ever drewe.

Explicit brevis processus de arsmetrica.

Incipit brevis tractatus de geometria.

283
Dame Geometrye her subtyl crafte oute ronge,   1975
And in her place as lady reverent
She sat at lust, with lynes large and long,
Compase, rule, plumbe, and many instrument,
With fygures queynte, and al to hir entent
Of every thyng to yeue the trewe mesure;   1980
This was her craft, her labour, and her cure.

284
She made cerculis, fygures, and spyres straunge,
Tryangles, quadrantes, wonderly y-wrought,
Layd lynes along, and ofte she dyd hem chaunge –
The pure mesure of every thyng she sought;   1985
And by her craft to pure knowlege she broght
How hye, how lowe, hou long, and how brode eke
Was every thyng; she had it not to seke!

285
Whiche is the poynt, the centre, or the pole
Ful craftely she taught of every spere;   1990
Whiche cercle is y-cut, and whiche is hole,

Whiche lyne is ryght, whiche perpentyculere,
Whiche circuler, and whiche dyametere;
And by this craft of al the erthes space
The veray mesure truly gan she trace.   1995

286
The erthes space how long it is aboute –
Arystotyl sayth that old clerkes sayne
That four and twenty thousand myle al oute
In his cercle he conteyneth certayne;
But Albert thynketh it is an errour pleyne,   2000
For in his tyme they couthe it not for clere
The quantite of his dyametere.

287
But other clerkes, sewyng Tholome,
Sayd that the erthe in his cyrcuyte round
Shold twenty thousand myle and fourty be;   2005
And thus one clerk another doth confounde
Soo that the trouthe by none of them is found.
'Gode thyng,' sayth Basyle, 'shold have remembrance,
And that shold passe which stondeth in doutaunce.'

288
With her dyvers clerkes of Egypte were   2010
(Whiche fyrst dyd fynde the crafte of geometry),
Eke Theodosius in his maner
With philosophres sate ful lustely,
Of that scyence tretyng ful craftely,
As good Euglyd, and many clerkes moo.   2015
Of theym no more, for ferther must I go.

Explicit de geometria.

Incipit de musica.

289
A lyte besyde within a place of blys
Dame Musyk sat, and with her ladyes thre:
The fyrst hyght Dame Armonyca, ywys,

The second Rethmica a lady free, 2020
The thyrd hyght Metrica ful of beauté,
The song she prycked, she numered notes trewe,
Theyr melodye formed an heven newe.

290
The fyrst delyted her in tunes mete;
The second mesured dyte with the note; 2025
The thyrd numered her songe with certeyne fete,
And whiche be her boundes ryght wel she wote;
And with them were good clerkis that thus wrote,
And sayd that musyk was the pure connynge
And veray wey of trewe parfyte syngynge. 2030

291
They wrote also who that fyrst musyk found:
Some sayd Tubal, some Linus Tibeus,
Some Zetus, Amphyon, as they dyd understond,
Some sayd also it was one Orpheus,
Some playnly said, for ought they coude discusse, 2035
That by the soune of hamers in a forge
Pyctagoras fyrst musyk ganne to forge.

292
Dame Musyk ganne on her craft to record,
And made a wey how folk shold fyrst begyn;
Her example was in a monycord – 2040
An instrument quadraunt, long, holowe within,
Of whiche the myd one strenge had with a gyn –
Oute of the whiche dyvers tunes she wrought,
And thus the ground of musyke first she sought.

293
She taught sex syllabes, whiche we notes clepe, 2045
And in her craft they necessary bene,
Whiche on an ympne thou mayst brynge to hepe,
If thou his metre can proporcyon clene:
Ut queant laxis is hit whiche I mene –
Ther mayst thou fynd ut, re, my, fa, sol, la; 2050
These syllabes sex useth Dame Musica.

294
She taught the notes by her monycord
As she the streng dyd touche or gan it pulle,
And, as she lengthed or shorted the cord,
Which hye, which lowe, which sharp and which is dulle   2055
Of al these notes taught she at the ful,
Theyr varyaunce, and theyr dyscencyon,
Theyr ordre eke, and theyr ascencyon.

295
A *gamma-ut* than wonderly she found –
Whiche is a rewle to teche them for to synge –   2060
And it to knowe she taught them on their hond,
By whiche they wote the ground of al syngyng:
The notes they knowe therby and theyr chaungyng,
And proveth eke whiche songe is fals or trewe;
To musyk thus she gan the wayes shewe.   2065

296
She taught them than whiche were tunes parfyte,
And yave hem lust to here theyr concordaunce,
Whiche tunes eke ben cleped inparfyte,
And whiche in song shold be theyr governaunce.
Proporcyon she had in remembraunce,   2070
Dyapason, and dyapente eke,
And dyatesseron nas not to seke.

297
Which large, which long, which breve or semybreve,
Mynym, crochet, in rule and eke in space,
Al this she taught; but, for I must be breve,   2075
In this mater I nyl no ferther trace;
For, though I wold, therto I have no space.
But whoso lust of musyk for to wyt
For veray ground to Boece I hym remyt.

298
And to a clerk whiche cleped is Berno,   2080
Johan de Muris, and John de Musica,
To Guydo eke in his *Metrologo*;

There mayst thou see of Dame Armonyca,
Of Dame Metryk, and of Dame Rethmica;
Of al musyke the veray ground parfyte   2085
There shalt thou fynd, with blysse and al delyte.

299
And these with Musyke were in joye and blysse
And helped her provynce with her armonye,
And with them was eche instrument, ywys,
That is of musyk and of mynstralcye: 2090
Harp, lute, pype, trump, fydel, ribibe, sautry,
The rote, the orgons, and the monycord,
The gyterne, symbale, and the clavycord.

Explicit tractatus de musica.

Incipit brevis processus de astronomia.

300
Than see I syt in place ful of plesaunce
The hevenly lady, Dame Astronomye,   2095
Whiche of the sterres the cours and governaunce,
Theyr fygures eke, descryveth craftely;
And with her was the mayd Astrologye,
Whiche somtyme is kyndely and precyous,
And otherwhyle overmoche superstyous.   2100

301
She is kyndely whan that she sheweth clere
The sonnes cours, the mone, the sterres eke,
And doth nothyng but as kynd doth her lere;
But whan she lust in sterres for to seke
The byrthe of man, whiche hole shal be, which seke,   2105
And wyl dyvyne, and preche thyng for to be –
Unkyndely than, and unleful is she.

302
Astronomye, that lady ful of grace,
Gan first dyvyne what thyng the world shold be,
What thyng heven is, his cours and his place,   2110

His poles eke, his partyes in degre,
His fourme, his spere, and eke his properte,
His syhte, his cours, his movyng at the best,
His yates twoo, whiche ben oeste and vest.

303
His hemyspery, and his cercles fyve,   2115
Theyr properte, and how they cleped bene;
The zodyak also she gan descryve,
The sonne, his cours and his effectes clene,
His magnytude, his nature wel besene;
The mone, her cours, her dyvers fourmes eke,   2120
And their eclypse; there was nothyng to seke!

304
She taught also how sondry sterres hyght,
And in what tyme they goo theyr cercules al,
Eke how the sonne the mone yeveth al her lyght,
Whiche Lucina we clepe in specyal;   2125
And how that fyre oute from the heven doth fall –
Lyke as the sterres fyl it is y-sene –
The cause of this, and what thyng it may mene.

305
And to eche sterre that cleped is a 'sygne'
(By syght of whiche, thyng to come men may gesse),   2130
A propre name she gan for to assygne,
As Arcton (Ursa – the more eke and the lesse);
Thus dyvers names gan she for to dresse:
As Tryones, Boetes, Yades,
Arcturus, Oryon, and Plyades,   2135

306
As Lucyfer, Cometes, Vesperus –
Theyr names old she told ful craftely;
The planetes seven she nevened unto us:
Saturne, Jove, Mars, Phebus, and Mercurye,
The moon, Venus, and what they sygnyfye,   2140
Their influence, and al theyr qualyte,
With cyrcumstaunce of pure solempnyte.

307
Twelve fygures than she told ryght wel arrayed:
The Ramme, the Bul, and eke the Gemelles to,
The Crabbe, the Lyon, and the sterell Mayd,   2145
The Balaunce, th'Archer, and the Scorpio,
The Gote, the Water-syre, the Fysshe also;
The planetes seven as they to this atteyne
So is eche tyme dysposed, soth to sayne.

308
And how eche sygne had of his properte   2150
A propre name, thus gan she to constrewe;
The gentyles eke, how that they blynded be
That lust honour, with worshyp fresshe and newe,
The planetes seven as parfyte goddes trewe;
Theyr rytes old and theyr ydolatrye   2155
She gan reherce, as techeth poeterye:

309
And how they clepe the Ramme the fyrst sygne,
For that in Mars, begynnyng of the yere,
The sonne in hym maketh his cours digne;
And howe they worshyp hym on theyr manere   2160
Bycause of Jove, whome in theyr temples clere
If they do paynte, a rammes hede they make
With hornes two for Jubyteres sake.

310
He come an oxe and took Europe, they sayd,
Wherfor the bole they worshyp of theyr grace;   2165
Castor, Pollux eke, when they dede were layd,
Among the sterres they demed have a place,
Whome they clepen the Gemelles with solace;
For Hercules eke slough the grete lyon
Hym for that sygne they worshyp with renoun.   2170

311
O mysbyleve, merveylous for to nevene!
O cursyd blyndenes of these gentyles al!
Whiche demyn fysshe and bestyal be in heven

For gloryfyed regnaunt perpetual –
As Rame, Bull, Crabbe, and Bere in specyal,   2175
Hound, Lyon, Swanne, the Egle eke in fere,
Whome they worshyp for Joves chyef squyer.

312
She told also of fatall destyne,
And how in sterres som men have such bileve
That in theyr byrth, ryght by necessyte,   2180
Ordeyned is al that hym shal please or greve;
This old errour oure doctours done repreve,
Socrates the same with Arystotyl sayth,
Notwithstondyng they were not of oure fayth.

313
For yf man were in his natyvyte   2185
Constreyned to his sondry actes al,
Theym for to doo ryght by necessyte,
Why shold good men have lawde in specyal?
Or myslyvers to punysshement be thral?
Good Isodore maketh this his reson   2190
In dampnynge of this fals oppynyon.

314
Astronomye the Egyptes fyrst dyd fynd
(Astrologye and her queynt observaunce
Folk of Caldee fyrst sought and brought to mynde)
Whom Abraham taught the Egyptes with plesance,   2195
As wryteth Josephus withoute doutaunce;
But they of Grece sayn this craft first was found
By one Athlant, and of hym had his ground.

315
And with this lady was Syre Tholome,
John de Hispayn, and Mysaleth also,   2200
With al other auctours in degre
That drewe of her, whoos names lete I go.
Thus in the sterres I wol cease and ho;
And, by the ordre of the artes seven,
Styre folk to leve the world and drawe to heven.   2205

Explicit de astronomia.

Incipit tractatus de fide.

316
Dame Feith than led us to her wonyng place,
Unto a towre solempne and gloryous,
Ful of al lust, comfort, vertu and grace,
Depeynted fresshe with colour precyous;
And in a parlour ful solacyous   2210
Th'appostles al were set with pure delyte,
And of oure feith the artycles they wryte.

317
They had byleve in God, fader of myght,
Maker of heven and erthe, and al that is,
Of vysyble and invysyble wyght;   2215
And in his sonne, Crist Jhesu, ful of blysse,
Before the world, whiche was alwey, ywys,
I-gete not made, and consubstauncyal
To his fader, of whome fourmed is al.

318
He cam from heven, and in the mayd Marye   2220
By inspyracyon of the Holy Goost
Mankynd he took, and borne was for to dye,
To wyn mans soule out from the fendes hoost;
And under Pylate set with Jewes boost,
Bounden and bete, crowned and crucyfyed,   2225
With watry woundes innocent he dyed;

319
For he was graven, man out from helle he broght,
and rose the thyrd day unto lyve ageyne;
Styed up to heven, his faders trone he sought,
From whens as kyng he shal come yet certeyn   2230
Bothe quyk and dede to deme to lyf or peyn –
The goode to blysse, the evyl to punysshement;
Hevene, erthe and helle shal quake in that jugement!

320
And in the Holy Ghoost byleve they had,
In holy chirche, baptysme, communyon   2235
Of sayntes eke, and to hold ferme and sad

Of al trespaas to have remyssyon,
And for to trowe the resurectyon
Of peple dede, and in lyf ay lastyng;
Unto the whiche almyghty God us bryng!   2240

321
These artycles, with other poyntes al
That longeth to the holy Tryntye,
Dame Feyth herself gan telle in specyal,
With al the secretes of the deyte
Whiche in Englysshe ought not reherced be;   2245
Suche thyng as shold be pryvate and occult
I rede we leve, and take *Quicumque vult.*

322
There was to Feyth doyng al reverence
The holy synner, Mary Magdalene,
Whiche by Dame Fayth hath geten indulgence   2250
Of al her synne, and was assoylled clene;
Good Martha eke by her grace gan optene
And brought to lyve her broder, Lazarus;
Soo was the sone also of Regulus;

323
There was the doughter eke of Canane,   2255
Whiche by her brought was fro the fendes bond;
Al other eke, that of infyrmyte
Thorugh Feyth was cured, with her see I stond:
Blynde, dome, and deef, and leprous fote and hond,
Whome Feith hath heled and brought unto grace,   2260
With al honour obeyed her in that place.

324
There was also the hooly confessours
That preched feyth whyle they were here on lyve,
Doctours, martyrs, and gloryous auctours
Wrytyng of feyth and her meryte blyve;   2265
And on this wyse they gan hyr to descryve
And sayd that Feyth is ground of al godenes,
Withouten whome lyf hath no sykernes:

325
'Unto al good she geveth strengthe and comfort,
And who troweth not, he falleth impotent;   2270
The sheld of feyth whoso lust to comport,
Al thyng overcometh as victoure reverent;
His thre enemyes, with theyr yrous entent,
Ayenst hym shal nevermore prevayle;
Aske and byleve: thyn askyng shal not fayle!   2275

326
She is ay one, for as the clerke sayth,
There is but one God, lord perpetual,
Pryncypally of whome preched is fayth;
Eke hole she is of her artycles al,
Trewe withoute errour outher grete or smal,   2280
Lyvely and quyck to do every good dede
For elles she were but as a body dede.'

327
There was the lady Clennesse wel arrayed,
Devocyon and Dame Vyrgynyte,
Dame Contynence, and Chastyte the mayd,   2285
Dame Loulynesse, and Dame Stabylyte,
Enlumyned fresshe echone in theyr degre;
These serven Fayth, and as they couthe devyse,
With blysse they song, and sayd upon this wyse:

328
'It better is to trowe in God above   2290
Than in mankynd, or any other thyng;
Who troweth in hym, for he can kepe and love,
Theyr lust fulfylle, and graunt them theyr askyng;
And in his Gospel eke, as worthy kyng,
He sayd hymself, "In me who lust byleve,   2295
Though he be dede, ywys, yet shal he leve!"

329
O cursed folk with youre idolatrye,
Whiche in fals goddes setten youre delyte!
Blynd, dome, and defe is al youre mametrye

Of stok and stone – men may suche karve and thwyte – 2300
Leve theym for fals, with sorow and despyte;
In our one God cast anker and byleve:
Though ye were dede, yet he can make yow leve.

330
He is al lyf whan youre goddes be dede;
They have a tyme, and he is sempyterne; 2305
They are but erthe, and brought as lowe as lede,
He regneth God above the heven superne;
Blyssed be he! For he no grace wyl werne
To them that wyl in hym set theyr byleve,
And though they dye, ywys, yet shal they lyve!' 2310

Explicit tractatus de fide et cantus familie sue.

Incipit de spe.

331
Forth went we thoo unto Dame Hopes place,
Elumyned fressh with beauté and plesaunce;
In whiche a table long with all solace
Depaynted was with Hopes governaunce,
And how that she, as grounde of all chaunce, 2315
Diffinid is, 'the certeyne abidynge
Of blis to man, and lyfe all way lastynge.'

332
'Thrugh grace and honest conversacion
Hope is engendred and made vertuous;
In woo, sekenes and tribulacioun 2320
She is comfort and medicyne precious;
Aye sure she is, and never ruynous;
Whos hert in Hope in God supportid is,
Go were he go, his wey lith never amys.

333
Resone will ask that fewe folkis desire: 2325
Thyng speciall that may them best susteyne;
O God, we that fellid bene with the fire

Of flesshly synne and of thoughtis unclene,
Why shulde not we than seche unto that quene,
Dame Hope, whiche is the parfite sustenaunce   2330
Of lyfe and soule, and salve of all penaunce?

334
She is the auctore of pure sikernes,
Whiche by no stormy blast may broken be;
She is the pollisshide myrroure of hevenlynes,
Light in derkenes, blis in adversite,   2335
Rest in laboure, pees aftir cruelte,
Parfite dulcor after all bitter breth:
Hir lady cure distroyeth ay lastyng deth.

335
Who servyth Hope, whether he route or goo,
Hym fayleth no strengeth, his labour nys but play;   2340
More stronge he is the more he suffreth woo,
His manly hert all penaunce doth away –
The high penaunce that servith Hope alway
So myghty is in his paynes temperall
That hir rewarde is blis perpetuall.'   2345

336
All this i-write was in the table forsaid,
In Hopis place, with goodly portreture;
And yongly ladies, fressh and well araid
Servid Dame Hope with lusty besy cure;
As Dame Gladnes, Dame Discipline also,   2350
Contricion and Contemplacioun,
Penaunce, Pacience, and Dame Confessioun.

337
And to a song moost hevenly ravisshyng
There angelike voice they gan to daunt,
And thus they seide, 'O myghty lord and kyng,   2355
O soverayne prince, O God invariaunt,
What wight may have grace more exuberant
Than with good Hope in the ther cost to fede?
Who trowith in the, heven shal be his mede!

338
What coward hert may fynde for to dispeyre   2360
That thyng to do the whiche possible is?
Who list his hope in God for to repeyre,
Aske what he will, he shall opteyne, iwis,
Through Hope he gete life, love, grace, lastyng blis;
Love hym, drede hym, trust hym, and thou shalt spede –   2365
Whoo trowith in God, mercy shall be his mede!

339
In whome shuld men trust but in God almyght,
Whiche may performe all possibilite?
No trespas eke may be in Godes sight
So moche of multitude ne quantite   2370
That yf Hope aske mercy of his pite
The trespassure is remyt, without drede –
Whoo trowith in God, mercy shal be his mede!'

Explicit tractatus de Spe et cantus familie sue.

[Here endith the boke of Sapience:
How man hadde first redempcioun,
The lapidarie with the seven science
Liberall, and eke the mansioun
Of Sapience, moost riall of renown;
Dame Feith, Dame Hope, with ther familitees,
Beestis and briddes with ther mery sowne,
Fissh, watir, erbe, spice, and trees.]

COMMENTARY

Commentary

1 The metre of this line is irregular in C, the only witness for this part of the *Court*. Perhaps 'laberous' should be read as a disyllable, as Spindler suggests, although the form 'labrous' is not recorded in *MED*, and the ō of Latin 'labōrōsus' persists in most of the English spellings. Perhaps the second 'the' should be omitted.

2 *syn firste regned nature*: 'from the time of the creation of the world'

4 The 'moost notable cure' of Sapience is the redemption of man by the Son of God, brought about by the advice of Sapience; see below, lines 498–602.

15 *Clyo*: Clio, one of the nine Muses, the Muse of history. Her aid is also invoked by Chaucer, *Troilus* ii 8–28, and Lydgate, *Troy Book* prologue 40.

19 *and*: Spindler's emendation. 'Hevenly' is invariably disyllabic in this poem.

35 *eche*: 'eke out,' 'extend,' 'amplify'

43–4 Compare the proverb, 'Sweet is sweeter after bitterness,' Whiting S944.

48 *soveraynte*: regularly pronounced as a trisyllable ('sovranty') in the *Court*

50 *Gower*: John Gower (d 1408), the English poet who ranked beside Chaucer in the opinion of their successors. Gower is among those to whom Chaucer's *Troilus* is dedicated.
   Chaucers: This form with final -s is recorded fairly frequently in the fifteenth century; see Caroline F.E. Spurgeon *Five Hundred Years of Chaucer Criticism and Allusion* (Cambridge 1925) 32, 36, 44, 46–8, 50–1.

51 *Ofthyrst of*: 'athirst for'

52 *successoures*: Spindler's emendation; 'successours' C

59 *hastyf dome*: 'initial hostile verdict,' 'hasty judgment'

68 *wyte*: 'blame'

73 *To purpoos late*: 'in my most recent intention,' 'to the new purpose'

75 *sequestracyon*: 'banishment,' 'exile'

78–119 Allegorical chess games are common in medieval literature; this one, like others, probably derives from Chaucer's *Book of the Duchess*, lines 618–64. The belief that chess was originally invented by a philosopher to teach a wicked king just government probably lies behind lines 92–4 of the *Court*; it derives ultimately from Jacobus de Cessolis, *Libellus de moribus hominum et officiis nobilium ac popularium super ludo scachorum* (ca 1290–1300). The queen was a much weaker figure in medieval chess than in modern chess: the modern moves developed at the end of the fifteenth century. See H.J.R. Murray *A History of Chess* (Oxford 1913; reprinted 1969) 529–63, 776–8.

Allegorically, the poet seems to mean that, having decided to 'give youth his head' and seek for enjoyment in life, he is in the position of the chess-player who wants to move his king without taking care of the pawns that block his way. When he thinks about the complexities of the game of life and his own lack of knowledge of the proper subordination of pleasures, he realizes that worldly happiness is controlled by Dame Fortune and he is driven to pray for wisdom. As in Boethius, the question, What is true happiness? is answered by Wisdom.

78, 84 *drawen, draught*: 'To draw' in this sense is 'to make a move' at chess, and a draught is a move; see *OED*, *draw* 73; *draught* 21.

80 *aulfyn*: This word derives from Arabid 'al-fil,' 'the elephant,' the name of the chess piece now called the bishop; see *OED*, *alfin*.

83 *eschekker*: 'chessboard'

93 *dyversyte*: This word could be pronounced with either three or four syllables in the fifteenth century. *MED* records the spellings *diversitee* and *diverste*; compare lines 1247, 1273, below.

99–103 In TH a Latin note to these lines is given; in T it runs as follows:

Policia secundum Aristotilem et Arnulphum (*De divisione scienciarum*), et Kylwarbi (*De ortu scienciarum*), et Isidorum dividitur in monasticam, iconomicam, et civilem, que authonomatice politica nominatur seu nuncupatur. Monastica ad regimen unius tantum pertinet, iconomica ad regimen famulie, politica ad regimen subditorum civitatis. Et hec politica continetur in tribus preceptis juris, que sunt: 'honeste vivere,' 'alterum non ledere sed juvare,' 'jus suum unicuique tribuere' (Justinianus *De justo et justicia et jure* civilis juris precepta).

Politics, according to Aristotle, Arnulphus (*On the Division of the Sciences*), Kylwardby (*On the Rise of the Sciences*), and Isidore, is divided into monastica, oeconomica, and civilis; the last of these is also called or named by this same name politica. Monastica refers to the self-government of a single man, oeconomica to the government of a household, and politica to the government of the subjects of a state. This same politica is contained in the three precepts of the law, which are: 'Live honestly,' 'Hurt no man, but help him,' and 'Give everyone his due' (Justinian [*Institutes* I i *Of Justice and Law*] the maxims of civil law).

This division of politics into three parts derives ultimately from Aristotle, *Nicomachean Ethics* I and *Politics* I; it is conveniently expressed in Isidore, *Etymologiae* II xxiv 16, where the terms 'moralis,' 'dispensativa,' and 'civilis' are employed. Robert Kilwardby (d 1272; see *DNB*) uses the terms 'monastica,' 'yconomica,' and 'pollitica' in his *De ortu scienciarum* (ms Merton, Coxe 261, f 69r). The same manuscript contains a work ascribed to Arnulphus Provincialis, entitled *De divisione scientiarum*; Lynn Thorndike and Pearl Kibre maintain that this is the same work as that of Kilwardby (see *A Catalogue of Incipits of Medieval Scientific Writings in Latin* rev ed [Cambridge, Mass 1963] cols 330, 1497). It is, however, clear from the length of the work of Arnulphus (six folios) that, if his work is related to Kilwardby's, it must be only an extract or abridgment. See the recent edition of Kilwardby, *De ortu scientiarum* ed A.C. Judy (Oxford and Toronto 1976).

110 All of the witnesses agree on this line. *DOST* records the forms 'againis' and 'aganist' for 'ayenst'; *Sir Gawain and the Green Knight*, 971, 1661, has 'ayaynes.' Such a pronunciation would account for the metre of this line and also lines 431, 1291, 2274.

114 *moble*: 'movable,' 'fickle,' 'unsteadfast'

116 *man*: 'chessman'

117 *a poynt*: C; 'oo poynt' TH; 'one poynt' P. These variants indicate that the author of the *Court* came from a northern region in which 'one' or 'ane' was used both for the indefinite article and the numeral. The witnesses are all southern and have chosen one or the other meaning. Similarly, in line 83, 'In one eschekker' might be read 'in an eschekker.'

137 Matt 7:14: 'How narrow is the gate and strait is the way that leadeth to life ...' *encomerous*: probably trisyllabic, as in the spelling 'encombrouse' in T

145 *Quyete*: Latin 'quies,' like the obsolete English meaning of 'quiet,' meant freedom from work or occupation; hence, the River Quyete stands for the opposite of 'dredeful worldly occupacyon' (line 163). The author may have had the closely associated Latin word 'requies' in mind; in the account of the exploits performed by Wisdom for the Israelites (Wisd 10–11) the image of the 'fountain of an ever-running river' occurs: 'They were thirsty ... and water was given them out of the high rock, and a refreshment [requies] of their thirst out of the hard stone' (Wisd 11:4, 7).

146–58 In TH a Latin note is added to these stanzas; in T it runs as follows (words in square brackets are supplied from H):

Sapiencia est res virtutis, Dei cognicio. Sapiens divinitatem rimatur, sed prudens ea que corporis sensubus experitur; vel sapiens in divinis, prudens in humanis; vel sapiencia secundum quosdam philosophos est rerum divinarum humanarumque sciencia. Et sic sapiencia, que juris prudencia, est rerum divinarum et humanarum noticia, justi et injusti sciencia (Justinianus *De justicia et jure* '[juris] prudencia'). Differunt tamen sapiencia, intellectus, et prudencia, quia sapiencia valet ad solius eterne veritatis contemplacionem et delectacionem, intellectus vel intelligencia ad creature vel creaturarum invisibilium speculacionem, sciencia ad rectam administracionem rerum temporalium et ad bonam inter malos conversacionem.

Et qualiter intellectus, sciencia, et sapiencia, qui [or 'que'] sunt dona Spiritus Sancti, differunt ab intellectu, sciencia, et sapiencia que sunt naturaliter in anima, vide per doctores et per Januensem, in suo *Catholicon* in verbo *sapiencia*.

Wisdom is a matter of virtue, the knowledge of God. The wise man searches into divinity, whereas the prudent man inquires into those things which are experienced by the bodily senses; or again, the wise man deals with divine things, the prudent one with human things; or again, according to some philosophers, wisdom is the knowledge of things both divine and human. Thus the kind of wisdom which is jurisprudence is defined as 'the knowledge of things divine and human, the science of the just and the unjust' (Justinian [*Institutes* I i] *Of Justice and Law* 'jurisprudence'). But wisdom, intellect, and prudence differ in that wisdom serves the contemplation of, and delight in, Eternal Truth alone; intellect or intelligence serves the contemplation of creation and invisible created beings; and science [or 'prudence'] serves the right administering of temporal things and the proper mode of living amongst the evil. And for the way in which the intellect, science, and wisdom which are the gifts of the Holy Spirit differ from the intellect, science, and wisdom which are in the soul by nature, see in the doctors and in Balbus, *Catholicon* sv *sapientia*.

The author takes these definitions of wisdom directly from the *Catholicon* of Balbus, except for the definition of jurisprudence, which he adds from Justinian's *Institutes*. Balbus uses the term 'doctores' vaguely, to mean any learned authority; when he has a specific source, he usually gives a more precise reference.

147 Beside this line in TH is written, 'Nota differenciam inter sapienciam, intellectum, et scienciam': 'Note the difference between wisdom, intellect, and science.

157–8 In TH, 'Nota quid est sapiencia,' 'Note what wisdom is,' is written beside this passage.

160 Possibly a reference to Prov 8:23: 'I [Wisdom] was set up from eternity, and of old before the earth was made.'

161 The Latin version of this proverb ('In senibus viget sapiencia') is given in the margin in TH.

162–3 In the margins of TH is written: 'Here discriveth the auctor the ferefull place thorough whyche the auctor came and lykenyth the place to the world.'

164–6 Possibly a reference to Prov 8:34–5, where Wisdom says, 'Blessed is the man that heareth me, and that watcheth daily at my gates, and waiteth at the posts of my doors. He that shall find me shall find life, and shall have salvation from the Lord.'

176 In T, 'Hic incipit processus hujus tractatus' is written beside this line. Both H and T give an English translation: 'Here tellith Sapience the proces of hir labour and eke hir besynesse' (H version).

For the story of the daughters of God, see introduction, pages xxvii–xxxii. *Rex et famulus* PL 94, col 505:

Fuit quidam paterfamilias, rex potens, qui quatuor filias habuit ... habebat etiam quemdam filium sapientissimum ... habebat etiam quemdam famulum servum, quem exaltaverat,

quem multo honore ditaverat ... dedit ei leve mandatum, dicens, 'Istud mandatum si custod-
ieris, ampliori honore honoraberis, si non pessima morte morieris.' Famulus, sumpto man-
dato domini sui haud mora transgressus est illud mandatum.

There was a powerful king, the ruler of a household, who had four daughters ... he also had a
very wise son ... He had, too, a certain household servant, whom he raised up and enriched
with much honour ... He gave to the servant an easy commandment, saying, 'If you keep
this commandment, you will be honoured with greater honours; if you do not, you will die
the worst sort of death.' The servant received the commandment of his lord, and, without
delay, broke it.

183–6 *Rex et famulus*:

Dominus ... quatuor vocavit tortores saevissimos, uni illorum praecipiens ut eum incarcer-
aret, alteri ut vivum decoriaret [Paris, ms lat. 5556, ed Creek; 'decollaret' PL text], tertio ut
eum jugularet, quarto ut eum devoraret.

The lord called to him four very cruel torturers, and bade one of them to imprison the
servant, the second to flay him alive, the third to kill him, and the fourth to devour him.

The four torturers are explained at lines 794–7 below.
188 TH have a note of the Latin names of the four daughters: Misericordia, Veritas,
Justicia, et Pax.
189–96 *Rex et famulus*:

Has vero famuli poenas audiens una de filiabus regis, scilicet Misericordia, veloci cursu currit
ad carcerem et introspiciens vidensque famulum tortoribus mancipatum, poenis affectum,
non potuit non misereri, quia Misericordiae proprium est misereri, laceratis ergo vestibus et
complosis manibus expansisque per colla capillis, ululans et clamans recurrit ad patrem et
ingeniculata ante pedes paternos, coepit simplici et gemebunda voce dicere ...

One of the king's daughters, namely Mercy, heard of the servant's penalties and ran swiftly
to the prison. When she looked in and saw the servant given up to the torturers, afflicted
with penalties, she was unable to refrain from mercy, because it is the property of Mercy to
be merciful. Therefore she tore her garments, beat her hands, scattered her hair upon her
neck, and ran crying and calling to her father; she knelt before his feet and began to say
openly, sighing as she spoke ...

197ff Mercy's speech is full of echoes of the Psalms and phrases from the liturgy. The
opening phrase suggests Ps 145:8 (Vulg 144:8): 'Miserator et misericors Dominus; patiens, et multum misericors' ('The Lord is gracious and merciful: patient
and plenteous in mercy').
  Mercy makes only one short speech in *Rex et famulus*; it is quoted in the introduction above, note 61.
198 One of the *Court's* rare examples of a Lydgatian type D (or 'headless') line; see
introduction, page xviii.

199 In TH the Latin version of this line, 'Cuius misericordie non est numerus,' is written in the margin; the phrase occurs in prayers in the Mass for the Dead. See *The Sarum Missal* 435, 438, 460.

201 The Latin of this line, 'Deus, cui proprium est misereri,' is also provided in the margins of TH. It is the opening phrase of prayers occurring in the Mass for the Dead (see *The Sarum Missal* 431, 438, 442n) and of one of the Orationes pro peccatis (prayers for sin) in the Sarum Use, which has been included among the 'Prayers and Thanksgivings' of the *Book of Common Prayer*: 'O God, whose nature and property is ever to have mercy and to forgive, receive our humble petitions ...' See *The Annotated Book of Common Prayer* ed J.H. Blunt (London 1869) 63 and note.

204 Ps 145:9 (Vulg 144:9): 'Suavis Dominus universis; et miserationes ejus super omnia opera ejus' ('The Lord is sweet to all: and his tender mercies are over all his works'). 'Misericordia Domini super omnia opera ejus' is written in the margins of TH.

208 Perhaps a reference to Ps 90:14 (Vulg 89:14): 'Repleti sumus mane misericordia tua' ('We are filled in the morning with thy mercy').

216 *in distraynte*: This is the reading of all three witnesses; but the noun 'distraint,' a legal term meaning 'restraint of liberty,' 'constraint,' is not recorded in MED, DOST, or OED before 1730. Either the poet borrowed the term from law French, or the witnesses are united in error, all reading 'in' for 'is.' The verb 'distreinen,' 'to restrain, take hold of, torment,' is quite common; reading 'is' for 'in,' the line would mean, 'My throat is tormented with sighs.'

224–35 *Rex et famulus*:

Taliter illa apud patrem argumentante, advenit soror ejus Veritas, et cur Misericordia fleret quaesivit a patre. Cui pater: 'Ista, inquit, soror tua Misericordia vult ut ego miserear illius superbi transgressoris cui poenam indixi.'

While she was asserting this before her father, her sister Truth came in and asked her father why Mercy was weeping. Her father said to her, 'Your sister Mercy wants me to have mercy on that proud traitor whose penalty I have pronounced.'

232 *pyteous*: to be pronounced as a disyllable throughout the *Court*, as in the spelling *pytous*, line 618

236 In *Rex et famulus* Truth is described as 'admodum stomachata,' 'very angry,' when she makes her reply.

238 *for any sute*: 'in spite of any petition,' 'disregarding all entreaty.' See OED, *for* 23; *suit* 11.

250 There seems to be one syllable too many in this line in all witnesses. Spindler suggests that there is an elision between 'unworthy ys.' OED records a not uncom-

mon medieval form of unworthy, *unworth*, which suggests that the line originally may have read 'unworth is that assent.'

253–6 The following note to this stanza is provided in TH:

> 'Misericordia Domini ab eterno, et usque in eternum manet.' Unde propheta, 'Domine, in celo misericordia et veritas tua usque ad nubes circuit orbem terrarum'; in psalmo, 'Quia magna super celos est misericordia et usque ad nubes veritas tua.'

> [Ps 103:17 (Vulg 102:17)]: 'But the mercy of the Lord is from eternity and unto eternity.' Whence the prophet [David] says [Ps 36:5 (Vulg 35:6)], 'O Lord, thy mercy is in heaven: and thy truth goes about the globe of the earth even to the clouds'; and in the Psalm [Ps 108:4 (Vulg 107:5)], 'For thy mercy is great above the heavens: and thy truth even unto the clouds.'

The distortion of the quotation from Psalm 36 has come about because the author of this note to the *Court* transcribed the Biblical verse from pseudo-Bonaventura (page 512) and inadvertently included the three words, 'circuit orbem terrarum' ('goes about the globe of the earth'), that form the beginning of the next sentence in pseudo-Bonaventura's version of the story.

258 *yone*: a northern form in ME and ModE. See Karl Brunner *An Outline of Middle English Grammar* 64.

263 'Truth seeks no herns (corners)' was a fairly well-known medieval proverb; see Whiting T512. A Latin version, 'Veritas non querit angulos,' is found in the margins of TH. *Legenda aurea* (page 183) contains another version: 'Veritas angulos non amat' ('Truth loves not corners'); and Balbus, *Catholicon* sv *clericus*, has 'Veritas angulum non habet.' This line may also contain a reference to the proverb, 'Truth is plain' (Whiting T503).

In TH a quotation from Ps 117:2 (Vulg 116:2) is also written in the margin: 'Veritas Domini manet in eternum' ('The truth of the Lord remaineth for ever').

267 'Quia non frangit votum qui mutat in melius' is written beside this line in TH. Including this saying, the sense of this difficult stanza might be given as follows:

> Even if you are thinking that God would not be breaking his word by exchanging vengeance for mercy, because of the principle that 'he does not break a vow who changes it for a better one,' you forget that God is one and consistent with himself. You would be requiring, at the least, that God be considered both ignorant of the future [since he gave a command and did not know that it would be broken], and hasty in judgment [since he promised a punishment and then remitted it]. You would deny to the same God both providence and foreknowledge [since the opposites, ignorance and foreknowledge, rashness and providence, cannot exist in the same subject]. Then, I might well ask, why did he command something when it would have been better if he had not done so?

The rules about exchanging vows may be found in Canon Law; see *Decretales*

Gregorii ix Lib ii, tit xxiv, ca iii: 'Non enim propositum aut promissum infringit qui in melius illud commutat' (Friedberg ii, col 360).

274 Pseudo-Bonaventura *Meditationes* ii 512: 'Ut quid ergo, Domine, me fecisti?' Pseudo-Bonaventura is summarizing St Bernard (ed Leclercq,24, line 10): ' "Utquid ergo," ait Misericordia, "utquid me genuisti pater, citius perituram?" ' (' "Why then," said Mercy, 'why then did you beget me, father, if I am to die so soon?" ')

280 Bühler (page 20) remarks upon the impropriety of Mercy's claim that the angels need her: 'The fallen angels ... were considered beyond the mercy of God ... it is clearly evident that the author, although not heretical, is at least unsound in his theological views.' Pseudo-Bonaventura repeats a statement from St Bernard (24, line 6) which may have given rise to this irregular view, 'Eget miseratione creatura rationalis' ('The rational creature needs mercy'). Mercy has already quoted this in lines 251–2; since angels are rational creatures too, she may just be expanding that statement here. It is also possible that the angels need Mercy because the divine mercy is necessary for the restoration of their ranks; see below, lines 652–72.

281 *adnychylate*: 'annihilated'

283 *royalme*: Caxton's most usual spelling for P's 'reaume' and T's 'reame'; he also uses 'reame,' 'royame,' and 'realme.' It is always monosyllabic. See *OED*, realm, royalme.

292–328 Justitia or Righteousness is barely mentioned in pseudo-Bonaventura and does not speak; in *Rex et famulus* she hears Misericordia and Veritas quarrelling and asks Veritas the reason. When she has heard the cause, she turns to her father 'inflato [or "inflammato"] vultu,' 'with enraged [or "inflamed"] countenance,' and makes a speech that parallels closely those of Misericordia and Veritas: 'Am I not thy daughter Justice, and art thou not called Just? ...'

304–7 See Gen 2:8, 1:28–30.

325 *subjecte to servytute*: '[now] subjected to slavery'

329–92 Pax (Peace) does not speak in *Rex et famulus*; in pseudo-Bonaventura she says only, 'Parcite vobis a verbis istis; virtutum non est honesta contentio' ('Don't say such things; it isn't fit for virtues to quarrel'). She is, however, clearly on Misericordia's side.

331 *patron of portature*: 'pattern for portraiture' – that is, ideal in beauty, 'let him paint her who can.'

332–3 The 'kiss of peace' was exchanged by priest and congregation during mass in the Middle Ages, a practice still found in some modern churches, although in the modern mass, members of the congregation usually shake hands.

336 *perfyte*: In ME this word could be stressed on the last syllable; see *OED*, perfect.

344–5 The Latin of this, 'Omne regnum in se divisum desolabitur,' is written in the margins of TH. It is a quotation from Matt 12:25, 'Every kingdom divided against itself shall be made desolate.'

349–50 In TH the Latin version of the same principle is written beside these lines: 'Pene pocius molliende sunt quam exasperande, De legibus et senatus vl. interpretacione.' The precise reference here is obscure; it may be that the titulus *De legibus et senatus consultis*, Justinian *Digesta* I 3, is intended, but this quotation does not appear there, although there are statements of similar import. The quotation does, however, appear in several other places: it may be found in *Digesta* xlviii xix 42; in Gratianus *Decretum* ii, causa xxxiii, qu 3, dist 1, ca 18 (Friedberg i, col 1162); and in Henry de Bracton *De legibus et consuetudinibus Angliae* ed G.E. Woodbine, trans S.E. Thorne, ii 299.

354–5 Beside these lines in TH is the following note: 'Nota hic stilum qualiter Deus vocatur princeps pacis, auctor pietatis, rex misericordie et Deus ['Dominus' H] bonitatis' ('Note this form of address, how God is called the Prince of peace, the Source of holiness, the King of mercy, and the God [or "Lord"] of goodness'). 'The Prince of peace' is the title foretold of the saviour in Isa 9:6; Mercy addresses her father by this title in line 210 above. See also line 897.

style: the proper title of a sovereign, which lists his dominions; after his victory at Bosworth in 1485 Henry vii styled himself 'Henry, by the grace of God, King of England and of France, Prince of Wales, and Lord of Ireland.'

357 A difficult line. TH read 'aquayle'; CP read 'batayle.' 'Aquayle' is perhaps a form of the verb 'aquellen,' meaning 'to slay, destroy, ruin' (see *MED*), although the vowel change is hard to account for. 'Perysshe' in its obsolete transitive meaning, 'to destroy, kill, wreck,' would then be a parallel verb, and the whole line would mean something like 'Strife and conflict destroy and ruin all things.' If 'aquayle' is derived from the verb 'quail' with the intensive prefix a-, it is not recorded elsewhere; it would give the perhaps better sense, 'Peace must reign; strife and conflict must pass away and come to nothing.'

358–9 In H a marginal note draws attention to this commendation of good kingdoms: 'Nota commendacionem bonorum regnorum.' Compare Ps 76:2 (Vulg 75:3): 'In pace factus est locus ejus' ('And his place is in peace').

369 *apryce*: 'value,' 'excellence.' See *OED*, aprice; *MED*, apprise. For this proverb, see Whiting s943.

383–5 'But Mercy, by her very nature, has no raison d'être without sin to pardon, and she derives all her power from pardoning sin, just as the moon derives her light from the sun.' See *OED*, property 5: 'an essential, special, or distinctive quality'; also *OED*, propriety 3.

yeveth: usually monosyllabic in the *Court*; see introduction, page xix.

389–91 A Latin proverb deriving originally from Sallust, *Bellum Jugurthinum* x 6: 'Nam concordia parvae res crescunt, discordia maxumae dilabuntur' ('For harmony makes small states great, while discord undermines the mightiest empires'). The Latin ('Concordia parve res crescunt, Discordia vero multa dilabuntur') is given in the margins of TH but assigned to 'Jeronimus'; this probably indicates that the author found the proverb in Balbus, *Catholicon* sv *pax*, where it is also ascribed to St Jerome.

414 In T there is a marginal note to this line which runs, 'Here declareth Sapience the processe of thys book of the whyche she spake of before.'

422 'Pierced through with bitter sickness'

424 *swonyd*: Caxton also spells this word 'swouned' (line 429). It is monosyllabic, 'swound,' a form of 'swoune,' which is represented by THP's 'sowne, swoune,' 'a swoon.' See *OED*, *swound*.
lytergye: a 'lethargy'; the word was used by medieval physicians to describe a comatose or insensible state, a swoon.

425 *extasye*: a stunned state of shock or bewilderment

425–97 There is no trace of Peace's farewell and exile in St Bernard and pseudo-Bonaventura; the author of the *Court* is here developing the hint given in *Rex et famulus* (PL 94, col 506A):

'And the maiden Astraea, last of the immortals, left the bloodstained earth' [Ovid *Metamorphoses* i 150], that is to say, Peace fled away to a distant region, for where there is strife and contention, there there is no peace.

The lament of Peace contains a number of formal rhetorical figures; I have named those which are described in the third section of Balbus' *Catholicon*.

428 The repetition of the word 'mercy' at the beginning and end of the line is a modified version of the figure epanalensis (the same word used at the beginning and end of a sentence).

430 The play upon the names of Trouthe and Right is the figure paronomasia.

431 See line 110n.

440 *clyppes*: 'eclipse'

441 The sharp contrast within this line is the rehetorical figure Balbus calls antitheca.
refuse: 'outcast'

442ff In TH a note on the angelic hierarchies accompanies these lines. In T it runs as follows:

Nomina angelorum. Tres sunt jerarchie, in qualibet jerarchia sunt tres ordines: in prima jerarchia sunt Cherubin, Seraphin, et Troni; in secunda sunt Dominaciones, Virtutes, et Potestates; in tercia sunt Principatus, Archangeli, et Angeli. Et dicitur 'jerarchia' a 'jeror' quod est 'sacrum,' et 'archos' quod est 'princeps,' quasi 'sacer principatus.' Hec ponit Dionisius.

The names of the angels. There are three hierarchies, and in each of the hierarchies there are three orders. In the first hierarchy there are Cherubim, Seraphim, and Thrones; in the second there are Dominions, Virtues, and Powers; in the third there are Principalities, Archangels, and Angels. And 'hierarchy' is derived from 'jeror' which means 'holy' and 'archos' which means 'prince'; hence it means 'holy principality.' This is from Dionysius.

Dionysius is pseudo-Dionysius the Areopagite (fifth century), author of a Greek treatise on the orders of angels called, in an early Latin translation, *De coelesti hierarchia*. When the *Court* was written, it was believed that this Dionysius was a contemporary of St Paul, and his works enjoyed great prestige in consequence. The note in TH probably derives more directly from Balbus, *Catholicon* sv *angelus*, where the information is attributed to Dionysius. The etymology of 'hierarchy' is given in the *Catholicon* sv *gerarcha*. However, all this information is also given in much the same words in *Legenda aurea* (page 644). See also below, lines 617–700 and notes.

442–5 These lines constitute a formal apostrophe to the angelic orders.

448 Balbus calls the immediate repetition of a word an epizensis.

449–52 These lines display the figure exclamatio.

453 *overset*: disyllabic; see introduction, page xix.

461 *sute*: The meaning here is obscure. Pees is saying that 'jugement may have no sute' unless it is carried out for the sake of peace. 'Sute' may be in the sense of 'legal process' (*OED*, *suit* 10), although it seems odd that Pees should argue that 'jugement' (rather than 'Sothfastnes' and 'Ryghtwysenes') should have no case; 'validity' would be a better meaning, but it is not recorded.

463–9 *Woo worth*: 'a curse upon,' 'may evil befall.'
These lines are a good (and much imitated) example of the figure anaphora combined with exclamatio: one is the repetition of the same words at the beginning of successive lines; the other is an exclamatory outcry of sorrow or joy. For this stanza, see introduction, pages xxiii–xxiv.

470–2 In H the Latin names of the seven planets are written in the margin: 'Saturnus, Jupiter, Mars, Sol, Venus, Mercurius, et Luna.'
Anaphora is also extensively used in this stanza.

472 This line makes use of the figure antonomasia: the moon is described, not named.

474–92 For the material in these lines the author is drawing on the entries in Balbus, *Catholicon* sv *Jupiter*, *cometa*. The planet Mars shared the inflammatory characteristics of Mars, the classical god of war.

475 *Jupyter*: Balbus records that the planet Jupiter is responsible for storms, thunder, and lightning on earth. These effects are aggravated when Jupiter is in conjunction with Mars; see below, lines 484–90.

477–8 Peace is using a metaphora.

481–3 The planet Mars is the lord of battles, and a comet is a sign of war, the death of princes, and confusion in the land. Balbus explains that both Mars and the comet are hot and dry and have an incendiary effect on mankind; this gives rise to wrath and tumults on earth.

484 Flora is the goddess of flowers; hence this whole line means 'in Spring.' The figure
is called periphrasis.
rydeth: The variant reading of HT is 'laughith,' indicating that 'rydeth' is derived
from Latin 'ridere,' 'to smile, laugh,' It is not otherwise recorded in English. It
must be monosyllabic: see introduction, page xix.

485–90 Balbus *Catholicon* sv *Jupiter*: 'Jupiter has the property of arousing very
powerful dry winds, especially when his power is in conjunction with Mars in the
northern signs [in signis aquilonaribus] in summertime. Then it can be predicted
with certainty that there will be much thunder and lightning in the air, so that
there will, in addition, be danger to men from the pestilence of the air. This
pestilence arises from the air's excessive corruption by the burning and pestiferous
vapours mixed with it: Jupiter, together with the sun, raises such vapours, and
Mars corrupts them by burning, and so the air becomes poisonous.'

486 *june*: 'join'; in this case, 'to come into conjunction'; see MED, *joinen* 7(d).
Aquylone: here, presumably 'the northern region of the sky'; see the Latin in the
preceding note.

489 Such a listing of opposites in one line is known as an antitheton.
This line is metrically a Lydgatian type D or 'headless' line; see introduction, page
xviii.

520 *incomerous*: 'difficult'; see MED, *encombrous*.

526–39 T has the note: 'Here speketh the kyngis sone to Sapience.'

533–5 The Latin is supplied in the margin of T: 'Pater est omnipotens, Filius est
sapiens, Spiritus Sanctus, pius, bonus, clemens' ('The Father is almighty, the Son
is wise, the Holy Spirit is gracious, good, and merciful').
    The association of these three qualities with the three persons of the Trinity is
very old: Bühler, *Sources of the Court of Sapience* 34, suggests that it goes back to
Origen (third century). An elaborate exposition of the idea is contained in Hugh of
St Victor, *De sacramentis Christianae fidei*, especially in i ii 6–7. Balbus *Catholicon* sv *pecco*, discusses these qualities in relation to man's sins. See also below,
lines 565–95 and notes.

535–6 The syntax of these lines is not clear. The most natural sense would be to take
'the blessyd hevenly lyght of al godenes' as the object of 'hath'; but P reads 'And'
for 'Of' (CT) in 535, and 'lux beatissima' ('most blessed light') is a periphrasis of
the Holy Ghost in the Sequence for Pentecost, so 'And al godenes the Blessyd
Hevenly Light, / The Holy Ghoost, hath to his propyrte' is also possible.

538 The metre of this line is defective in all three witnesses; a syllable is missing in the
last foot. Spindler suggests 'may thys acorde [well] make.' Perhaps 'accord' should
be emended to 'accordaunce' or 'accordement,' both of which mean a 'formal
agreement of reconciliation.'

539 *treuse take*: 'arrange the truce,' 'make peace'; see OED, *take* 54. The spelling of
TP, 'trewes' or 'trewis,' suggests that the word is to be read as a disyllable.

547–53 In T a long Latin note follows line 546. The first part of it runs as follows (the rest of the note has been moved in this edition to lines 554n and 582n):

Nota quod Sapiencia probat triplici racione quod filius, non pater nec spiritus sanctus, erat redempturus genus humanum. Prima racio quia, ut dicit Bernardus in quodam sermone mellifluo de incarnacione filii 1. 9. [?] cardinalis Bonaventure, 'quod misericordia et veritas et virtutes predicte concesserunt precipue in persona filii; nam persona patris aliqualiter videtur terribilis, et sic suspicari quodammodo potuissent pax et misericordia; persona spiritus sancti benignissima et sic suspicari poterant veritas et justicia. Unde persona filii tanquam media persona accepta est michi in remedium fiendum.'

Note that Sapience proves with three reasons that the Son, not the Father nor the Holy Spirit, must be the redeemer of the human race. The first reason is that which St Bernard gives in a sweet sermon on the incarnation of the Son, quoted by Cardinal Bonaventura: 'Mercy and Truth and the other virtues agreed chiefly on the person of the Son, for the person of the Father seems in some manner stern, and thus Peace and Mercy could have mistrusted him in some degree; the person of the Holy Spirit seems most gentle, and thus Truth and Justice could have mistrusted him. Hence the person of the Son, as a mean between them, was acceptable to me as the remedy.'

This quotation comes from pseudo-Bonaventura, *Meditationes* ii 512. The author of the *Court* is wrong in ascribing it to St Bernard: it comes from the sentence immediately following pseudo-Bonaventura's long quotation from Bernard.

554–60 The marginal note in T to these lines runs:

Secunda racio quare oportet filium genus humanum redimere et sorores concordare. Scutum patris: omnipotencia; scutum filii: sapiencia; scutum spiritus sancti: bonitas sive clemencia.

The second reason why the Son must be the redeemer of mankind and reconcile the sisters. The shield of the Father is omnipotence; the shield of the Son is wisdom; the shield of the Holy Spirit is goodness or clemency.

This is expanded in the second part of the long note written beneath line 546 in T, which runs as follows:

Secunda racio: Adam percussit personam secundam, cui appropriatur [Spindler's emendation; 'appropriatus' T] sapiencia, in medio celestis exercitus (ie in medio trinitatis), cum voluit Deo per sapienciam comparari. Et quia sic scutum suum Dei sapientiam affectando percussit, ideo ipsum filium ad modum militis respondere oportebat, ipsum redimendo et quod in eum commissum fuerat penitus dimittendum. Hec doctores.

The second reason: Adam struck at the second person, to whom wisdom is assigned, in the midst of the celestial army (ie the Trinity), when he wished to be like God in wisdom. And because he struck the Son's shield in aspiring to the wisdom of God, it behoved the Son, in the fashion of a knight, to respond by redeeming him, discharging utterly what had been done against him. This is in the doctors of the Church.

I do not know the origin of this quotation. The reason derives from the rules of chivalry: striking a shield was a conventional way of expressing a challenge. Man challenged God, not for power or love, but for wisdom ('... you shall be as gods, knowing good and evil,' Gen 3:5); hence it must be the Son who responds. Similar accounts of the three shields of the Trinity and the challenge to God are found in Robert Holcot, *Moralitas ix*, and *Gesta Romanorum* ed H. Oesterley, cxiii 454–5.

561–7 *Tercia racio quare*: 'The third reason why' is written in the margin in T beside this stanza, but a much longer Latin note about the third reason follows line 602. As it seems to belong more properly at this point, it is given here:

Tercia racio quare secunda persona (scilicet filius Dei) erat redempturus genus humanum: quia terra de qua Adam formatus erat erat incorrupta et virgo, quia nec se ad bibendum humanum sanguinem apparuerat, nec ma勒勒勒勒... maylediccionem spinarum accepit, nec hominis mortui sepulturam habebat, nec serpenti fuerat ad edendum. Oportuit ergo ex virgine Maria novum Adam fieri juxta historiam: 'Ecce virgo concipiet et pariet filium etc.' Ut sicut serpens natum ex virgine vicerat, sic a nato de virgine vinceretur. Cum ergo qui redimet genus humanum filius esset virginis incarnatus et nisi unicus in trinitate est, ipsum ergo filium, non patrem nec spiritum sanctum, oportuit incarnari et generis humani facere redempcionem. Hanc racionem ponit Silvester, ut in vita eius cantum est.

The third reason why the second person, namely the Son of God, was to be the redeemer of mankind: because the earth of which Adam was made was uncorrupted and virgin, because it had not drunk human blood, nor had it received the curse of bearing thorns [Gen 3:18], nor had it become the sepulchre of man, nor was it to be eaten by the serpent [Gen 3:14]. Therefore it was necessary for the new Adam to be born of the virgin Mary, according to the account [Isa 7:14]: 'Behold, a virgin shall conceive and bear a son, etc.' And as the serpent overcame one born of a virgin, so it should itself be overcome by one born of a virgin. Since therefore he who is to be the redeemer of mankind has to be a son incarnate of a virgin, and there is only one Son in the Trinity, therefore the Son himself, not the Father nor the Holy Spirit, must be incarnate and bring about the redemption of the human race. Silvester gives this reason; it is in the story of his life.

This passage ('terra ... vinceretur') is a quotation from the life of St Silvester in *Legenda aurea* (page 75). Hugh of St Victor develops the argument that there may be only one Son in Trinity in *De sacramentis*, II i 2: 'The Son of God was made Son of Man that He might make sons of men sons of God, and that the name of son might not pass over to another person, and there be two sons in the Trinity and the distinction of the Trinity be confused' (trans Deferrari, 206).

568 T notes: 'Here speketh the auctor of the boke to Sapience askyng oon question.'

582–95 The marginal note in T runs: 'Here rehersyd ys the cause that in kynde, wherfor the Fadyr in Trinite ys clepyd myghty, the Son wytty, the Holy Gost full of goodnes – that hit be nat supposyd the same in the Trinite that ys in kynde.'

A more detailed explanation is given in the third part of the Latin note written under line 546 in T, which runs as follows:

Nota quod in rerum natura patres solent debiles esse et impotentes, non ita creditur in trinitate; et ideo appropriato vocabulo patri attribuitur omnipotencia. Filii solent esse insipientes quia juvenes; et ne putetur hoc in trinitate, ideo attribuitur filio sapiencia. Spiritus est nomen crudelitatis et erroris [tumoris?], ne ergo credatur in trinitate, ideo appropriato vocabulo attribuitur spiritui sancto bonitas, pietas, sive clemencia. Tamen in potencia, bonitate, sapientia sunt equales, consubstanciales pater et filius et spiritus sanctus.

Note that in the nature of things fathers are usually feeble and powerless, but this is not to be believed of the Father in the Trinity, and therefore omnipotence is appropriately attributed to him. Sons are usually foolish because of their youth, and hence wisdom is the attribute of the Son, lest the same weakness be thought to be in the Trinity. 'Spirit' is a word meaning 'cruelty' or 'error' ['pride'? as in Hugh of St Victor]; so that it should not be thought to be so in the Trinity, goodness, kindness, or clemency are fittingly attributed to the Holy Spirit. Nevertheless, Father, Son, and Holy Spirit are equal and consubstantial in power, goodness, and wisdom.

This theory of the qualities of the Persons of the Trinity is outlined in Balbus *Catholicon* sv *proprietas*. There is a much more elaborate version of it in Hugh of St Victor, *De sacramentis Christianae fidei* I ii 8, I iii 26. The author of the *Court* is not quoting directly from either of these works.

For 'spirit' in this sense see OED, *spirit* 12, 13; Lewis and Short *spiritus* II A.

592 The metre of this line is defective in all witnesses, although P's 'is in kynde' would work if final -e were sounded. Since final -e is mute everywhere else in the poem, it seems most likely that a syllable has dropped out here. Perhaps 'knyt' was originally 'y-knyt' as in line 1694.

603 *conclude*: This form of the past tense of the verb 'to conclude,' 'to come to a decision,' survives in T but is 'corrected' to 'concluded' in CP. The metre seems to require it, and DOST records the same form in a text of about the same date (Hary's *Wallace*). There are also parallels in *Sir Gawain and the Green Knight*; see the edition by J.R.R. Tolkien and E.V. Gordon: 'Weak verbs having stems in *d* or *t* sometimes do not add any suffix in the past tense or past participle' (page 132). See also *Court*, lines 325, 779, 1671.

607–16 In T a quotation from the beginning of pseudo-Bonaventura is added to the long note written below line 602 (removed in this edition to line 561). The quotation from pseudo-Bonaventura belongs more properly to these stanzas. It runs as follows:

Dicit Bonaventura Cardinalis in libro *De meditacionibus eorum que precedunt incarnacionem Christi*: Quod cum per longissima tempora ultra spacium quattuor milia annorum et amplius miserabiliter jaceret [Spindler's emendation; 'jacere' T] genus humanum, et nullus propter peccatum primi parentis ascendere posset ad patriam, beatissimi angeli spiritus compacientes tante ruine de sua restauracione solliciti, licet eciam pluries primo tamen adveniente plenitudine temporis devocius et instancius totaliter supplicarunt Domino, procedentes in faciem et simul omnes congregati in unum, ut hic canetur in effectu.

Cardinal Bonaventura, in his book *Meditations on the Matters Preceding the Birth of Christ*, says that when mankind had lain in misery for a very long time, four thousand years and more, and no one, because of the sin of our first parent, was able to ascend to our heavenly home, the most blessed angelic spirits felt pity for this great disaster and concern about the restoration of their ranks. They had made supplication to the Lord many times before, but especially when the fullness of time came did they cast themselves on their face, and all together with one voice said what follows in these verses.

The first chapter of pseudo-Bonaventura, *Meditationes vitae Christi*, is entitled 'De meditationibus eorum que precedunt incarnacionem Christi' in some of the early editions. All texts that I have been able to look at give the period of man's exile as five thousand years, instead of the four thousand which the author of the *Court* gives here and in line 666. The figure of four thousand years is not uncommon elsewhere; see, for example, the lyric 'Adam lay I-bowndyn,' *Religious Lyrics of the xvth Century* ed Carleton Brown (Oxford 1939) 120.

607 The author of the *Court* develops the idea of the compassion of the angels for man from pseudo-Bonaventura; see below, lines 607–700 and notes. Pseudo-Bonaventura seems himself to have developed this episode from St Bernard's citation of Isa 33:7: 'angeli pacis amare flebunt' ('the angels of peace shall weep bitterly') ed Leclercq, 23, line 10; Bernard reads 'flebant.'

614 *carybde*: Charybdis, the name of a famous whirlpool on the Sicilian side of the Straits of Messina; see *MED*, *Caribdis*; Balbus *Catholicon* sv *Caribdis* ('*periculum marinum*').

617–22 In T the following note precedes this stanza:

Seraphin, Cherubin, et Troni sunt in prima jerarchia secundum Dionisium. Et hii per assimile tribus potestatibus comparantur, hiis qui immediate operantur circa personam regis, ut cubicularii, consiliarii, et assessores. De secunda jerarchia vide infra.

According to Dionysius, Seraphim, Cherubim, and Thrones are in the first hierarchy. These are compared in likeness to three kinds of powers who perform functions about the person of the king, such as chamberlains, counsellors, and assessors [advisers to a judge]. For the second hierarchy, see below.

As the author says (see lines 673–9n), this quotation comes from the chapter on St Michael in *Legenda aurea* (page 644); and almost the same words are to be found in Balbus *Catholicon* sv *angelus*. Balbus, however, omits the word 'consiliarii.' See also above, lines 442–52.

628-9 The speeches of the hierarchies in the *Court* appear to be elaborated from the speech of the angels in pseudo-Bonaventura (page 511). The words of the first hierarchy develop the idea in the words, 'Mementote quod ad similitudinem vestram creastis eos' ('Remember that you created them [the human race] in your own likeness').

638 The metre of this line seems to be defective in all witnesses.

645-51 In T the following note precedes this stanza:

Dominaciones, Virtutes, et Potestates secundum Dionisium sunt in secunda jerarchia, et simulantur hiis in terrenis potestatibus qui habent officia ad regimen regni in communi, non deputati huic vel illi provincie, ut principes milicie et judices curie. De tercia jerarchia vide infra.

According to Dionysius, Dominions, Virtues, and Powers are in the second hierarchy. These are likened to those earthly powers who hold positions in the government of the realm in general, such as military commanders and justices of the high court, who are not delegated to this or that province. For the third hierarchy, see below.

This quotation is also taken either from *Legenda aurea*, page 644, or Balbus, *Catholicon* sv *angelus*.

652-72 The prayer of the second hierarchy develops the words of pseudo-Bonaventura (page 511):

Domine, placuit majestati vestrae, et rationalem creaturam, scilicet hominem, creare propter vestram bonitatem, ut ipse esset hic nobiscum, et ut nobis ex ipso nostrarum contingeret restauratio ruinarum. Sed ecce pereunt omnes, et nemo salvatur, et in tot annorum curriculis hoc videmus, quod de omnibus hostes nostri triumphant, et de ipsis non nostrae ruinae sed tartareae speluncae replentur. Ut quid ergo, Domine, nascuntur? Quare traduntur bestiis animae confitentes tibi?

O Lord, it pleased your majesty to create, of your goodness, man, a rational creature, to be here with us, and through whom our own fall should be repaired. But, behold, they all perish, and no one is saved; in the course of so many years we have seen that our enemies triumph over all of them, and, instead of repairing our fall, the caves of hell are filled with them. Why, O Lord, were they born? Why are souls confessing you given up to wild beasts? [Ps 73:19 Vulgate only]

657-8 1 Pet 5:8: 'The devil as a roaring lion, goeth about seeking whom he may devour.'
lake: MED, *lake* 3: 'a pit, shaft, hole; a lion pit; the pit of hell.'

673-9 In T the following note precedes this stanza:

Principatus, Archangeli, et Angeli sunt in tercia Jerarchia. Et simulantur hiis in terrenis potestatubus secundum Dionisium qui preponuntur ad regimen alicujus partis regni, ut prepositi et ballivi, et hujusmodi minores officiales. De ista materia vide Dionisium et

Januensem in suo *Catholicon* in verbo angelus; et in *Legenda aurea*, capitulo de Sancto Michaele.

Principalities, Archangels, and Angels are in the third hierarchy. According to Dionysius, they are like the earthly powers who are set in charge of governing some part of the realm, such as captains and bailiffs, and minor officials of this sort. For this material see Dionysius, Balbus (*Catholicon* sv *angelus*), and *Legenda aurea* [cxlv] 'St Michael' [pages 644–5].

680–700 The speech of the third hierarchy develops the theme of the refrain to all three prayers. Pseudo-Bonaventura (page 511):

Et si secundum justitiam vestram hoc fiat, tamen misericordiae tempus est. Et si primi parentes vestrum mandatum incaute transgressi sunt, subveniat misericordia vestra. ... Oculi omnium spectant ad vos, sicut oculi servorum ad manus dominorum suorum, donec misereamini et subveniatis remedio salutari humano generi.

If this is done according to your justice, yet now is the time for mercy. And if the first parents heedlessly broke your commandment, let your mercy remedy it ... The eyes of all look to you, as the eyes of servants to the hands of their masters, until you have mercy [Ps 123:2 (Vulg 122:2)] and provide a remedy to save the human race.

691 Ps 89:49–51 (Vulg 88:50–1): 'Ubi sunt misericordiae tuae antiquae, Domine ... Memor esto, Domine, opprobrii servorum tuorum' ('Lord, where are thy ancient mercies? ... Be mindful, O Lord, of the reproach of thy servants').

694–700 In the margin of T is a slightly altered quotation from Ps 102:13 (Vulg 101:14), which runs as follows: 'Tu exurgens Domine misereberis Sion quia tempus miserendi eius quia tempus venit' ('Thou shalt arise and have mercy on Sion: for it is time to have mercy on it, for the time is come').

698 *playne indulgence*: a plenary indulgence, full remission of the punishment for sin; see *OED, plain* a².

720 A reference to the proverb 'Smite [now 'strike'] while the iron is hot' (Whiting 160).

732–5 On the right of these lines in T is written, 'Here expowneth the autour the text penitet me fecisse hominem.' On the left is the note, 'Penitet me fecisse hominem. Id est, Penitenciam me agere oportet, quia feci hominem' ('It repenteth me that I have made man. That is, I must do penance, because I have made man'). The quotation is a reference to Gen 6:6–7, where God, observing the sins of man, repents of having created him. The author of the *Court* is probably using pseudo-Bonaventura (page 512) at this point; pseudo-Bonaventura is himself abridging St Bernard's slightly longer exposition of the same verse (St Bernard 28, lines 4–6).

745 The variant 'emperyce' in TP is probably to be preferred to C's 'pryncesse'; compare line 1519.

751 *Your lyf, your lust, your love*: C; 'Youre loue youre lust your spouse' TP. TP are probably right. Perhaps the poet was influenced by the language of the Song of Songs, 4:8 to 5:2 ('my sister, my spouse'); the speaker of this passage was identified as Christ in the *Glossa Ordinaria*.

763 *you at lust*: 'according to your wish'; see *MED*, *lust* 1b, 'You' must be an example of the rare use as a possessive, 'your'; see *OED*, *you* 8.

764 *Revygure*: 'revive,' 'be restored to vigour and life'

780 The 'doughter of Syon' is the title given to the mother of the Son of God by St Bernard and pseudo-Bonaventura in reference to the prophetic verse of Zach 9:9: 'Rejoice greatly, O daughter of Sion, shout for joy, O daughter of Jerusalem: behold, thy King will come to thee, the just and Saviour.'

787–8 The syntax is unclear: 'His swete breth' could be either the object of 'enspyre' or the subject of 'gan fille.'

792–8 The Latin note in T to this stanza runs as follows:

> Nota primo homo torquetur in carcere presentis vite; secundo labore et miseria mundi dedecoratur [*originally* 'decoriatur'?]; tercio moritur; quarto quis vermibus devoratur, quia ex quo quis moritur [Spindler's emendation; 'meritur' T] vermibus esca datur. Hec Lincolniensis super 'Misericordia et veritas obviaverunt simul.'

> Note that first, man is tormented in the prison of this present life; secondly, he is disgraced with [flayed by?] the labour and wretchedness of the world; thirdly, he dies; fourthly, he is devoured by worms, since anyone who dies is given as food to worms. Thus says Robert Grosseteste, Bishop of Lincoln, on the text, 'Mercy and truth have met each other.'

> This statement derives most probably from the anonymous *Rex et famulus*, to which it has strong verbal resemblances. The ascription to Grosseteste (d 1253; see *DNB*) may have come about because Grosseteste's most famous work, *Le Chasteau d'Amour*, also contains an account of the four daughters of God.

795 *unhele*: 'sickness,' 'wretchedness,' 'disease'

799–805 A marginal note in T runs: 'Here fulfylleth the Son in hys personne the sentence yeven for mannys syn.'

802 *A monyment*: 'a grave'

809–10 This seems to be a reference to the antiphon 'Salve regina,' where Mary is addressed as 'mater misericordiae,' 'mother of mercy.' See *Analecta Hymnica Medii Aevi* ed Clemens Blume and Guido Dreves (Leipzig 1907) volume 50, pages 318–9. (The editors' note that the word 'mater' is a sixteenth-century interpolation is incorrect: at least two fifteenth-century English lyrics based on the antiphon contain the word; see *Religious Lyrics of the xvth Century* ed Carleton Brown, numbers 25 and 26.) See also the note to lines 827–9 below.

814–19, 883–94 This passage appears to be based on *Rex et famulus*:

[Filius] famulum duplicato honore in patriam reduxit, dans ei stolam immortalitatis. Hos videns Misericordia non habebat unde conquereretur, quia vidit famulum duplicato honore reversum, stola immortalitatis indutum. Veritas non inveniebat causas querelae, quia pater inventus fuerat verax, jam famulus omnes poenas exsolverat. Justitia similiter jam nihil conquerebatur, quia in transgressore fuerat justitia, et sic qui perierat reinventus est. Videns igitur Pax sorores suas concordantes, reversa est et eas pacificavit.

The Son brought the servant home with double honour and gave him the garment of immortality. When she saw these things, Mercy had no reason to complain because she saw the servant return, wearing the garment of immortality. Truth found no cause for complaint because her father was proved to be truthful, now that the servant had fulfilled all his penalties. Justice similarly now complained of nothing because justice had been done on the transgressor. Thus he who had perished was restored. When, therefore, Peace saw her sisters in agreement, she returned and made peace between them.

825–68 Mary's speech interceding for man is not paralleled in either of the known sources. There are, of course, many lyrics in which Mary is besought to intercede for Christ's 'brothers'; see, for example, *Religious Lyrics of the xvth Century* ed Carleton Brown, numbers 11, 13, 15, 19, 25, 35, etc.

827–9 The Latin note to this stanza in T runs as follows:

Hic mater misericordie provocat filium suum Christum ut misereatur homini cum ipsemet homo sit, et omne simile sui similis compati et misereri naturaliter obligatur.

Here the Mother of Mercy calls upon her son Christ to have mercy on man since He himself is man, and everyone has a natural duty to have mercy and compassion on those who resemble him.

This appears to be a reference to the proverb 'like to like,' or 'kind to kind': Whiting L272, K29.

833 The proverb 'Where once is lief let never be loath' is recorded in Whiting L232; see also L562.

834 'Here reherseth Cryst to Mercy how hys moder shall come with Mercy to pray for man yef he offende' T.

839–40 Beside these lines in T is the following statement: 'Nota quanto preciosior est res, tanto et major diligencia servanda est' ('Note that the more precious a thing is, the more carefully should it be kept').

841–7 In T, the following note is written above this stanza:

Nota Christum multiplicem titulum proprietatis habere ad hominem: primo, quia hominem creavit et sic ejus est creator; secundo quia ad imaginem sui creatus est homo et racionem sibi tribuit; tercio quia omne bonum sibi administrat, quia 'omne donum optimum desursum est a patre luminum'; quarto quia hominem dampnatum proprio redemit sanguine.

Note that Christ has a manifold title of ownership in man: firstly, because he created man and is thus his creator; secondly, because man is created in his likeness and owes him his reason; thirdly, because Christ administers all good things, because 'every best gift is from above, from the Father of lights' [James 1:17]; and fourthly because he redeemed man with his own blood when man was condemned.

863 In T, 'Nota bonum verbum' ('Note this good saying') is written beside this line, and again beside line 875.

864 This is a reference to Simeon's prophecy, Luke 2:35.

879–80 *and ofter syth hym kyst / Than tonge can telle*: 'Ofter syth' is an emendation; CT read 'after syth'; P reads 'oft'; P has 'Than' for CT's 'That.' 'Than' seems clearly required by the sense, and in its turn requires a comparative; the variants suggest 'ofter,' 'more often.' For 'syth' ('times'), see *OED, sithe* 4.

895 *owne*: most probably to be read as a disyllable; the usual late-medieval spellings were 'owen' or 'owyn.'

896 *And Ryght and*: Spindler (page 76) argues that the nonsensical T reading, 'And ryghtyng,' suggests a northern exemplar in which the present-participle form ended in -and instead of the southern -ing. The scribe, mechanically changing -ands to -ings throughout, misread the two words 'ryght and' for a participle form, 'ryghtand,' and changed it too.

The speech of Sapience ends at this line. The concluding stanza of the first book is the narrator's epilogue.

Explicit: 'Here ends the first book of *The Court of Sapience*: how "Mercy and Truth have met each other: Justice and Peace have kissed" [Ps 85:10 (Vulg 84:11)].'

In T, the Latin version of this verse is also written in the margin beside lines 895–6.

907 CP read, 'Whos Cyte is sette in al perfectyon.' The metre would be correct if 'cyte' were regarded as a scribal correction of the word 'seat,' since both words could be spelled 'sete' in fifteenth-century English. The T reading of 'feete' would then be a result of the confusion between f and long s. However, the T reading makes sense as it stands: the whole line may be based on such Biblical phrases as Ecclus 51:20: 'My heart delighted in her [wisdom], my foot walked in the right way' ('Ambulavit pes meus iter rectum').

910 For Minerva, goddess of wisdom, see below, lines 1744–88.

914 *t'apere*: to appear, present oneself formally

923 *thou lust*: The verbs 'list' and 'lust' are very confused in later Middle English, and both can take a personal or an impersonal construction. The variant readings to the lines in the *Court* containing these verbs suggest that the poet used the impersonal construction, writing 'thee lust' or 'thee list,' and the scribes subsequently altered 'thee' to 'thou' or misread 'thee' as 'ye' (the Middle English letter

thorn, which stood for th, is indistinguisable in some hands from y). Since the author of the *Court* is quite consistent in his use of singular and plural forms of address, 'ye' readings in 'thou' passages are clearly incorrect and indicate the presence of a lost 'the(e).' But there is no 'ye' variant for this line, and I have let 'thou' stand, although I suspect that it should be emended to 'thee lust' to bring the construction into line with the poet's usage of this verb elsewhere. See lines 677, 731, 1102, 1922, and their variants.

925–8 Beside these lines in T is written 'Sciencia et intelligencia famule sunt Sapiencie' ('Science and Intelligence are handmaids of Sapience').

932–3 T contains the remark, 'Nota hic de rivo vocato Quies juxta manerium sapiencie' ('Note here the river named Quiet, beside the manor house of Sapience').

939 *Nota de ponte*: 'Note the bridge' is written beside this line in T.

941 *alured*: furnished with a covered passage or gallery; see OED, *alure*.

944–5 A reference to Ps 111:10 (Vulg 110:10): 'Initium sapientiae timor Domini' ('The fear of the Lord is the beginning of wisdom'). The Latin is added in the margin in T.

949 Either a monosyllable is missing between 'world' and 'wyde,' or 'world' is to be read as a disyllable; OED records *warlede*, *wordel*, and *wardle* as fifteenth-century spellings.

952–1106 Bühler has shown that the whole of this section of the poem is derived from book XVI of Bartholomaeus Anglicus, *De proprietatibus rerum* (*Sources of the Court of Sapience* 41–59; see also introduction, pages xxxii–xxxiii). The author of the *Court* used the Latin text of Bartholomaeus, not the English translation that had been made by John Trevisa in 1398.

In T, a list of the Latin names of all but four of the stones mentioned in the verses is placed between lines 952 and 953. These Latin names will be given here in the notes to the individual stones.

952 *is*: C. The TP reading of 'thyk' is probably to be preferred.

953, 960 *alabastyr* or *alabaustrum*: alabaster; Bartholomaeus (XVI iii) quotes Dioscorides in saying that it gives victory.

953, 962 *electorye* or *allectoria*: a stone said to be found in the gizzard of a fowl; Bartholomaeus (XVI xvii) says that it has the properties of arousing desire ('excitat Venerem') and of reforming or reconciling friends ('amicos reformat'). See MED, *alectorie*.

954, 965 *aurypygment* or *auripigmentum*: a mineral described by Bartholomaeus (XVI vi) as having the natural properties of heat and dryness. It is in fact trisulphide of arsenic, the 'King's Yellow' of painters, known today under the French term 'orpiment': see OED, *auripigment*, *orpiment*.

954, 961 *argeryte* or *argerita*: a silvery stone, which, according to Bartholomaeus (XVI xv), had the property of restraining wrath. See MED, *argirites*.

955 *asteron* or *astrion*: probably the asteriated sapphire; see *OED*, *astrion*. Bartholomaeus (XVI xvi) says, quoting Isidore, that in the centre of the asteron a star shines.

956, 963 *adamante* or *adamas* ('Admante' C): the loadstone; Bartholomaeus (XVI ix) calls it 'the gem of reconciliation and love.' Medieval writers explained the etymology of the word from 'adamare,' 'to have an attraction for'; see *OED*, *adamant*.

956, 963–4 *asteryte* or *asterites*: a stone that Bartholomaeus (XVI xviii) describes as having a light, like a star, moving around within it. See also *OED*, *asterite*.

957, 966 *amatyst* or *amatistes*: the amethyst. Bartholomaeus (XVI x) says that it confers good intellect.

957–8 *amatyte* or *amatites*: Bartholomaeus (XVI xix), quoting Isidore, tells how this stone resists heat and becomes brighter when exposed to it. *MED* identifies the *amatite* and the *amatist*.

959 Perhaps, 'No one could ask for a better sight than this'; see *MED*, *desiren* 3.

967–8 *byrel* or *berillus*: the beryl. Bartholomaeus (XVI xxi) describes it as like a pale emerald and lists its pacifying properties, its power to heal 'moist eyes' and to stimulate conjugal love.

969–70 *selydon* or *celidonius*: a precious stone said to be found in the belly of a swallow. Bartholomaeus (XVI xxx) says that it is good against insanity and 'old weakness' ('valet … contra insaniam et antiquum languorem'); this shows that the reading of PT is correct in line 969, and of CP in line 970. See *OED*, *celidony*; *MED*, *celidoine*.

medycyn: disyllabic; compare lines 1064, 1239, 1290, 2321; contrast line 1010.

971–2 *carbuncle* or *charbunculus*: a precious stone famous for its power of shining like a light in darkness. See Bartholomaeus XVI xxvi; also *OED*, *carbuncle*.

972–3 *crisolyte* or *crisolitus* (T does not give the Latin name): This stone's power to frighten demons is mentioned by Bartholomaeus, XVI xxix; see also *OED*, *chrysolite*, 'a green stone.'

974 *calcydone* or *calcidonius*: a stone referred to in the Bible (Rev 21:19), but otherwise obscure; see *OED*, *chalcedony*. Bartholomaeus (XVI xxviii) mentions its hardness and says that it also has the power to combat diabolic illusions.

975 *chrysopasse* or *crisopassus*: Bartholomaeus (XVI xxvii) says that this is a golden-green stone that shines in the night but is hidden by day. See also *OED*, *chrysoprase*.

976 *crystal* or *cristallus*: crystal, which was believed to be snow or ice frozen for many years; see Bartholomaeus XVI xxxi. A Latin quotation from this chapter of Bartholomaeus is written beside line 976 in T; it runs as follows: 'Cristallus in potum sumptus valet contra colicam et visceram passionem, si non assit constipacio' ('Crystal taken in liquids is good for colic and troubles of the bowels as long as there is no constipation').

977 *corall* or *corallus*: Bartholomaeus (xvi xxxiii) explains that red coral is good for all kinds of bloody flux; the Latin of this statement, 'Valet contra fluxum sanguinis corallus,' is written beside line 977 in T.

978 *ceranne stone* or *cerauneus*: a stone said to fall from the sky in thunderstorms; Bartholomaeus (xvi xxxii) adds that the stone protected its bearer, if chaste, from lightning. See MED, *ceranius*.

979 *calcophan* or *calcephanus* (elsewhere 'kalcophanus' – the C reading of 'Caleophan' must be a misprint): according to Bartholomaeus (xvi lix), a black gem that clears the voice and protects the throat from hoarseness ('a raucedine'). See MED, *calciphane*. The reading of T, 'voyces hoorse,' may be preferred, but the CP reading is also possible. The origin of the variants may have been a word in Northern dialect resembling Henryson's 'hoir' in *Testament of Cresseid*, 338, where it must mean something like 'rough,' 'hoarse.' See Henryson *Testament of Cresseid* ed Denton Fox, line 338n.

980 *cabiate* or *cabrates* (elsewhere 'kalbrates'): Bartholomaeus (xvi lviii) says that this stone is like crystal, and it is thought to bestow honour and eloquence. In C, line 980 runs, 'Al these doon bote without offence'; the text here is supplied from PT.

981 *dyadek* or *diadocos*: according to Bartholomaeus (xvi xxxvi), a pale stone which is good for obtaining responses from demons. See MED, *diadocus*.

982 *dyonys* or *dionisius*: according to Bartholomaeus (xvi xxxv), a black stone streaked with red that makes water smell like wine but prevents drunkenness. See MED, *dionise*.

983 *eschyte* or *echites* (the Latin is not given in T): Bartholomaeus (xvi xxxix) says that there is a male and female of this stone and that it is a great help in parturition: eagles cannot breed without them; hence both are often found in eagles' nests. See MED, *etites*; OED, *echites*.

985 *emachyte* or *emachites*: haematite or iron ore. Bartholomaeus (xvi xl) mentions its property of staunching blood.

986 *elytrope* or *elitropa*: According to OED, *elitrope, heliotrope*, this is green quartz with veins of red jasper. Bartholomaeus (xvi xli) repeats the medieval etymology that interprets 'eliotropa' as 'turning away the sun' and mentions among its properties the power to repel venom.

988 *enydros*: according to Bartholomaeus (xvi xlii), a little stone that perpetually drips water without itself ever dissolving or becoming smaller. Bartholomaeus quotes two lines of verse from the *Lapidarium* (see below, line 1093n), which are added in the margin of T:

Perpetui fletus lacrimas distillat enydros,
Qui velut ex plenitudine fontis scaturigine manat.   Hoc in *Lapidario*

The enydros drips tears of perpetual weeping, which flow as if from the fullness of a fountain. The *Lapidarium*

See MED, *enydros*.

991 Metre defective in all three witnesses. Spindler reads 'seyth [that] hit hyght.'

992 *epystyte* or *episterus*: Bartholomaeus explains (XVI xliii) that this stone is 'frendful to corn' because it keeps away locusts, birds, and hail from crops.

993 *excolycerose* or *excolerius* (also 'excoliceros'): Bartholomaeus says (XVI xliv) that this small stone comes from the Troglodytes of Libya and that it has forty colours. See MED, *excolericus*.

995–9 *gagates*: jet; see OED, *gagate*; MED, *gagates*. Bartholomaeus (XVI xlix) gives an account of its use in this virginity test.

997 The metre of this line is defective in all witnesses.

1000–1 *galachyte* or *gagachites*: see OED, *galactite*; MED, *galactiles*. Bartholomaeus (XVI l) describes it as a pale stone, which, when hung around the neck, aids mothers in lactation.

1002 *Geratycen* or *geraticen*: Bartholomaeus (XVI lii) praises this black stone for its power to make a man lovable. In the margin of T a quotation from Bartholomaeus records the source for lines 1005–6:

> Geraticen. Unde de illo metrice scribitur,
> Quo prius abluto, si quis gestaverit ore
> Dicere mox poterit quid de se cogitat alter.

> Geraticen. Whence of this stone there is a verse:
> 'If anyone should first wash this stone, and then carry it in his mouth, he would soon be able to say what others thought about him.'

See MED, *garant* n (2).

1006 *jaspre* or *jaspis*: the jasper, but not, however, the modern stone; see OED, *jasper*. Bartholomaeus (XVI liii) says that it cures fevers if the wearer is chaste.

1009 *jacynct* or *jacinctus*: the medieval jacinth, a blue stone; see OED, *jacinth*. Bartholomaeus (XVI liv) notes its efficacy against pestilences of the air and mentions its 'virtus comfortativa,' 'strengthening power.'

1010 *pestylence*: A disyllabic form, *pestlens*, is recorded in OED.

1011 *adachyte* or *idachites*: another stone that sweats water; Bartholomaeus (XVI ci) suggests that it may be the same as 'enydros' (see line 988n). He also records that it has another stone inside it, which can be heard tinkling when the adachyte is shaken. See MED, *idachytes*.

1014 *jerachyte* or *irachiten*: a stone briefly mentioned by Bartholomaeus (XVI cii) as having the power to protect from biting insects and to prevail against poison. See MED, *irachite*.

1016–17 *irys* or *iris*: a prismatic crystal; see OED, *iris* 3a. Bartholomaeus (XVI lv) explains that it helps women in childbed either by making them give birth quickly or by making them more able to endure the pain.

chyldbed: A monosyllable seems to be missing in all versions. The word 'childing' occurs in ME from 1300, and compounds such as 'childing-pine,' 'chiltyng-state,' exist, but 'childing-bed' does not seem to be attested. See OED, *childing*; MED, *childinge*; DOST, *childyne*.

1018 *jena*: a precious stone said to be taken from the eye of the hyena; see OED, *hyena* 4. Bartholomaeus (XVI lvi) repeats the belief that, if it is hidden under a man's tongue, it will make him prophesy. See MED, *hiena*.

1019 *camen* or *camena*: a stone having layers of different colours, often carved and polished; see OED, *cameo*; MED, *cameu*. Bartholomaeus (XVI lvii) ascribes to Dioscorides the statement that it is good for dropsy.

1021–2 *lygurius* or *ligurius*: a stone that supposedly hardened from the urine of a lynx; see OED, and MED, *ligure*. Bartholomaeus (XVI lx) says that it restores lost colour.

1023–6 *Lipparia*: a fabulous stone whose power to attract wild beasts is recorded in Bartholomaeus, XVI lxi

1027 *alabandyne* or *alebandina*: the stone now called almandine, a kind of garnet; see OED, *alabandine, almandine*; MED, *alaba(u)ndine*. Bartholomaeus says (XVI xiv) that it increases the blood.

1028 *abisate* (T) or *abisatus*: according to Bartholomaeus (XVI xiii), a stone that, when heated, retains the heat for seven days. See also MED, *absictus*. C's reading, 'abatystus,' and P's 'abistist' are both unmetrical.

1030 *margaryte* or *margarita*: the pearl. Bartholomaeus (XVI lxii) in his account of the generation of pearls says that they are formed in oysters by dew. He adds that the whitest ones are the best and lists their medicinal qualities; above all, they have the power to give strength ('habent autem virtutem confortativam').

1032–3 *magnes*: the magnet or loadstone; see OED, MED, *magnes*. Bartholomaeus (XVI lxiii) explains that in some cases the 'vertu attractyf' ('virtus attrahens') is so strong that magnets as big as mountains will wreck ships by attracting the nails out of them. The attracting power extends to reconciling husbands and wives. CP's 'yeveth grace and delyte' translates 'auget gratiam et decorem in sermone.' 'Yeveth,' here as elsewhere in the *Court*, is monosyllabic; see introduction, page xix.

1034 *mellanyte* or *mellanites*: a green and yellow (or honey-coloured) stone, supposed to shed a sweet juice; see Bartholomaeus XVI lxiv. This virtue is probably derived from the supposed (but false) etymology from Latin 'mel,' 'honey.' See OED, *melanite*.

exceptyf: C; 'acceptive' PT. Neither word is to be found in the medieval dictionaries, but OED records 'acceptive' in 1596 and gives the meaning, 'fit for acceptance.' It was perhaps coined here for the sake of the rhyme.

1036 *myryte* or *mirrites*: murrhine stone; see OED, *myrrhite*. Bartholomaeus (XVI lxvi) states that it has a scent like that of nard when pressed.

1037 *stone memphyte* or *memphites*: Memphian stone; see *OED, Memphian*. This stone is described by Bartholomaeus (XVI lxv) as originating in Egypt; he says that it was used as an anaesthetic.

1037 *melochyte* or *melochites*: malachite, or hydrous carbonate of copper, a green mineral; see *OED, malachite; MED, molochites*. The statement about its use as a protection for infants is from Bartholomaeus (XVI lxviii), who is citing Dioscorides.

1040 *nitrum*: natron, or washing soda; see *OED, natron*. Bartholomaeus (XVI lxx) elaborates on its cleansing powers.

1041 *medus*: a stone supposed to be found in Media; see *OED, mede* 2. Bartholomaeus (XVI lxvii) mentions its power to cure blindness.

1042 *noset*: the stone said to be found in the head of a toad. Bartholomaeus (XVI lxxi) says that it gets so hot near poison that it burns the fingers of anyone touching it.

1044–6 *onychyne* and *onyx*, or *onichinus* and *onix*: Bartholomaeus (XVI lxxii) treats these two as one; he says that onichinus is the Greek word for a fingernail, which the onyx resembles. They come from India or Arabia and may be polished until their surfaces reflect like a mirror.

1047 *Optallyus* or *optallius* (or 'opallus'): the opal. Bartholomaeus (XVI lxxiii) mentions its various colours and explains that it is good for thieves because it renders its wearer practically invisible.

1049–50 *oryte* or *orites*: a stone that, according to Bartholomaeus (XVI lxxiv), protects against bites from animals or reptiles, acts as a contraceptive, and procures abortions

1051 *paryus* or *parius*: Parian marble. In T, the following note is written in the margin beside line 1051: 'Parius: de isto lapide dicitur in lapidario: Utile nil affert, nisi quod viret et decet aurum' ('Parius: Of this stone the *Lapidary* [see line 1093n] says, "It is of no use, unless it is green, and adorned with gold" '). This statement is not found in Bartholomaeus' chapter on parius (XVI lxxvi) but in the following one, on 'prassius.'

1051–2 *prassyus* or *prassius*: a kind of quartz; see *OED, prase*. Its name is derived from the Greek for leek. Bartholomaeus (XVI lxxvii) says that it is as green as a leek and strengthens weak sight.

1053–4 *pyrryte* or *pirites*: 'fire-stone,' a mineral that may be used for striking fire; see *OED, pyrites*. Bartholomaeus (XVI lxxviii) repeats the belief that it burns the hand that presses it, and his statement is added in the margin of T: 'Pirrites: de isto dicitur in lapidario: tangi vult leniter, blandaque manu retineri, nam pressus nimium digitos tangentis adurit' ('Pyrites: Of this stone it is said in the *Lapidary* [see line 1093n], "It wishes to be touched lightly, and held in a gentle hand, for if it is pressed too hard, it burns the toucher's fingers" ').

1055–7 *ponyte* or *pomites*: pumice? Bartholomaeus (XVI lxxix) records the belief that it reproduces itself; hence it is good for pregnant women.

1058–9 *quyrryne* or *quirinus*: an unknown stone that, according to Bartholomaeus

(XVI lxxxiii), makes a sleeper say what he dreams about if it is placed at his head when he is asleep

dremeth: monosyllabic

1059–60 *quandras*: a stone, said to be found in the head of a vulture, that aids in lactation; see Bartholomaeus XVI lxxxiv.

1061 *ruby*: Bartholomaeus (XVI lxxxv) says that it staunches blood.

1062–4 *reben*: T and Latin; 'Rebe' C; 'ruben' P. According to Bartholomaeus (XVI lxxxvi), this is a stone found in the head of a crab; it heals the bites of rabid dogs and is good for wounds.

medycyne: disyllabic, as in 970

1065–71 *saphyre* or *saphirus*: the sapphire, best of all precious stones according to Bartholomaeus (XVI lxxxvii, where all these qualities are recorded). The following verses are written beside these lines in T:

> Saphirus. De isto dicitur in Lapidario:
> Sudorem stringit nimio torrente, scitote;
> Tollit et ex oculis sordes, de fronte dolorem;
> Et plusquam reliquas amat hanc idromancia gemmas,
> Ut divicia queant per eam responsa mereri.
> Hic lapis ut perhibent, educere carcere vinctos,
> Obstrusosque flores et vincula tacta resoluit;
> Sed qui gestat eum, castissimus esse videtur.

The sapphire. Of this stone the *Lapidary* says: 'Know that it checks the excessive flow of sweat, takes impurities from the eyes, and pain from the forehead; and diviners love this more than other gems, because they are able to get divine [reading "divina" for "divicia"] responses through its means. They say this stone takes captives from prison – it opens closed doors [reading "obstrusasque fores"] and loosens chains by its touch, but he who carries it is bidden to be most chaste [reading "jubetur" for "videtur"].'

These verses are dispersed through Bartholomaeus' account of the sapphire and, as the note in T says, are taken from the *Lapidary* (see line 1093n). The variant readings are from the printed text of Bartholomaeus.

1072–3 *smaragde* or *smaragdus*: the emerald; see OED, *smaragd*. Bartholomaeus (XVI lxxxviii) lists these properties; 'fantasye' translates 'phantasmata daemonum' ('diabolic illusions').

1074–5 *sardonyx* or *sardonix*: a kind of onyx containing layers of sard; see OED, *sardonyx*. Bartholomaeus (XVI xc) says that it expels lechery and makes a man humble and modest.

1076 *sardius*: a kind of cornelian, a red, yellow, or orange stone; see OED, *sardius*, *sard*. Bartholomaeus (XVI lxxxix) says that it increases joy, decreases fear, and renders men bold.

1077 *sonnes gemme* or *solis gemma*: See *OED, sunstone*; a white stone that throws out rays like the sun (Bartholomaeus XVI xci).
gemme: probably disyllabic

1078 *serenyte* or *serenites*: selenite, or 'moonstone,' a kind of gypsum; see *OED, selenite, selenites*. Bartholomaeus (XVI xcii) describes its potency in reconciling lovers.

1079–81 *Topacius* or *topasion vel topasius*: The topaz is famed, according to Bartholomaeus (XVI xcvi), for its efficacy against lunacy, wrath, sorrow, and frenzy.

1082–3 *turkoys* or *turgogis*: turquoise, which according to Bartholomaeus (XVI xcvii) is good for strengthening the sight and for making men cheerful

1083 *zemeth* or *zimeth*: Bartholomaeus (XVI ciii) says that this stone is the same as lapis lazuli and that it has virtue against melancholy and many other passions.

1084–5 *zyngynt* or *zinguntes*: According to Bartholomaeus (XVI civ), this is a stone the colour of glass that, hung round the neck, restrains haemorrhages and keeps a man in his right mind.

1092 *them*: should perhaps be 'him' ('hem'); compare line 2181n.

1093 The *Lapidarye* has been identified by Joan Evans, *Magical Jewels of the Middle Ages and Renaissance* (Oxford 1922), as the *Liber lapidum* of Marbod, a versified Latin lapidary which was very well known. Marbod was appointed bishop of Rennes, Brittany, in 1096 (see Sarton i 764–5). The author of the *Court*, however, probably knew the *Lapidarye* only from the quotations from it that occur in Bartholomaeus Anglicus: at all events, the passages from it that are given in the margins of T may all be found in Bartholomaeus.

In T, a Latin note beside this line runs, 'Nomina auctorum tractancium de lapidibus et naturis eorundem' ('The names of authorities on stones and their natures').

1094 *Isodore*: Isidore of Seville; see introduction, pages xxxiv–xxxv. In this case the poet is probably relying on the citations from Isidore in Bartholomaeus.
Dyascorydese: another authority cited frequently by Bartholomaeus. The work in question is the *Materia medica* of Dioscorides of Anazarbos, a first-century pharmacologist, the last book of which contains an account of the properties of stones and minerals. The work cited by Bartholomaeus, however, is only remotely derived from the treatise of Dioscorides: over the centuries it had been much altered by translation from Greek into Latin, rearrangement, and expansion and contamination from other sources; see Pauly-Wissowa *Dioskurides* 12; Bühler *Sources of the Court of Sapience* 47–59.

1095 *Platearye*: Platearius is another author cited by Bartholomaeus on the properties of stones. He is probably to be identified with Matthaeus Platearius (d 1161), a physician of Salerno, author of a work on drugs called *De simplici medicina* and a commentary on the *Antidotarium* of Nicholas of Salerno, either of which could be the source of Bartholomaeus' quotations. See Sarton ii 241.

1095 *Barthylmewe*: Bartholomaeus Anglicus; see introduction, page xxxii, and line 952n.

Explicit: 'Here ends the description of the stones lying at the edge of the river.' Compare line 952 above.

1107–48 The whole of this passage is translated from the introductory chapter of book xiii of Bartholomaeus; Bartholomaeus is at this point making a long quotation from the *Hexaemeron* of St Basil (fourth century), whom the author of the *Court* acknowledges at line 1156.

1109 *moyst and cold*: These are the distinguishing properties of water, as those of earth are cold and dry, of fire, dry and hot, and of air, hot and moist.

1110–13 Bartholomaeus xiii: 'Aquae enim sunt omnium nascentium causa, quia fruges gignunt, arbores et plantas producunt, sordes detergunt, peccata diluunt, potum cunctis animantibus tribuunt' ('For the waters are the cause of all things that are born, because they generate fruits, bring forth trees and plants, cleanse filth, wash away sins, and give drink to all living things').

1116–18 Barthomaeus xiii: 'Aqua ... aerem suis vaporibus incorporat et condensat' ('Water ... with its vapours gives body to the air and makes it thick').

1119–20 Bartholomaeus xiii: 'Scandit in sublime et coelum sibi vendicat' ('[Water] mounts up to the heights and lays claim to heaven').

1121–7 Bartholomaeus xiii:

Est enim aqua terrae conjunctiva, penetrativa, repletiva, caloris caelestis nutritiva, omnium inferiorum temperativa, nisi enim haec inferiora suis exhalationibus temperaret, omnia in conflagrationem vi caloris verterentur.

Water joins the earth together; it penetrates, fills, and nurses the heat of heaven; it tempers all the lower world, for if it did not moderate the lower world with its exhalations, all things would be burnt up with the force of heat.

fallith: probably monosyllabic

1128–34 Bartholomaeus' quotation from St Basil runs:

Haec [aqua] sui diffusione per interiores partes terrae facit partium eius unionem, terra enim propter intensionem siccitatis dissolveretur in pulverem, nisi pars cum parte humorositate aquea uniretur.

By its diffusion through the interior parts of the earth, water makes a union of those parts. For the earth would dissolve into dust through intense dryness if one part were not joined to another by the wetness of water.

The theory is based on the belief that the four elements, earth, water, air, and fire, maintain the precarious balance of the natural world through their opposing qualities: thus the moistness of water counteracts the dryness of earth and fire, and water's coldness balances the heat of fire and air.

1130 *The partes of the erthe*: The variant readings 'parties' (T) and 'portyse' (P), together with the metre, suggest that C's 'partes' represents the plural of 'party' rather than that of 'part'; see *OED, party; DOST, partie*.

1135–6 Bartholomaeus XIII: 'Haec [aqua] piscibus dat spiraculum, sicut aer animantibus praebet vitam et animationem' ('Water gives breath to fish, just as air gives life and living to breathing creatures').

1139–40 Bartholomaeus XIII:

Et ideo quia superficiem habet specularem, per actionem reflexi luminis rerum obiectarum imagines in se repraesentat, et intuentium facies ad modum speculi manifestat.

And therefore, because it has a mirroring surface, water represents in itself images of things before it, through the action of reflected light, and it shows the faces of those looking into it just like a mirror.

speculer: having the properties of a mirror; see *OED, specular*.

1142–5 Bartholomaeus XIII:

Haec movetur a fundo sive a centro ad circumferentiam, nec sistitur donec aequetur ejus superficies secundum aque distantiam a centro terrae.

Water is moved from the earth's foundations or centre to its circumference, nor does it stand still until its surface is level, according to the distance of the water from the centre of the earth.

In T, 'equidistancia a centro terre' is written over 'dystaunce.'

1148 *natures four*: In T, 'quattuor elementa,' 'the four elements,' is written in explanation over these words.

1156 See above, line 1107n.

1170 *Physon*: the first of the four rivers of Paradise mentioned in Gen 2:11 (spelled Pison in AV); it is described in Bartholomaeus, XIII iii, and identified with the Ganges.

Tygrys: the third river of Paradise (Gen 2:14), still called the Tigris; in AV it is called the Hiddekel. See Bartholomaeus XIII v.

Gyon: the second river of Paradise (Gen 2:13), identified in Bartholomaeus, XIII iv, with the Nile. The Vulgate form of the name is Gehon; in AV it is Gihon (Genesis) and Geon (Ecclus 24:27).

Eufrates: the Euphrates, the fourth river of Paradise; see Gen 2:14; Bartholomaeus XIII vi.

1171 *Doryx*: This is Bartholomaeus' River Dorix (XIII vii). It is not one of the 'floodys of Paradys' mentioned in Gen 2; its identification as such may be found in the

Glossa ordinaria on the Vulgate of Ecclus 24:41: 'Ego [Sapientia] quasi fluvii dioryx, et sicut aqueductus exivi de paradiso' (Douai: 'I [Wisdom] like a channel of a river, and like an aqueduct, came out of paradise'). The rare Latin word 'dioryx' (transliterating the Greek for 'canal') is misunderstood in the *Glossa* and treated as a proper noun, and 'paradisus,' which means 'garden' or 'park' in Greek, is read as the Paradise of the Garden of Eden. (There is no Hebrew text for this part of Ecclesiasticus.) Bartholomaeus records that the River Dorix had been identified with the River Araxes (the modern Aras) of Armenia.

1172 *Jordan*: The River Jordan is described by Bartholomaeus, XIII viii.

Cobar ('Chebar' AV): mentioned by name in the Bible (Ezech 1:1); it is also identified in Bartholomaeus (XIII ix) as the 'waters of Babylon' by which the Israelites sat and wept (Ps 137 [Vulg 136]).

Edapces or *Hydaspes*: described in Bartholomaeus (XIII ix), where it is identified with the River Gasan or Gozan of 2 Kings 18:11 (Vulg 4 Reg 18:11). It is a tributary of the Indus.

1173 *Danybyus*: The River Danube is mentioned by Bartholomaeus (XIII ii).

Pharphar: another Biblical river, generally coupled with Abana; see the next line.

1174 *Abana*: Abana and Pharphar are the rivers in Syria mentioned in 2 Kings 5:18 (Vulg 4 Reg 5:18). The detail about their watering the gardens of Damascus is taken from Bartholomaeus (XIII viii).

1177–8 References to all these European rivers may be found scattered through Bartholomaeus, book xv 'Of Provinces' (book XIII deals mainly with Biblical rivers), but the author of the *Court* would scarcely need a source for most of them. 'Tybre' is the Tiber; 'Rodan,' the Rhône (Latin 'Rhodanus'); 'Yber,' the Iberus (modern Ebro); 'Leyre,' the Loire; 'Sayne,' the Seine; 'Geron,' the Garonne; 'Ryne,' the Rhine.

1180 The three continents of the known world. In T, 'Nota de tribus partibus mundi, Asia, Affrica, et Europa' ('Note the three parts of the world, Asia, Africa, and Europe') is written in the margin beside this line.

1189–90 The whole of book xv of Bartholomaeus is devoted to descriptions of the provinces and countries of the world; the names of various rivers are given if they are especially noteworthy or if they provide boundaries to the areas under discussion. In T, the note 'ac eciam in libro suo xiii' ('and also in his book XIII') has been added, correctly indicating the source of lines 1170–6, as noted above.

1195 *Isidore*: Isidore of Seville, *Etymologiae* XIII xxi; Isidore is frequently cited on rivers by Bartholomaeus.

1198–1200 The author is indebted to Bartholomaeus, XIII xxvi, for these lines:

Piscis natans pennulas movet a parte posteriori in anterius, et quasi quibusdam brachiis aut remis aquas amplectens et retinens in anterius se extendit.

> A fish in swimming moves its fins forward from the rear, and extends itself forward by embracing and holding the water as if it had some kind of arms or oars.

1203 *overthwert*: The metre requires either the northern pronunciation of 'over' as a monosyllable, or that 'overthwert' has been substituted for 'athwert.'

1206 Spindler suggests that 'attend' has been substituted for the aphetic form, 'tend'; but it is also possible that the author used an elision (t'attend') similar to 't'apere' in line 914.

1207–8 This seems to derive from Bartholomaeus, XIII xxvi:

> Dum piscis natat contractione corporis in minorem se colligit longitudinem, et iterum se extendens aquae innititur.

> When a fish swims, it draws itself into its shortest length by a contraction of its body, and then it extends itself again and pushes against the water.

1210 See variant readings. CT are both unmetrical unless 'aferd' is a substitution for the aphetic form, 'ferd.' P's line, ending 'yet they ferth,' is metrical but meaningless. CT's 'were' should perhaps be negative, 'nere.'

1211 *joye*: C; 'heven' PT. 'Heven' is probably the true reading: it would fit in with the paradisal and 'heavenly' language of this section of the poem.

1212–28 Most of these fishes are to be found in Isidore, XII vi, and in Bartholomaeus, XIII xxvi; Bartholomaeus quotes Isidore frequently, but he does not include all the fishes mentioned by him. The author of the *Court* must have consulted Isidore as well as Bartholomaeus.

1212 *The whale, the dolphyn, and escaryus*: all described by both Isidore and Bartholomaeus; the escaryus (Latin 'escarus,' 'escarius') is said by Isidore to be the only fish which chews the cud. The word 'escarius' in classical Latin means 'pertaining to bait'; the fish is perhaps simply a misreading of the word.

1213 *carabo*: Bartholomaeus mentions this creature as an example of the eat-and-be-eaten law of the sea: a carabo eats big fishes and is then itself eaten by others. A carabo or carabus was a kind of crab.

effimeron: Bartholomaeus describes this fish on the authority of 'Jorath' (the author of a treatise on natural history recording a number of fabulous tales about mysterious creatures; see Thorndike ii 423–4: Jorath's work appears to be no longer extant); he says that it reproduces without coition and lives only three hours. (Latin 'effimeron,' 'ephemeron,' 'effumeron'; see *MED, effimeron*).

1214 *cakodryl*: the crocodile ('cocodrillus'); both Isidore and Bartholomaeus classify it as an amphibious fish, like the seal and the hippopotamus.

uranoscopus: an emendation; 'vratynstopus' C; 'vrounscopus' P; *om*. T. The uranoscopus is a fish described by Isidore (XII vi 35) as having a single eye on the top of its head; see *OED, uranoscopus*.

1215 *The see-swyn*: The 'porcus marini' or sea-swine is mentioned by both Isidore and Bartholomaeus, who comment on its habit of rooting in the mud, just like its terrestrial counterpart.

fascolyon ('fascalion' PT): The fuscaleon is mentioned by Bartholomaeus (from Aristotle) as the only fish that does not eat its kind in spawning time.

This line is defective in CP, and the whole stanza is confused in T. An adjective describing the see-swyn is perhaps missing.

1216 *The myllago*: Isidore (XII vi 36–7) describes the millago, a fish that 'flies out of the water' ('evolat super aquam'). Beside this line in T is written, 'Quando volitat super aquam significat tempestatem' ('When it flies above the water, it signifies a storm'). Although 'fleten' can mean 'to fly' (of chaff or arrows), its usual meaning is 'to float'; 'flien' is the usual verb used for birds and other flying things. Hence I have accepted P's 'fleieth' for CT's 'fleteth' here. The words may very easily be confused in manuscript.

1217 *The hamio*: from Isidore, XII vi 33; it is so called because it can be caught only with a fish-hook (Latin 'hamus'). CPT all read 'hamo', but both the metre and the source seem to require Spindler's emendation, 'hamio.'

1219 *myllamur*: Isidore (XII vi 27) describes the 'melanurus,' so called because it has a black tail and fins and black stripes (Greek 'melan': 'black').

castor: the Latin name for the beaver. Isidore mentions beavers with the other animals (XII ii 21); Bartholomaeus puts them among the amphibia and mentions them in his list of fishes, while also including them in XVIII xxviii with the other animals.

ypotamus: the hippopotamus, classed by both Isidore and Bartholomaeus as an amphibious fish. The medieval Latin spelling of the word was 'ipotamus.'

1220 *Auronnea*: A fish mentioned by Isidore (XII vi 18), it is so called because it 'stings with gold' (Latin 'aurum': 'gold').

phager: This must be Isidore's 'pagrum' (XII vi 22) and Bartholomaeus' 'phagion,' an unknown fish that has two teeth for crunching up oysters.

serra: the sawfish. Isidore (XII vi 16) says that it swims under boats and cuts through the bottoms.

1221 *The conger*: Bartholomaeus includes a quotation from Pliny describing the skill of the 'congrus' at gnawing bait off hooks without getting caught. The fish is the conger eel, or great sea eel; see *OED*, *conger*.

corus ('cocus' T): most probably Isidore's 'aphorus' (XII vi 40), the fish so small that it cannot be caught with a hook. The same fish appears in Bartholomaeus; Trevisa translates it 'affocus.'

1222–8 For the remainder of the fishes it seems unnecessary to indicate a precise source. 'The luce' is another name for the pike.

1223 A syllable seems to be missing in all witnesses.

1225 *The flouk*: another name for the flounder, or perhaps a similar kind of flatfish; see *OED*, *fluke* sb¹.

1226 *craveys*: the crayfish or crawfish. At this period the word is often used vaguely to mean any kind of shellfish: see *OED*, *crayfish*.

1230 *stewe*: an artificial pond, used for keeping fish for the table

1254–60 All these 'clerkes' are cited by Bartholomaeus as the authorities on fish and water in book XIII of *De proprietatibus rerum*. Aristotle's *Book of Beestes* is his *Historia animalium*.

1255 *Jorath*: See line 1213n above.

Ysydore: See introduction, page xxxiv.

Plenius: Pliny the Elder (d 79 AD), author of *Naturalis historia*, is one of Bartholomaeus' authorities.

1256 *Avycen*: Avicenna, Latinized form of ibn Sīnā (980–1037), Arabian philosopher and doctor; see Sarton i 709–13. Avicenna is cited by Bartholomaeus as an authority on the edibility and nutritious value of fish.

Barthylmewys gestys: *De proprietatibus rerum*

1257 *Constantyn*: Constantinus Africanus (d 1087). Bartholomaeus quotes (XIII x) his *De aquae potu* on the various types of wholesome water and the different fish produced in standing and flowing water.

Basylyus: St Basil the Great (d 379). His *Hexaemeron*, nine homilies on Genesis 1, was a very influential work, containing much popular knowledge of natural history. The *Hexaemeron* was translated from Greek to Latin circa 440.

1258–9 St Ambrose (d 397), one of the Fathers of the Church, wrote a *Hexaemeron* based upon the work of St Basil.

1270 'The Goddes of flowres' is written beside this reference to Flora in T.

1273 *dyversite*: probably to be read here as a trisyllable, 'dyverste'; compare line 93n, but contrast line 1247.

1282–1386 The catalogue of flowers and trees is based largely on Bartholomaeus, book XVII, although some of the common English flowers (for example, the primrose, daisy, gillyflower, lines 1296–7) are not mentioned there. Detailed references will be given in the individual notes.

1282–8 This stanza may have been suggested by Bartholomaeus' words (XVII lxxiii), 'Inter alios flores praeponuntur liliorum flores, rosas, et violas' ('Lilies, roses, and violets are valued above other flowers').

1285 *asure*: lapis lazuli, a bright blue stone; see *OED*, *azure*.

1289–95 *The purpyl two*: must be the rose and the ruby; 'purpyl' in ME is crimson or dark red, the colour of venous blood (see *OED*, *purple* 2d, B1, *purpur* 3). Both roses and rubies were held to be efficacious in stopping haemorrhages (Bartholomaeus XVI lxxxv, XVII cxxxvi).

The two laughyng (PT; 'langyng' C): the lily and the pearl ('margaryte')?

Bartholomaeus attributes many medicinal properties to both (xvi lxii, xvii xci). I do not know why the two white ones should be described as 'laughyng'; meadows are said to laugh – according to Bartholomaeus (xiv l), 'propter vernantem et virentem quam praetendunt pulcritudinem' ('on account of the green and springing beauty they show forth') – but this does not seem relevant to whiteness. See *OED*, *laugh* 1c, and line 1461 below.

The hevenly two: the violet and the sapphire. PT read 'hete' for 'payne' (C) in line 1291, and they are probably correct: the chief virtue of violets is their cooling power (Bartholomaeus xvii cxci), and sapphires too were held to be efficacious against unnatural heat (xvi lxxxvii).

The information in this stanza may all be found in Bartholomaeus; I am grateful to Ian McDougall for help with this passage.

1291 For the metre, see line 110n.

1292–4 Perhaps based on Bartholomaeus, xvii lxxiii:

> Flores, ut dicit Isidorus lib 18, dicuntur quasi fluores, eo quod cito defluunt et solvuntur, in his tamen multiplex est gratia, scilicet odoris, saporis, et coloris ... nam odore recreant et etiam delectant spiritum, sapore quidem immutant gustum, colore alliciunt visum.

> Flowers, as Isidore says in book xviii, are so named from flowing, because they swiftly pass away and dissolve. But in them there is a threefold pleasure, namely of perfume, taste, and colour ... They relax and delight the spirit with their perfume; they transform taste with their flavour; they entice the sight with their colour.

1294 Candied violets are still used for decorating cakes.

1296 *jacynct*: jacinth, a plant described by Bartholomaeus, xvii lxxxvi. It has been variously identified; see *OED*, *hyacinth* 2a.

1297 *dayse*: daisy; trisyllabic, as in Chaucer
gylofur: gillyflower, a name given to a variety of flowers; perhaps here the clove-scented pink. See *OED*, *gillyflower*.

1299 *gendren*: T; 'gendreth' CP. The present indicative plural does not usually end in -eth in this poem, but see 1315n.

1300–1 *Agnus castus*: a shrub renowned for its alleged anaphrodisiac qualities; see Bartholomaeus xvii xv; *OED*, *agnus castus*.

1301 *saffron*: Latin 'crocus'; Bartholomaeus xvii xli

1302 *tyme*: thyme; Bartholomaeus xvii clxxi
mynte: mint; Bartholomaeus xvii cvi
rewe: rue; Bartholomaeus xvii cxli

1303 *rosemary, sawge, savery*: These common herbs are not found in Bartholomaeus.

1304 *Arystologye*: Bartholomaeus (xvii xiv) describes two kinds of aristolochia, the

long and the round. This herb is known in English as birthwort; see *OED*,
aristolochia.

1305 *annys*: The medicinal properties of anise are described by Bartholomaeus, XVII x.
bete: Bartholomaeus (XVII xxii) records that the beet is very good for troubles of
the head, from earache to hair loss and nits.

1306 *dyten*: dittany, famous for its power of expelling arrowheads, etc, from wounds;
see Bartholomaeus XVII xlix; *OED*, *dittany*.

1307 *selydon*: the celandine, so called because it appears at the time of the swallows'
return (Greek 'chelidōn': 'swallow'); compare the stone 'selydon,' line 969n.
Bartholomaeus XVII xlvi; *OED*, *celandine*.

1308 *century*: centaury, a plant said to have been discovered by Chiron the centaur;
see Bartholomaeus XVII xlvii.
fumytere: fumitory, from Latin 'fumus terrae,' 'smoke of the earth,' because its
growth resembles smoke on the ground; see Bartholomaeus XVII lxix.

1309 *malve*: mallow (Latin 'malva'); Bartholomaeus XVII cvii
dok: dock; not in Bartholomaeus
dragaunce: dragonwort; see *OED*, *dragons*; Bartholomaeus XVII l.
brere: briar or brier (Latin 'sentix'); Bartholomaeus XVII cli; however, Trevisa also
translates as 'brere' the Latin 'tribulus' in XVII clxx.

1310 *marygold*: Heliotrope was formerly another name for the marigold (the modern
calendula); Bartholomaeus XVII liv.

1311 *bure*: burdock; Bartholomaeus XVII xciii
fenel: feniculus or fennel; Bartholomaeus XVII lxx
percele: petrosilinum or parsley; Bartholomaeus XVII cxxx

1312 *letuse*: Bartholomaeus (XVII xcii) explains that the lettuce ('lactuca') is so called
from the abundance of milky ('lacteus') fluid in its leaves.

1313 *coryandre*: Bartholomaeus (XVII xxxix) says that coriander seed acts as an aphro-
disiac on men but is poisonous to dogs. The variant reading, 'houndes' (TP), would
require a trisyllabic pronunciation for 'coryandre'; it may well be correct.

1314 *plantane*: plantain or waybread, a powerfully medicinal herb; see Bartholomaeus XVII cxxix.
mandrage: mandrake or mandragora, famous for its narcotic powers; Bartholomaeus (XVII civ) says that it is used as an anaesthetic and discusses the notion that it
promotes conception in women.

1315 *groweth*: the reading of all witnesses. The present indicative plural does not end
in -eth elsewhere in the poem; here it is probably a scribal alteration of 'growen.'

1328–30 *cedre tre*: The cedar is described by Bartholomaeus, XVII xxiii. He calls it
'omnium arborum domina et regina,' 'mistress and queen over all trees.' The
author of the *Court* is mindful of the natural hierarchies here and elsewhere: the
whale is the first of fish, the rose of flowers, the cedar of trees, and the lion of

beasts; the eagle does not have first place in the list of birds, but when it does appear, it is called 'soverayne of fowles al' (line 1415). The sapphire is 'most noble and moost digne of al stones' (line 1065–6) and has more space devoted to it than any other stone.

1331 *palme*: Bartholomaeus (XVII cxvi) remarks on the height of the palm tree.
cypresse: See Bartholomaeus XVII xxiv.

1338 *peretre*: the pear; see Bartholomaeus XVII cxxiv.
olyve: the olive; Bartholomaeus (XVII cxi) remarks on the multitude of its boughs.
appyltree: the apple; see Bartholomaeus XVII xcviii.

1341 *almond tree*: Bartholomaeus (XVII iii) includes the almond; in XVII ii he describes how it emits gum if nails are driven into the trunk. A 'jardyn' is a Jordan almond, the best kind of almond; see *OED*, *Jordan almond*; *MED*, *jardyn*.

1343 *fyrre*: Bartholomaeus (XVII iv) gives Isidore's derivation for the fir: it is called in Latin 'abies,' from 'ab eundo,' 'from going,' because it grows higher than other trees.

1344 *amonum*: Bartholomaeus XVII viii. This is an aromatic plant, not identified with any certainty; see *OED*, *amomum*.

1344 *rede*: Bartholomaeus (XVII vii) describes a reed of India, from the root of which may be squeezed a sweet juice.

1345 *aloes*: an aromatic tree, described by Bartholomaeus, XVII v; see also *OED*, *aloe*.
canne: Bartholomaeus gives an account of the sugar-cane in XVII cxcvii.

1346 *marugh*: The variant reading of P, 'marche,' and the metre suggest that the monosyllabic pronunciation recorded in Middle English and common in Middle Scots is to be used here. Recorded spellings are *SND*, *mergh*; *DOST*, *merch*, *march*; *MED* (sv *marwe*), *mergh*, *margh*, *margth*. See also *OED*, *marrow*.

1347–8 *balsamum*: Bartholomaeus (XVII xviii) describes the balsamum shrub, which produces balm; see *OED*, *balsam*, *balm*.

1349 *cynamom*: cinnamon. Bartholomaeus (XVII xxvi) describes 'cinnamomum' as a small shrub with slender branches and a most sweet smell.

1350 *spyknarde*: spikenard, or nard, an herb described by Bartholomaeus, XVII cx; it has many medicinal properties.
mastyk, the gum rosyn: Bartholomaeus (XVII xc) explains that the tree called 'lentiscus' exudes a gum or resin from its bark, and this gum is called 'mastix'; he also deals with resin separately in XVII cxxxix. Perhaps this should be punctuated: 'mastyk; the gum rosyn.'

1351 *Olybanum, thure*: frankincense. Bartholomaeus describes frankincense (Latin 'thus,' gen 'thuris'), in some detail in XVII clxxiii. He says that 'thus' is a gum that comes from the tree called 'libanus'; hence physicians and natural philosophers call it 'olibanum.'

1352–8 The author of the *Court* is fond of this device of listing and then combining elements in a stanza; see lines 1282–95 above. Here the 'first two' and the 'fyrst' are obviously grapes and honey, and 'the other' or 'second' are frankincense and herbs; presumably the first 'they' in line 1358 refers again to grapes and honey and the second 'they' to herbs and incense.

1361–72 These lines may owe something to Bartholomaeus, XVII cxlii:

Item ad sylvas aves confugiunt et apes, illae ut nidificent, istae ut mellificent, aves ut ab aucupe tueantur, apes ut mellis favos in arborum concavitatibus componentes secretius abscondantur.

Birds and bees take refuge in the woods, the birds to build their nests, the bees to make honey; there the birds go to protect themselves from the fowler and the bees that they may be hidden away more secretly while they make honeycombs in the cavities of the trees.

1368–9 Perhaps, 'The root beneath made spring up abundantly the moist and cool refuge of all the earth [ie water].' 'Refreshment' would give a better sense than 'refuge' for 'refuyte,' but it is not recorded.

1372 *electuarye*: 'a medicine in which the ingredients are combined with honey or syrup to form a paste,' MED

1373 *oke*: See Bartholomaeus XVII cxxxiv.
asshe: Bartholomaeus XVII lxii. The 'chattes' in the next line are the keys or seeds of the ash; see OED, *chat* sb³.
plum tree: Bartholomaeus (XVII cxxv) mentions that the most medicinal of plums is the 'prina Damascena' or 'damecyne,' the damson, mentioned in the next line. A syllable seems to be missing from this line.

1375 *frutes*: C; frute PT. PT are probably correct, for metrical reasons: everywhere else in the poem (except for here and lines 1797, 1939) the plural -es of a monosyllabic word in this position in a line is syllabic: see introduction, page xviii.

1376 *rampe*: 'rhamnus' or buckthorn in Bartholomaeus, XVII cxxxviii, but Trevisa takes it to be cammock or rest-harrow, a low-growing plant. Probably buckthorn is correct here, as the author is talking about trees in the rest of the stanza.
more: the mulberry tree. See OED, *more* sb²; Bartholomaeus XVII c.
laurer: the bay-tree, or bay laurel, used for crowning poets and victors; see Bartholomaeus XVII xlviii, lxxxix.
pyne: See Bartholomaeus XVII cxxi.

1377 *cherubynte*: the terebinth or turpentine tree; Bartholomaeus (XVII clxiv) says that it produces the best kind of resin. The initial c of cherubynte probably arises originally from the confusion in manuscript between c and t; but as it is found clearly as c in all three witnesses, I have let it stand.

1378 *byrche*: Bartholomaeus XVII clix

box: the box-tree; Bartholomaeus XVII xx

alme: the elm; Bartholomaeus XVII cxcii

sycomore: Bartholomaeus XVII cxlviii

1379 *fyge*: the fig; Bartholomaeus XVII lxi

vyne: vine; Bartholomaeus XVII clxxvii

1381 *mace*: Mace, used as a spice, is the outer covering of a nutmeg; OED, *mace* sb²; Bartholomaeus XVII cix.

gynger: ginger; Bartholomaeus XVII cxcv

clowe: clove; Bartholomaeus XVII lxxix

1382 *Peper*: Bartholomaeus XVII cxxxi

greynes: more fully, 'grains of Paradise,' the name by which the seeds of 'amomum meleguetta' were known; see OED, *grain* sb¹ 4; *cardamom* b.

1385 *casia*: Bartholomaeus (XVII xxvii) says that cassia resembles cinnamon (of which it is in fact a variety) and remarks that the word should properly be spelled with only one s (XVII xxviii).

1393 *Sanctus*: 'Holy, Holy, Holy, the Lord God of hosts,' is the hymn sung by the seraphim before the throne of God (Isa 6:3) and repeated at the beginning of the canon of the mass.

1394 All these birds, except for some of the better-known ones (for example, the lark and parrot), are to be found in Bartholomaeus, book XII, though some are mentioned only in passing in the prefatory chapter.

1394 *throstel-cok*: the male song-thrush, mentioned by Bartholomaeus only in the introductory chapter to book XII

1395 *nyghtyngale*: mentioned by Bartholomaeus in the introductory chapter to book XII

1396 *swan*: described in Bartholomaeus, XII xi, as totally white, 'for no-one ever found a black swan'; hence, he says, it derives its Greek name, 'olor,' from the Greek for 'all.'

1406 The metre is irregular in all witnesses. Although trisyllabic forms of 'among,' such as 'amonges,' existed in Middle English, it is more likely that 'all' has dropped out after 'them'; compare lines 609, 1181.

1408 *pecok*: Bartholomaeus (XII xxxi) says that the peacock lifts up his tail feathers like a circle or a wheel in order to admire their beauty, but often, when he catches sight of his ugly feet, he lowers his tail again in shame.

1415 *egle*: Bartholomaeus (XII i) says that the eagle is known as queen amongst birds ('regina inter volucres').

1416 *gooshauk*: the goshawk; Bartholomaeus XII ii

faucon: the falcon; Bartholomaeus XII iii. Both of these are birds used for 'dysport royal,' or hawking.

1419 *dowve*: the dove; Bartholomaeus (XII vi) speaks much of its gentleness and affectionate nature.

1420 *turtyl*: The turtle-dove, in contrast to the dove, was famous for its chastity and
fidelity to its mate: Bartholomaeus (xii xxxiv) says that if one turtle-dove dies, its
mate will never seek another, but live alone.

fenyx: the fabulous phoenix, 'syngulere' because there is only one of them in the
world; Bartholomaeus (xii xiv) records the belief that every three hundred years
this bird is renewed by immolating itself in a nest made of spices, set on fire by the
sun's heat.

1422 *pertryche*: the partridge, an edible bird. Bartholomaeus (xii xxx) remarks on its
libidinous habits.

pellycane: Bartholomaeus (xii xxix) repeats the legend that the parent pelican
sheds its own blood to bring its children to life.

1423 *sparowes*: Bartholomaeus xii xxxii. T gives the reading 'sparow,' but the plural
of CP has been kept because Bartholomaeus' chapter is headed 'De passeribus.'

plover: the lapwing or plover; Bartholomaeus xii xxxvii. (This chapter is about the
'upupa' or hoopoe, but Trevisa translates it as 'lapwing.')

pye: The magpie is mentioned only in passing by Bartholomaeus in the prefatory
chapter to book xii.

1424 *popyngay*: The popinjay or parrot is not mentioned by Bartholomaeus.

roke: C; 'coke' PT. Both are possible, and perhaps 'coke' is to be preferred since
Bartholomaeus includes a chapter on the cock (xii xvi) and does not speak of the
rook; but both are common birds, and there is perhaps no need to invoke dependence on Bartholomaeus at this point.

henne: Bartholomaeus xii xviii

crane: Bartholomaeus xii xv

1431 *gyler*: C; 'gyldyr' T; *om.* P. A 'gilder' (also recorded as 'giller'), is a snare for
catching small birds; a northern word, it survives in Scots and northern dialects.
See OED and EDD, *gilder*.

1436 *lyon, leonesse*: The catalogue of animals begins appropriately with the lion and
lioness, the king of the beasts and his mate; Bartholomaeus xviii lxiii, lxiv.

1437 *unycorn*: identified with the rhinoceros: Bartholomaeus xviii lxxxviii

olyfaunt: the elephant. Bartholomaeus devotes three chapters to elephants, xviii
xli–xliii.

1438 *The leopard, the wolf, the bere*: Bartholomaeus xviii lxv, lxix, cx. 'Leopard' is
trisyllabic.

1440 *herte, hynd*: The hart or stag and hind are the male and female of the red deer;
Bartholomaeus xviii xxix.

buk, doo: Buck and doe are the male and female of smaller deer; Bartholomaeus
xviii xxxiv.

1441 *bole, oxe, cowe, caulf*: Bartholomaeus xviii xii, xcviii, cvii, cix

1447–9 *Jak-napys nyce*: the foolish ape. This is the earliest recorded use of the nickname Jack applied to an ape; see introduction, pages xxii–xxiii. Bartholomaeus

describes the ape in xviii xciv. 'Mynstralcye': 'entertainment'; 'counterfete': 'imitate.' Bartholomaeus lays emphasis on the ape's imitative nature: he says that hunters often catch apes by leaving shoes for them, knowing that they will be unable to resist putting them on as men do; they are captured while tying the shoelaces.

1450 *brocke*: the badger; Bartholomaeus xviii ci
pantere: the panther; Bartholomaeus xviii lxxx
dromydare: the dromedary; Bartholomaeus xviii xxxv

1451 *asse*: the donkey; Bartholomaeus xviii vii
camyl: the camel; Bartholomaeus xviii xviii
lynx: Bartholomaeus xviii lxvii; an animal whose keenness of sight was, and is, proverbial; see OED, *lynx* lb.

1452 *bore*: the boar or wild pig; Bartholomaeus xviii vi
swyne: the pig; Bartholomaeus xviii lxxxv
whesel: the weasel (Latin 'mustela'); Bartholomaeus xviii lxxii
hare: Bartholomaeus xviii lxvi

1453 *foxe*: Bartholomaeus xviii cxii
tyger: Bartholomaeus (xviii cii) says that the tiger is remarkable for its courage and its speed.

1454 *hound*: the dog; Bartholomaeus xviii xxiv
whelpe: the puppy; Bartholomaeus xviii xxvii
ermyn: the ermine or stoat. This seems to be the animal included by Bartholomaeus (xviii lxxii) under 'weasel': 'It has a red back and a white belly, but it changes its colour; for in some regions, at a certain time of the year, the whole of its coat except for its tail becomes white.' But the author of the *Court* may have taken xviii lxxiii, 'De mygale' (translated by Trevisa as 'fyrette,' or ferret), to be either the weasel or the ermine. all these animals are of the same family and are easily confused.

1455 *squerel*: The squirrel does not appear to be in Bartholomaeus.
myse: mice. Bartholomaeus (xviii lxxi) often mentions the mouse in the plural; however, the reading of P is 'mule' and that of T 'mowlle' (mole), both of which are described by Bartholomaeus (xviii lxx, c). Either of these may be preferred.
cat: Bartholomaeus xviii lxxiv
ramme: Bartholomaeus xviii ii

1456 *ghoot, kyd, hors, shepe, lamme*: These common domestic animals hardly need a learned source, but they are all in Bartholomaeus, xviii lviii, xliv, xxxviii, lxxix, iii.

1457–8 'To be concise, that meadow sustained all the animals in creation ...' Line 1458 lacks a syllable in all witnesses.

1464 In T, 'Recapitulacio omnium premissorum' ('Recapitulation of all the foregoing things') is written beside this line.

1476 *towres seven*: This detail is ultimately taken from Prov 9:1: 'Wisdom hath built herself a house: she hath hewn her out seven pillars,' a verse that was commonly taken, from as early as Cassiodorus (d 583), to refer to the seven liberal arts that comprised all learning (see below, lines 1541–6; 1807–2205). The author of the *Court*, however, prefers to relate the seven towers of wisdom to another well-known 'seven': the seven principal virtues (faith, hope, charity, prudence, fortitude, temperance, and justice), who 'live' in the towers; see lines 1499, 2206–7.

1485 The castle of Sapience is like that of the wise man in the parable, 'that built his house upon a rock. And the rain fell and the floods came and the winds blew; and they beat upon that house. And it fell not, for it was founded on a rock' (Matt 7:24–5).

1487 *kirnell*: indentation in a wall, battlements; see *OED*, *kernel* sb².

1495 *Ther*: 'where'; see *OED*, *there* 9.

1499–1505 The 'seven ladyes' make up one famous medieval group of major virtues. Feyth, Hope, and Charyte are the theological virtues, whose authority derives ultimately from 1 Cor 13:13. Prudence, Fortytude, Temporaunce, and Ryghtwysenes (Justice) are the cardinal virtues, for it was said that all other virtues turned upon them (Latin 'cardo': 'hinge'). These four derived from the classical tradition; see, for example, Cicero *De inventione* II liii–liv, and lines 1604–10 below. The virtues are discussed in Rosemond Tuve, *Allegorical Imagery* (Princeton 1966) 57–76. A note in T above this stanza gives the Latin names of the seven virtues.

1506–33 There are many medieval classifications of the major virtues with their 'handmaids,' or lesser ancillary virtues; see A. Katzenellenbogen *Allegories of the Virtues and Vices in Medieval Art* (London 1939). The scheme in the *Court* seems to be remotely related to that devised by pseudo-Hugo of St Victor, *De fructibus carnis et spiritus* PL 176, cols 998–1006, where each major virtue has seven ancillary virtues, except for Charity, which has ten. The arrangement of the virtues in the *Court* is still closer to that shown in a diagrammatic 'tree of virtues' contained in British Museum ms Arundel 83 (fourteenth century) f 129r, where each major virtue or branch has seven leaves inscribed with the names of lesser virtues. An almost identical 'tree' appears in Bodleian ms Laud, misc 156, f 62v.

In T, the Latin names of nearly all the virtues mentioned in the text are written above these stanzas.

1506–8 T lists the Latin names of the 'servientes Fidei' as Mundicia, Virginitas, Continencia, Devocio, Humilitas, and Castitas. In Arundel 83, Simplicitas (Honesty) takes the place of Humilitas, and Puritas (Purity) is added to make up the full seven. The author of the *Court* does provide Feyth with a seventh handmaid, Stabylyte, in line 2286; however, in line 1528 Stabylyte appears as one of the maids of Fortytude. Perhaps Stabylyte in line 2286 is an error for Simplicity.

Clennes is purity or innocence; Contynence is bodily self-restraint in all things, while Chastyte is restraint in sexual behaviour. Stabylyte is steadfastness. These handmaid virtues are often hard to distinguish from one another; they are perhaps to be seen rather as aspects or manifestations of the major virtue than as distinct and separate parts.

1510–12 Balbus, sv *castitas*, mentions that chastity is a virtue of the married and widowed as well as of virgins. See also Morton W. Bloomfield '*Piers Plowman* and the three grades of chastity' *Anglia* LXXVI (1958), especially pages 230–1.

1513–16 T names the handmaids of Spes as follows: Leticia, Contricio, Disciplina, Paciencia, Confessio, Contemplacio, and Penitencia. The same seven appear in Arundel 83. Penytence or Penaunce (line 2352) is the repenting of sins done, while Confessyon and Contrycyon (regarded as parts of the sacrament of penance) are respectively the acknowledging of one's sins and heartfelt sorrow for them. Discyplyne is the correction or chastisement undergone in repentance for sin.

1517–19 In T, Caritas comprises Gracia, Indulgencia, Pax, Concordia, Pietas, Compassio, and Misericordia. The same seven appear in Arundel 83. Grace and Indulgence are qualities that show unasked and generous favour and forbearance; Acord is reconciliation or harmony. Pyte, Compassyon, and Mercy are closely related aspects of charity: Compassyon feels for the sufferings of others; Pyte is a holy concern for the wretched, and Mercy forgives wrongdoers. On the literal level it is confusing that the author introduces Mercy here both as a handmaid to Charity and as 'emperesse of al renoun' in her own right; perhaps he was influenced here by the role of Mercy in the first part of his poem.

1520–3 The handmaids of Prudencia in T are Consilium, Racio, Timor Domini, Tractabilitas, Diligencia, Discrecio, and Providencia. All seven are the same in Arundel 83. Counceyl and Drede of God derive ultimately from Isa 9:2. Provydence is proper foresight, from classical times a traditional aspect of prudence.

1524–6 In T Temperancia comprises Benignitas, Moralitas, Modus, Tollerancia, Sobrietas, and Sufficiencia; in both the Latin and the English there are only six handmaids here instead of seven. Perhaps, as in the case of Dame Feyth, the seventh would have been named at the second appearance of Temporaunce. Arundel 83 provides a slightly different list here: Modus and Sufficientia are absent, and Jejunium (Fasting), Modestia (Modesty), and Contemptus mundi (Scorn for this world) make up the number. Maner here means moderation; Suffysaunce is contentment.

1527–31 The entry for Fortitudo in T runs: 'Perseverancia, Quies, Silencium, Stabilitas, Non extolli in prosperis nec deici in adversis.' The Arundel manuscript may reflect the original seven more clearly in its list: 'longanimitas, silencium, stabilitas, requies, perseverancia, non deici in adversis, non extolli in prosperis.' The author of the *Court* has doubled Quies (or Requies) in 'Rest and Quyete' and omitted Longanimitas (Forbearance); and in line 2286 he also gives Stabylyte to Dame Feyth. The last two aspects of Fortytude should perhaps be written 'Never-

proude-for-no-prosperyte' and 'Nother-yet-grutchyng-for-adversyte' since they
are compond abstractions like some of Langland's.

1532–3 T lists the servants of Justicia as Lex, Correctio, Rectitudo, Judicium, and
Execucio, omitting Veritas (Trouthe). The Arundel manuscript has all these except
Execucio, adding Juris observancia (Observance of the law) and Severitas (Stern-
ness). Ryghtwysenes lacks a handmaid at this point in the *Court*. Dome is that
aspect of Justice which passes judgment on right and wrong; Execucyon is the
fulfilling of the dictates of Justice.

1534–47 *ladyes seven*: here, the seven liberal arts, which are treated more extensively
below, lines 1807–2207. The belief that the seven arts served theology was traditional; see, for example, Vincent of Beauvais *Speculum quadruplex*, generalis
prologus viii.

1537 *gan to lowte*: C; 'gan hir lowte' PT. Both readings are possible, but PT are
probably right.

1539 The metre is defective in all witnesses; Spindler supplies '[lust and] grace.' The
missing word may have been 'hevenly,' which dropped out because it appeared in
the line below; this author does sometimes repeat a word in the next line – for
example, lines 1415–6 (but see variant readings).

1548 *dongeon*: the donjon or keep, the great central tower in the inner court of a
castle; see *OED*, *dungeon*.

1550–4 Isidore (II xxiv 3) had explained that the word 'philosophy' meant 'love of
wisdom' ('amor sapientiae').

1555–1652 As Bühler points out in his notes to these stanzas, they consist of a loosely
allegorized translation of sentences from Isidore, II xxiv 'De definitione
philosophiae.'

1555–8 These lines translate Isidore II xxix 1: 'Philosophia est rerum humanarum
divinarumque cognitio cum studio bene vivendi coniuncta.'

1557 *sad*: 'serious'

1559 *probable connyng*: 'probabilis scientia' (Isidore II xxiv 9). Philosophy embraces
not only what can be certainly known, but also 'probable' or speculative matters;
see lines 1564–75 below.

1562–3 Isidore II xxiv 9: 'Philosophia est ars artium ... est meditatio mortis.'

1565 *scyence, oppynacyon*: These terms correspond to Isidore's 'scientia,' 'knowledge,' and 'opinatio,' 'opinion, conjecture.' Scientia deals with material which can
be proved, opinatio with unprovable speculations, such as those about the structure of the heavens in stanza 225 below.

1569–73 These speculations translate Isidore II xxiv 2:

Utputa sol utrumne tantus quantus videtur, an maior sit quam omnis terra: item luna
globosa sit an concava ... caelum ipsum qua magnitudine, qua materia constat: utrum
quietum sit et inmobile, an incredibili celeritate volvatur.

> For example, whether the sun is as big as it seems to be, or is bigger than the whole earth; or whether the moon is a solid sphere or a concave hollow; ... or what size the heavens are, and what they are made of; or whether the heavens are still and immobile, or whether they whirl round at an unbelievable speed.

1573 *holowe*: The metre requires either an elision or a monosyllable: perhaps some form similar to the Middle English 'holw' or Scottish 'holl' was in the original; see MED, DOST. Compare line 2041.

1581 *sustres thre*: Isidore first divides philosophy into natural philosophy or physics, moral philosophy or ethics, and rational philosophy or logic; these are then further subdivided as in lines 1602–3, 1609–10, 1616–7.

1590–1 Isidore II xxiv 3: 'Physica ... in qua de naturae inquisitione disseritur' ('Physica, which treats of inquiries into natural things')

1592–3 Isidore II xxiv 3: 'Ethica ... in qua de moribus agitur' ('Ethics, which deals with morals')

1594–6 Isidore II xxiv 3: 'Logica ... in qua disputatur quemadmodum in rerum causis vel vitae moribus veritas ipsa quaeratur' ('Logic, which discusses in what manner the real truth should be sought for in the causes of things and the conduct of life')

1597 *Millesius*: Thales of Miletus (Thales Milesius in Isidore; fl ca 585 BC), one of the 'seven sages' of Greece. He founded a school of philosophical speculation about questions of natural science and is mentioned by Aristotle.

1601 *Plato* (d 347 BC): He is credited by Isidore with having defined the four disciplines of the quadrivium – arithmetic, geometry, music, and astronomy – on the basis laid by Thales.

1605 *Socrates* (d 399 BC): correctly celebrated here (as in Isidore) for his inquiries into ethics; the establishment of the four cardinal virtues, however, is more probably to be attributed to Aristotle, who sets them out at length in the *Nicomachean Ethics*.

1611–15 The Latin makes these lines a little clearer. Isidore II xxiv 7: 'Logicam ... Plato subiunxit, per quam, discussis rerum morumque causis, vim earum rationabiliter perscrutatus est' ('Plato added Logica, in which, after the causes of things and of morals have been examined, their force is analysed according to the rules of reason').

1618–24 Isidore (II xxiv 8) explains that these three kinds of philosophy can be exemplified by certain books of the Bible: Genesis contains natural history; Proverbs dispenses moral advice, and the Song of Solomon (Vulgate, Canticum canticorum) argues the love of God.

1625–52 Here the author of the *Court* confusingly adds Isidore's second scheme of the divisions of philosophy, where some of the same terms are used in different combinations. In this scheme philosophy is divided primarily into the study of abstract things ('inspectiva') and the study of practical living ('actualis').

1632–8 *Inspectiva*: subdivided into 'naturalis,' which teaches the nature of the things (line 1636) in the natural created world; 'doctrinalis,' which is concerned (lines 1639–45) with the abstractions of quantity (arithmetic), magnitude (geometry), mobile magnitude (astronomy), and numerical relations (music); and 'divinalis,' which deals with invisible beings – God and the angels (line 1638). See Isidore II xxiv 11–15.

1646–52 *Actualis*: the philosophy that deals with the practical matter of living and corresponds to 'policia' (see line 99n), the science of the management of life. 'Moralis' is 'monastica,' the ethics by which an individual lives; 'dispensativa' is 'iconomica,' the rules by which households are to be governed; 'civilis' is the art of government of cities or states – politics in its modern sense.

1653–87 The first court is that of Sapience's handmaid, Dame Science, who deals with 'thynges temporal' (see lines 153–4 and note). Her concern is 'the proper administering of all earthly things'; hence her court is painted with pictures of men, plants, and animals, and her companions are the natural and moral philosophers, the authors who provided Bartholomaeus with materials for his *De proprietatibus rerum* (see 1674n).

1653 The metre of this line seems defective in all witnesses.

1669 *The philosopher*: usually Aristotle; he is named in line 1674 below with the rest of the company of natural philosophers.

1671 *clerk note*: famous scholar; see *MED, noten* v (2), 2c. Since this is a past participle of a verb derived from Old French, it should perhaps be written 'clerk noté'; this would, however, produce a metrical pattern not found elsewhere in the poem.

1674–9 The author of the *Court* appears to derive his list of authorities on natural philosophy from the much longer list which appears (often in slightly differing forms) in Bartholomaeus Anglicus, *De proprietatibus rerum*. It constitutes a list of the sources on which Bartholomaeus claims to base his work and is usually divided into two parts, one list of theologians, one of philosophers. All the names in this passage of the *Court*, as natural philosophers, are taken from the philosophical list.

Arystotyl: Aristotle (384–22 BC), the Greek philosopher; he is frequently cited by Bartholomaeus as an authority on natural history.

Averous: Averroes (1126–98), an Arabian philosopher and doctor of Muslim Spain, most influential as a commentator on Aristotle. He is probably the 'Commentator' mentioned by Bartholomaeus, VIII ii. See Sarton II 355–61.

Avycenne: Avicenna (see above, line 1256n) is frequently cited as a medical authority by Bartholomaeus.

1675 *Algazel*: al-Ghazzālī (1058–1111), another Arabian philosopher; he taught at Baghdad. Some of his works were translated into Latin; Bartholomaeus (XIX x) cites him on vision. See Sarton I 753–4.

Galyene: Galen of Pergamon (d ca 200 AD), the last of the great physicians of the classical period; see Sarton i 301–7. Many of his works were known in the later Middle Ages through translations from Arabic versions; Bartholomaeus quotes him frequently.

Appollynus: There is an Appollonius in Bartholomaeus' list of sources, but I am unable to identify him with any certainty. Thorndike (*History of Magic* i 267, 723) says that several medieval works are ascribed to an unknown Appollonius in manuscripts, among them a *Liber de principalibus rerum causis*. A treatise on cautery also exists, which is ascribed to the joint authorship of Galen and Appollonius.

1676 *Pyctagoras*: Pythagoras of Samos (d 496/7 BC); see Sarton i 73–5. Bartholomaeus (III iv) cites the Pythagorean view that the soul is harmony. The legendary association of Pythagoras with mathematics and music is mentioned below, lines 1970, 2037.

Plato: the Greek philosopher (also mentioned in lines 1601, 1611). Bartholomaeus (II xix) quotes his *Timaeus*.

1677 *Macrobius*: Ambrosius Theodosius Macrobius (fl ca 400 AD), author of *Commentarii in somnium Scipionis*, a neo-Platonist work that was exceedingly popular in the Middle Ages. Bartholomaeus quotes it frequently; see XIII xxi.

Cato: Probably what is intended here is the collection of moral distichs that passed under the name of Cato throughout the Middle Ages. Bartholomaeus would have regarded him as a moral philosopher.

Boecius: Anicius Manlius Severinus Boethius (d 524 AD), most famous for his *De consolatione philosophiae*. He also wrote works on arithmetic, music, and geometry (see lines 1972n, 2079n), translations of Aristotle, and theological works. Bartholomaeus (I iii) quotes him on the Trinity.

1678 *Rasus*: Razes, the Latin name of Abū Bakr Muhammad ibn Zakarīyā al-Rāzī, an Arabian physician who flourished in the early part of the tenth century. See Sarton i 609–10.

Isake: Isaac Judaeus (d ca 932?), a Jewish physician of Egypt who was famous for his elaborate treatise on urology; see Sarton i 639–40. Bartholomaeus quotes this in v xlv.

Calyxte: 'Kalixtus Graecus sive Atheniensis' appears in Bartholomaeus' list; I cannot identify him or find a precise citation from him in *De proprietatibus rerum*.

Orbasius: Oribasius, physician to the emperor Julian (fourth century); see Sarton i 372–3.

1679 *Salustius*: Gaius Sallustius Crispus, known as Sallust, the classical historian. Bartholomaeus mentions him in xv viii.

Theophyl: Theophilos Protospatharios, a Byzantine imperial physician of the seventh century. Bartholomaeus cites his influential work on urology. See Sarton i 478.

Ypocras: Hippocrates of Cos (fifth century BC), associated with the founding of Greek medicine. He is frequently quoted by Galen and other later medical authorities; Bartholomaeus mentions him frequently.

1688–1722 The second court is that of Dame Intellygence, who deals with the invisible creation; see above, line 146n. She is concerned with heaven, hell, angels, and devils – knowledge that goes beyond what can be perceived with the five senses.

1694 *jerarchyes*: See above, lines 442n, 617–73n.

1697 *ypyphanye*: Dionysius says that the first hierarchy is called 'epiphania'; the term is explained as meaning 'the highest showing forth' in *Legenda aurea*, page 644. The author could also have found the term in Bartholomaeus, II vii.

1709 The 'clerkes' with Dame Intellygence are all authors of works that deal with 'invysyble creatures' – heaven and the angels.

Denyse: pseudo-Dionysius, the authority on angels; see above, line 442n.

Bernard: St Bernard of Clairvaux (d 1153), the ultimate source for the story of the daughters of God. Bartholomaeus quotes Bernard's description of God in I xvii.

Bede: the Venerable Bede (d 735); Bartholomaeus quotes him on bad angels (II xix).

Barthilmew: Bartholomaeus Anglicus; he devotes the second book of *De propriet-atibus rerum* to angels good and bad.

1710 *Bonaventure*: St Bonaventura (d 1274), philosopher and author of several devotional and mystical works. The author of the *Court* believed this St Bonaventura to be the author of *Meditationes vitae Christi*, on which he drew for the account of 'the pryvy counceyl of the fyrst nature' in the first part of his poem.

1712 Written above the word 'nature' in T are the words, 'Scilicet dei nature naturantis': 'Namely, of God as Nature Naturing.' The term 'nature naturing' applied to God had been current in philosophy since the twelfth century; for its use see Henry A. Lucks 'Natura Naturans, Natura Naturata,' *New Scholasticism* IX (1935) 1–24; *OED*, *nature* v[1].

1732 *Pryamus*: King Priam of Troy; Ilyon or Ilium is another name for Troy. The author of the *Court*, however, like Lydgate, holds that Ilyon was the name of the splendid palace or hall built by Priam in the city of Troy; see Lydgate's *Troy Book* ii 927–83. (Lydgate is following Guido delle Colonne on this point.)

1736 *As for a maystry ...*: 'As a work supreme in appearance'?

1739–43 These four books constitute the 'wisdom literature' of the Vulgate Bible: the 'Parables' or Proverbs ('Parabolae Salomonis' i 1); Eclesiastes; the 'boke of Sapyence' or Wisdom; and Ecclesiasticus. The latter two are relegated to the Apocrypha in the Authorized Version.

1744–57 The author of the *Court*, as Bühler pointed out (*Sources of the Court of*

Sapience 15–16), takes his description of Minerva from the little treatise called *De deorum imaginibus libellus*, which usually goes, erroneously, under the name of Albricus Philosophus. It is printed in *Fulgentius Metaforalis* ed Hans Liebeschütz (Leipzig 1926) 117–28. See also Jean Seznec *The Survival of the Pagan Gods* 167–79. Both Liebeschütz and Seznec assign the *Libellus* to a date near 1400.

1747–9 *Libellus* viii:

> Minerva, dea sapientie ex cerebro Jovis nata, alio nomine Palas dicta est. Hec enim pingebatur a poetis in similitudinem unius domine armate ... cuius caput yride circumcinctum erat ipsamque cassis cum crista desuper contegebat.

> Minerva, goddess of wisdom, was born from the brain of Jupiter; she is also called Pallas. She was painted by the poets in the likeness of an armed woman ... whose head was girdled about with a rainbow; a helmet with a crest on top covered her. [ed Liebeschütz, 119–20]

The detail about the rainbow is not found in the other mythographers; 'yride' is 'corrected' to 'viri' or 'viride' in earlier printed texts of the *Libellus*.

1749–52 *Libellus* viii:

> Ipsa autem lanceam tenebat in dextera. In sinistra vero scutum cristalinum habebat, quod caput monstruose gorgonis cerviciis [sic] serpentibus continebat.

> She held a spear in her right hand, but in her left she had a crystal shield, which contained the monstrous head of the Gorgon with its snakes at the neck (?). [ed Liebeschütz, 120]

The text of the *Libellus* is corrupt at this point. The author of the *Court* seems either to have misunderstood the image or to have had an even worse text before him: these lines attribute to Minerva herself the snakes that grew instead of hair upon the head of the Gorgon, Medusa, which Minerva carried on her shield.

1753–7 *Libellus* viii:

> Hec igitur oculos habebat splendidos. Triplici colore palium induebat distinctum ... Juxta se habebat olivam viridem pictam et desuper avem que dicitur noctua volitantem.

> She had bright eyes. She wore a garment adorned with three colours ... Next to her was painted a green olive tree, and flying above the bird which is called the night-owl. [ed Liebeschütz, 120]

1759–78 Sapience's interpretation of the figure of Minerva appears to be taken from Petrus Berchorius, *De formis figurisque deorum*, which has been edited by the Instituut voor Laat Latijn der Rijksuniversiteit Utrecht (1966), with an introduction by J. Engels. The *Libellus* attributed to Albricus in fact derives from Berchorius, omitting the moralizations (see Seznec 170–9), but Berchorius does not have the detail about the rainbow (*Court* lines 1748, 1766), so the author of the *Court* must have used both works.

1763 The opening verse of the book of Ecclesiasticus, 'Omnis sapientia a Domino Deo est' ('All wisdom is from the Lord God'), is written beside this line in T. This verse is quoted by Berchorius, page 31.

1765 Berchorius 31, lines 36–7: 'Sapientia ... debet habere multiplicem armaturam virtutum' ('Wisdom ... ought to have the manifold armour of the virtues').

1767–71 Berchorius 31, lines 57ff:

[Scutum] debet esse ymago id est timoris divini habere ymaginacionem et paviditatem, quia scilicet sapiens semper debet timere, et timorem Domini et ymaginem Gorgone id est mortis vel dyaboli, in corde suo pictam habere ut sic per timorem Domini possit a viciis declinare.

[The shield] ought to be an image, that is, it ought to have the imagining and dread of the fear of the Lord, because in truth a wise man should always fear, and have the fear of the Lord and the image of the Gorgon (that is, of death or the devil) pictured in his heart, so that in this way, through the fear of the Lord, he may be able to abstain from vices.

1772–8 All these qualities (except those in line 1776) appear in Berchorius, pages 31–2.

1774 The metre of this line seems defective. 'Tholyve' is the C reading; P has 'The lyue' and T 'Tholyng,' which suggests that the elision in C is correct. Spindler supplies 'set' after 'nyght-crowe.' A more drastic emendation would be to read 'noctua' for 'nyght-crowe': it is the Latin name of the night-crow, used by Berchorius.

1779–85 The form of this reference suggests that the author means not the *Mythologicon* of Fabius Planciades Fulgentius (ca 480–550) but the *Fulgentius metaforalis* of John Ridevall (written by 1333–4). Ridevall's work is a rearrangement and allegorization of part of the *Mythologicon*. It contains six chapters; the first is introductory and discusses idolatry; the next five are devoted to Saturn and his four children, Jupiter, Juno, Neptune, and Pluto. Saturn is interpreted as prudence, and his children are the four parts of prudence: benevolence, memory, intelligence, and foresight. (Fulgentius interprets Saturn as time and his children as the four elements.) For Ridevall, see Beryl Smalley *English Friars* 109–32.

The author of the *Court* may have omitted Jupiter (benevolence) deliberately: the classical division of prudence gave it three parts: memory, intelligence, and foresight, and most medieval authors followed this scheme. See Cicero *De inventione* II liii 160; Erwin Panofsky 'Titian's Allegory of Prudence: a Postscript' *Meaning in the Visual Arts* (1955; reprinted 1970) 184–6.

1792 The wisdom of King Solomon was proverbial: see 1 Kings 3:5–14, 4:29–34 (Vulg 3 Reg 3:5–14, 4:29–34); Whiting s460.

1794 This line is defective in all witnesses. Perhaps 'her' should be supplied after 'torned.'

1796–7 *The doctours four*: the doctrinal authorities of the Latin Christian Church, St Gregory the Great (d 604), St Augustine of Hippo (d 430), St Jerome (d 420), and St Ambrose (d 397)

1797 *thynges*: CP; 'thyng' T. The T reading is probably correct; see 1375n.

1800 *Holcote*: Robert Holcot (d 1349), an English Dominican friar, author of a famous commentary on the Book of Wisdom (Sapyence); see Beryl Smalley *English Friars* 133–202.

1801 *Notyngham*: William of Nottingham (d 1251), a Franciscan friar, author of a commentary on the Gospels; see the article by A.G. Little in DNB.

1802 *Mayster of Sentence*: The scholastic theologian Peter Lombard (d ca 1160) was known as the Magister Sententiarum or Mayster of Sentence from the title of his most famous work, *Sententiarum libri* IV. This line is either a Lydgatian type C line, or a syllable has been lost in all witnesses.

1803 *Seynt Thomas*: St Thomas Aquinas (d 1274), the famous theologian most venerated by the friars of his own Dominican order

1804 *The Mayster of the Storyes* (or Magister Historiarum): Peter Comestor (d 1179 or 1189), author of the widely popular *Historia scolastica* (a retelling of Biblical history). 'Story' is an aphetic form of 'history.'

1805 CP; the reading of T is smoother: 'And many mo good clerkis and dyuyne.'

Incipit ...: Caxton omits this incipit. P adds 'Explicit processus de tercia curia' immediately before it; but neither T nor C terminate the procession of Sapyence's courtyard here. Since Grammar and the other liberal arts are part of the train of Dame Theologye, I have assumed that P added the explicit here in error. Neither C nor P has a general explicit between Astronomye and Feith, where it might be expected.

1807–41 The liberal art of grammar is the study of Latin grammar, essential for all other learning. The author of the *Court* takes his account from the grammatical treatise provided by Balbus at the beginning of his *Catholicon*; the four ladies are the four parts of grammar, which are defined at the beginning of the treatise.

1808, 1814 *Ortographye*: The first part of the *Catholicon* is devoted to 'orthographia: de recta scriptura litterarum et syllabarum' ('of the correct writing of letters and syllables'). It deals mainly with the alterations in spelling of Latin words when they undergo grammatical modifications.

1810, 1815–17 *Ethymologye*: Balbus explains that this word is derived from the Greek for 'true speech'; his use of the word is equivalent to the modern grammatical term 'accidence' – that is, it deals with the different parts of speech, the declension of nouns, the conjugation of verbs, and so on.

1811, 1818 *Dyasyntastica*: Balbus' 'diasyntastica' is the modern 'syntax'; he deals with etymologia and diasyntastica together in one tractatus as the accidence and syntax of Latin grammar.

1811, 1819 *Prosodye*: Prosodia was the part of grammar that assigned the correct accent and quantity ('tyme') to the syllables of Latin words and hence provided the foundation for an understanding of quantitative verse.

1815 *the partes of reson*: 'parts of speech'; see OED, *reason* 3c. For 'partes' see the same word in line 1130 and note.

1823 *reson*: 'a sentence'; see OED, *reason* sb 4; compare line 1857.

syllable: probably to be pronounced here as the disyllable 'syllabe,' as in lines 2045, 2051. See OED, *syllab*.

1825–7 Grammar is traditionally 'the ground, the yate [gate] the entryng' (Isidore's 'origo et fundamentum') because she teaches the Latin language in which all the other arts are written. Hence they are 'made specyal' or acquire their individual distinguishing features only after a study of Latin grammar; see OED, *special* 3.

entryng: here presumably pronounced 'entering' to rhyme with 'consyderyng,' although the more usual form in the fifteenth century is disyllabic

1828 *Moyses, Cadmus, and Carmenta*: the traditional inventors of letters. Moses was held to have invented the Hebrew alphabet, Cadmus to have brought these letters to Greece (via Phoenicia), and Carmenta (also called Carmentis and Nicostrata) to have taken the Greek letters to Italy when she emigrated there with her son, King Evander (*Aeneid* viii 333–6). See Isidore I iii 5–6, I iv 1.

1829 *Ebrard*: Eberard of Béthune (northern France), whose versified Latin grammar, the *Graecismus*, was written in 1212. See Curtius *European Literature* 43.

Ferryn: unidentified. PT read 'Ferrum' or 'Ferrun.'

Johan Gerlond: John Garland, author of several grammatical works, an Englishman who taught at the University of Paris during the first half of the thirteenth century; see DNB. His *Scolarium morale*, *Synonoma*, and *Equivoca* were among the earliest books to be printed.

Donate: Aelius Donatus, a fourth-century grammarian, whose *Ars minor* (often known as 'the donet') had to be learned by heart by medieval students at the beginning of their training in grammar. See Curtius 43–8.

1830 *Prescyane*: Priscianus Caesariensis or Priscian (fl ca 500), author of *Institutiones grammaticae*, a large and influential Latin grammar; see R.H. Robins *Ancient and Mediaeval Grammatical Theory in Europe* (London 1951) 67.

Petyr: identified by a note in T ('Helias, qui compilavit Memoriale minor') as Petrus Helias, a Frenchman who taught at Paris circa 1142. He was the author of a versified *Grammatica* based on Priscian.

Thomas de Hennaya (or Thomas Hanney): began his grammatical treatise entitled *Memoriale juniorum* or *De quattuor partibus grammaticae* at Toulouse in 1313 and finished it later in England. It survives in manuscript in the Bodleian Library (ms Bodl 643; ms Auct F 3 9); see DNB, *Hanney*. His grammar deals with the same 'four parts' as those in the *Catholicon*.

1831 *Lambart Papy*: must be Papias of Lombardy, an eleventh-century grammarian, the author of a *Vocabularium*, frequently quoted by Balbus, which was printed several times in the fifteenth century. In T 'Achos' is written over Lambart and 'Pictaviensis' ('of Poitiers') over Papy; it is hard to make sense of these notes. Bühler (*Sources of the Court of Sapience* 70) suggests that Achos Pictaviensis should be read as 'Abbas Pictaviensis': he argues that the annotator must have confused Peter Helias with one Helias, abbot of Poitiers, and that the note should therefore appear over 'Petyr' in the line above.

1832 *The Januens*: Balbus ('Januensis': 'of Genoa'), author of the *Catholicon*; see introduction, page xxxv.

1834 *Paryarmonyse*: a garbled version of the Greek title, *Peri hermeneias* (*On Interpretation*), of Aristotle's introduction to logic. Perhaps the work is found in Dame Gramer's parlour because it starts by considering language and the logic that governs it.

1835 *Hugucyon*: Uguccio of Pisa, bishop of Ferrara, canonist and lexicographer (d 1210). His dictionary, entitled *Derivationes*, was based largely on Papias and used extensively by Balbus.

1839–41 Since grammar is 'the ground, the yate, the entryng,' her pupils are 'babes,' first-grade schoolchildren, who must master Latin before proceeding to the next art, logic, whose instruction is given entirely in that language.

1847–8 The definition of Dialectic as the art that distinguished between truth and falsehood in reasoning is traditional; compare Isidore II xxii 1: 'Dialectica ... docet enim in pluribus generibus quaestionum quemadmodum disputando vera et falsa dijudicentur' ('Dialectic teaches how to distinguish the true from the false in many kinds of questions by the method of disputation').

1850, 1852 *dyffert, scire, incipit, desinit*: typical logical terminology. 'Differt,' Latin for 'it is different from,' and 'scire,' 'to know,' are perhaps just examples of words frequently used by logicians; 'incipit' ('starts') and 'desinit' ('stops') are words that feature in a group of logical problems and paradoxes ('sophysmes,' line 1851) concerning statements about things in flux. See Walter Burleigh (b 1275) *De puritate artis logicae tractatus longior* ed P. Boehner, tr II, tertia pars, iv.

1853 *The Comune Treatys*: unidentified. In T, 'the somies [sonnes?] of art' is written above '*comone tretyse*.' It seems possible that the book could be the logical treatise of Peter of Spain, which was originally entitled *Tractatus* but which had acquired the title *Summulae* by the fifteenth century. Most of the terms used by Dame Dyaletica can be found conveniently in Peter of Spain's work, but its most recent editor, L.M. De Rijk, believes that the *Tractatus* was not popular in England. He maintains that the logical treatise *Cum sit nostra*, called in one manuscript *Summule ad modum Oxonie*, was the text most frequently used there. *Cum sit nostra* also contains most of the terms used in the *Court*, but since this material must have been common to many similar introductory texts, it is impossible to prove dependence.

1854–5 *proposicion*: a proposition in the logical sense, a statement that affirms or denies a relation between its subject and predicate – for example, 'homo currit,' 'the man is running.' Medieval students learned to define the kind of proposition they were dealing with by asking a / 'Que?' ('Whiche?' line 1854), to which the answer was either 'categorical' or 'hypothetical'; b / 'Qualis?' ('whatkyns?' of line 1854, 'of what kind?'), to which the reply was either 'affirmative' or 'negative'; and c / 'Quanta?' ('how great?' perhaps 'what?' of line 1854), to which the answer was 'universal,' 'particular,' 'indefinite,' or 'singular' (see below, lines 1858–60n). See Peter of Spain *Tractatus* I 7–10; and the interlinear notes, appendix 2.

1856 *subject, couple, and predicate*: the subjectum, copula, and predicatum that make up a categorical proposition; see Peter of Spain I 7.

1857 'And how the proposition must be a sentence in the indicative'; see Peter of Spain I 6.

1858–60 Peter of Spain divides propositions first into universalis, particularis, indefinita, singularis (I 8) and then into affirmativa and negativa (I 9). A universal proposition is one of the kind 'omnis homo currit' ('every man is running'); 'aliquis homo currit' ('someone is running') is particular; 'homo currit' ('a man is running') is indefinite; and 'iste homo currit' ('that man is running') is singular. These in turn can be classified as affirmative ('homo currit') or negative ('homo non currit').

1861–2 *subalterne, contradictyon, contrarye*: These terms classify the relationships between different propositions using the same terms. For example, 'every man runs' and 'no man runs' are contrary propositions: one is a universal affirmative and the other is a universal negative of the same subject and predicate. 'Every man runs' and 'a certain man does not run' are contradictory (universal affirmative and particular negative); and 'every man runs' and 'a certain man runs' are subaltern (universal affirmative and particular affirmative). The author of the *Court* leaves out the fourth term, 'subcontrary' (particular affirmative and particular negative). These may be found, with a diagram, in Peter of Spain, I 12.

1863 *Equypollens*; equipollence, equivalence between two propositions couched in different terms. For example, 'not every man is running' is equipollent to 'a certain man is not running.' See Peter of Spain I 14, 18.
conversyon: transposition of the terms of a proposition – for example, 'no man is a stone' and 'no stone is a man.' See Peter of Spain I 15.

1864 *Sylogysmus*: syllogism. Peter of Spain (IV, v 2) considers 'sillogismus' to be a subdivision of 'argumentum' (maner of arguyng').

1865–6 *to make an oblygacyon*: to construct an argument so well that one's opponent is obliged to grant or deny a conclusion against his intentions. Walter Burleigh wrote a treatise on obligations; see *Logica Modernorum* ed De Rijk, II i 40, and the definition on pages 83–4.

1867 *dysputen*: Spindler's emendation; 'dyspute' CPT. The metre would seem to require some emendation, and the third-person indicative plural in this text frequently has the ending -(e)n.

1868 *comonyng*: 'debating'; see *MED, communing* 4a.

1868–9 *sophyms*: sophisms, sophistries, specious arguments used to display skill in reasoning. Such arguments were occasionally cast in such a way as to 'prove' that the opponent is a donkey ('Tu es asinus,' 'Thou art a donkey'). See, for example, Walter Burleigh's *De puritate artis logicae tractatus brevior*, pages 223, 228, where he discusses the sophisms 'Non aliquid es, et tu es asinus' and 'Nullo currente tu es asinus.'

1870–2 This seems to be a list of textbooks on logic, although it is not possible to identify all of them with precision. The *Topykes* and *Elynks* are presumably Aristotle's *Topica* and *Sophistici elenchi*, and the *Predycamentes* may probably be identified with his *Categoriae*, as this work sometimes went under that title in the Middle Ages; see *Logica Modernorum* II ii 421. A treatise entitled *De universalibus* (*On the Universals*) is mentioned in *Logica Modernorum*, II i 53. I cannot identify the *Natures Good* or the *Pryncipals*.

1877–90 Medieval writers often tended to speak of logic as if it could be identified with philosophy; Isidore places his definition of philosophy (given above, lines 1555–1652) in between his definition of logic and his account of that art (II xxii–xxxi). The English logical text *Cum sit nostra* defines 'dialectica' as 'ars artium,' a term more usually reserved for 'philosophia' (see above, line 1562). The author of the *Court* appears to think that all philosophers can be regarded as logicians; hence he takes the list of authorities on logic in these lines from the list of philosophers conveniently provided by Bartholomaeus Anglicus (see above, line 1674n). The result is odd: many of these 'philosophers' are natural scientists or medical authorities whose connection with logic seems remote indeed.

1881 *Alfred*: Alfred of Sareshel (fl ca 1200), also called Alfred the Englishman. He wrote a treatise on the action of the heart. Bartholomaeus made use (XVII xx) of Alfred's translation and commentary on the Aristotelian work called *De vegetabilibus*. See Sarton ii 561–2.

Haly: Alī ibn Abbās, known to the west as Haly Abbas (d 994/5), an Arabian physician who worked in Baghdad and a famous medical authority; see Sarton i 677–8. Bartholomaeus uses his work in book v.

Jorath: an authority on fish; see line 1255n.

Juvenal: the Roman satirist who wrote in the late first century AD; Bartholomaeus quotes a line from him in XIX cxlv.

1882 *Eraclius*: probably the Eraclitus from Bartholomaeus' list, perhaps to be identified with Heraclitus the philosopher (fl ca 500 BC), cited in *De proprietatibus rerum*, III iv (where Bartholomaeus repeats an opinion of Heraclitus which he found quoted in Aristotle's *De anima*). A.G. Rigg has drawn my attention to a

medieval Eraclius, the obscure author of some items in prose and verse in ms
Bodleian Library Add A 44; see André Wilmart 'Le Florilège Mixte de Thomas
Bekynton' *Mediaeval and Renaissance Studies* I (1943) 48, note 1, and items
14–17, 77.

Affricane: Scipio Africanus in Bartholomaeus; probably Africanus Minor is
intended, for he was well known to medieval readers for the part he plays in the
dialogue in Cicero's *De re publica*. The commentary of Macrobius on that fragment of Cicero's book that deals with Scipio's dream was widely celebrated; Bartholomaeus quotes it frequently (for example, in VIII ii).

Demostene: Demosthenes, the Greek orator (d 322 BC); Bartholomaeus mentions
him in XV viii.

1883 *Mercurius*: Hermes Trismegistus, the supposed author of *Asclepius*, an astrolog-
ical treatise on the divine origin of man and the mysteries of Egyptian religion.
Bartholomaeus quotes Mercurius on the threefold world in VIII i.

Damascene: St John of Damascus (Joannes Damascenus), a Christian Arab who
wrote in the early part of the eighth century. Part of his major work was translated into Latin by 1154 and entitled *De fide orthodoxa*. He is the only author in
this section whose name is taken from Bartholomaeus' theological list; this may
be explained by the fact that he is quoted in almost every book of *De proprietatibus rerum* since his work covers natural history as well as theology.

1884 *Gyles*: Giles of Corbeil (Aegidius Corboliensis, d 1220–4), author of a versified
treatise on urines. Bartholomaeus includes a quotation from this work in XIX xiv.

Euclide: Euclid (fl ca 300 BC), the classicial geometer. See also below, line 2015.

Rufus: Rufus of Ephesus, physician (fl ca 100). His works were known to the
Arabian medical writers, who cite him frequently as an authority. Bartholomaeus
(IV viii) mentions him as an authority on blood.

Cythero: Marcus Tullius Cicero, quoted by Bartholomaeus in V xxviii. See also
lines 1886n, 1919n.

1885 *Democritus*: Democritus of Abdera (ca 460–ca 370 BC), the classical philosopher;
he is quoted by Bartholomaeus, III iv.

Physyologus: in fact not an author but the title of a book. The *Physiologus* is a
bestiary, or treatise on the symbolic properties of animals; it is very old, and its
origins are obscure. See Thorndike I 497–503.

1886 *Syr Theoprasse*: Theophrastus (d 288/285 BC), botanist, peripatetic philosopher,
and successor to Aristotle. See Sarton I 143–4. 'Sir' was frequently added to
classical names as an honorific; see *OED, sir* 2; and below, lines 1888, 2199.

Tytus: Titus Livius or Livy (d 17 AD), Roman historian

Cipio: must be Scipio Africanus, as in line 1882 above. The name is spelled 'Cypio
affricanus' in the list of authorities in the first edition of the English translation of
Bartholomaeus (Westminster, Wynkyn de Worde 1495?). The list in that edition

makes two people out of Cicero, naming him once as 'Cithero' and again as 'Tullius' (compare *Court*, lines 1884, 1919); perhaps the doubling of Scipio (and of Sallust? *Court* lines 1679, 1889) came about in a similar way.

1887 *William Conches*: William of Conches (d 1154?), philosopher and teacher, associated with the university at Paris. See *DNB* William of Conches.

Zeno: Probably Zeno of Elea (b ca 490 BC). Bartholomaeus quotes a saying of Zeno, which had been transmitted by Aristotle. However, Zeno could also be Zeno of Citium (335–263 BC), the founder of Stoicism.

Johannycus: Johannicius, the Latin name of Hunain ibn Isháq (ninth century, a famous translator of Greek scientific works into Arabic; see Sarton i 611–3). His name was attached to various medical writings that circulated in Latin translations; Bartholomaeus cites him frequently.

1888 *Syr Tholome*: Claudius Ptolemaeus, the classical astronomer; see below, lines 2003n, 2199n. Bartholomaeus quotes him frequently in VIII.

Varro: Marcus Terentius Varro (116–27 BC), Roman scholar; his works are extant only in fragments. Bartholomaeus mentions one of his definitions in v xliii.

Plinius: Pliny the Elder (d 79), Roman encyclopaedist. His *Naturalis historia* was used extensively by Bartholomaeus. See also above, line 1255.

1889 *Salustyane*: most probably a second appearance of Sallust; see above, lines 1679n, 1886n.

Permenides: Parmenides of Elea (fifth century BC), the Greek philosopher. Bartholomaeus quotes a definition of his in III iv; he derived this from Aristotle's *De anima*.

1891 *Rethoryke*: 'The art of speaking well' is by this date reduced mainly to a list of ornaments with which both prose and verse may be decorated. The author of the *Court*, as he says himself (lines 1916–18), takes the few technicalities of rhetoric that he mentions from the fourth treatise of Balbus' *Catholicon*, which contains a long catalogue of the faults and figures of speech in prose and poetry.

1903 *facund*: 'eloquence' (Latin 'facundia')

1904 *Cacephaton*: Cacephaton or cacophony is the second of the ten faults or 'vicia' ('vyces' in line 1906) of speech listed by Balbus. As the term itself implies, it is the 'ugly sound' produced by the unskilful placing of words so that the syllables clash unharmoniously together.

1905 *endytyng*: 'composition'; see *OED*, indite 3.

1907 *colours*: The 'colours' of rhetoric are the different figures by which speech might be adorned; they include such devices as alliteration, repetition, metaphor, apostrophe, and so on. The term is taken over from the Latin rhetorical textbooks. See *OED, colour* 13.

1909 *poynted*: 'punctuated.' A short note on punctuation is given by Balbus as the end of his treatise on figures.

1910 *Dystynctyon*: 'Distinctio' is the term used by Balbus for the division of a sentence into clauses by punctuation.

1911 *coma*: the sign used to perform the function of a modern comma; Balbus describes it as a point with a tail going upwards.

colym (Latin 'colum'): the sign that corresponds to the modern semicolon; it had the appearance of a full stop (period).

periodus: the period or full stop; it was shaped like a modern comma.

These are the only marks of punctuation described by Balbus.

1914–15 *Galfryde*: Geoffrey of Vinsauf, who wrote his versified treatise on rhetoric, *Poetria nova*, circa 1210. Geoffrey also wrote a prose treatise covering much the same ground as *Poetria nova*; this is known as *Tria sunt*, after its opening words. See E. Faral *Les Arts Poétiques du xiie et du xiiie siècle* 15–33, 194–327.

Written over 'Tria sunt' in T are the words, 'id est ad librum qui incipit "Papa stupor mundi."' ('That is, to the book which begins, "O Pope, the wonder of the world!"') Geoffrey wrote two sets of verses with this beginning, *Poetria nova* itself and a plea to the pope on behalf of England. It seems most likely that the former of these is intended here by the author of the note, who must have been confused about the relationship between the prose *Tria sunt* and the verse *Poetria nova*. See the introduction, page xvi, for the interlinear glosses.

1916 *Januens*: See lines 1832n, 1891n.

1919 *Tullius*: Marcus Tullius Cicero (d 43 BC). Two treatises on rhetoric were assigned to Cicero during the Middle Ages: one, the *De inventione*, is a genuine work; the other, *Rhetorica ad Herrenium*, is no longer ascribed to him. Both works were exceedingly influential.

1923 *the Code*: the *Codex constitutionum* of the Emperor Justinian, one of the major compilations of Roman law. The 'Dygestes thre' refers to the *Digesta* of Justinian; the Glossarists (jurists at the law school of Bologna in the eleventh to the twelfth centuries) divided the *Digesta* into three parts called *Digestum vetus*, *Infortiatum*, and *Digestum novum*. These two books, together with Justinian's *Institutes* (see above, line 146n) and his *Novellae*, constituted the Corpus Juris or body of civil law on which most of the legal systems of Europe were based.

1924 *bookes ... of physyk*: medical textbooks. Legal and medical books seem rather odd sources of 'ornate speche' and 'gay thinges,' but both contained numerous extracts from a variety of authors and would be sources of illustrative anecdotes and impressive vocabulary.

1928 *Blesens*: Petrus Blesensis, Peter of Blois (fl 1190), author of a large collection of letters and sermons and of a work on the rhetorical art of letter-writing ('ars dictaminis'); see N. Denholm-Young *Collected Papers on Mediaeval Subjects* (Oxford 1946) 32, 51; *DNB* Peter of Blois.

Richard de Pophis: a Roman notary of the later thirteenth century, author of a collection of letters extant in nine manuscripts in England; see Denholm-Young 52.

1929 *Farrose pystyls*: This work was identified by James J. Murphy ('Caxton's Two Choices' 250) as the *Somnium morale Pharaonis* of John of Limoges (Joannes Lemovicensis, fl 1208). Also entitled *Epistolae Pharaonis* in some manuscripts, this little work is a retelling in model epistolary form of the story of Pharaoh's dream in Genesis 41. It is not as rare as Murphy's remarks suggest: it survives in at least two manuscripts at Oxford and many more in Europe; it was printed at least once. It has been published in *Johannis Lemovicensis opera omnia* ed C. Horvath (Veszprém 1932).

1931 The classical poets Ovid, Homer, Virgil, Lucan, and Horace traditionally represented the poetry of the ancient world; Chaucer gives a similar list in *Troilus*, v 1792.

1932 *Alane*: identified by a note in T as 'Alanus de Insulis,' or Alain of Lille (d 1202), author of *De planctu naturae*, a well-known and influential allegory in alternating prose and verse, and of *Anticlaudianus*, a poem in dactylic hexameters
Bernard: In T the word 'Silvestris' is written over 'Prudencius' instead of over Bernard; it identifies Bernard as Bernardus Silvestris (fl ca 1150), author of *De universitate mundi*, a work in prose and verse.
Prudencius: Prudentius Aurelius Clemens (b 348), a Christian Latin poet, author of the allegorical poem *Psychomachia*
Stace: Publius Papinius Statius (ca 45–96 AD), author of the *Thebais*, an epic poem

1933 *Arsmetryke*: This version of the word 'arithmetic' is common in the late Middle Ages; it was based on a false etymology, as if the word came from 'ars metrica,' 'art of measuring.' The account of this art in the *Court* is based largely on Isidore, III i–iv.

1939 Arithmetic is necessary to all the arts because, according to the Bible, nothing was made without number; see line 1954n. Hence ignorance of the properties of numbers would affect the understanding of both written works and the whole natural creation; see lines 1940–60 below. The 'sex artes' are of course the 'ladyes al' of line 1933: arithmetic traditionally had the middle place in the seven arts. For this line P reads, 'Withoute hir ben the six artes vsure,' and T reads, 'Without hir byn so syx artes vnsure.' It seems likely that 'Without' should be preferred to C's 'Withouten,' since 'artes' in this position must be disyllabic. See line 1375n.

1940–6 There are more scriptural examples here than there are in Isidore, but the principle is the same. Isidore (III iv 1–4) argues that arithmetic is necessary in order to understand the Bible, for there are many things in scripture that are expressed by numbers used mystically: for example, the days of creation are six because that number signifies perfection. Classical arithmetic concerned itself not with techniques such as multiplication or addition but with the properties and significances of the different numbers; medieval Christian writers adapted this to the explication of symbolic passages in Christian writings.

1945 *Moyses*: Moses; Exod 24:18

Ely: Elijah (Vulg, Elias); 1 Kings 19:8 (Vulg 3 Reg 19:8)

Cryst: Matt 4:2

1954–5 Wisd 11:21: 'Thou hast ordered all things in measure, and number, and weight.'

1958–60 Isidore III iv 3–4:

Datum est etiam nobis ex aliqua parte sub numerorum consistere disciplina, quando horas per eam dicimus, quando de mensuum curriculo disputamus, quando spatium anni redeuntis agnoscimus.

For it is appointed to us in some part to live under the discipline of numbers whenever we tell the time by them, or reckon up the course of the months, or know the time-span of the returning year.

The syntax of the lines in the *Court* is rather obscure; perhaps they should be read, 'When it is uncertain what hour, week, month, or year it is, we can arrive at true knowledge by studying their courses, times, and duration with the help of Lady Arithmetic.'

1962–6 The techniques mentioned here – addition, subtraction, division, multiplication – formed no part of classical arithmetic; they belong to 'algorist' arithmetic, which was introduced into Europe from the East during the twelfth century with the translation of the treatise of al-Khowarizmi (the author's name was corrupted into a title, 'The *Algorism*'). The 'ten fygures of augrym [algorism]' are the Arabic numerals (counting the zero), which were introduced at the same time, radically simplifying arithmetic and making possible better ways of computing calendars, etc. See Guy Beaujouan 'L'Enseignement de l'Arithmétique élémentaire à l'Université de Paris aux XIII⁰ et XIV⁰ siècles' *Homenaje a Millás-Vallicrosa* I (Barcelona 1954) 93–124; see also *OED*, algorism.

dymynew: 'subtract'; see *MED*, diminuen; *DOST*, diminew.

1969 The definition is given in Isidore, III iii 1: 'Numerus autem est multitudo ex unitatibus constituta.'

1970 *Pyctagoras*: Pythagoras, like all these companions of Arsmetryke, is from Isidore, III ii. He is the philosopher Pythagoras of Samos who was said to have instituted the study of number as the key to all things; see also line 1676n above.

1971 *Nychomacus*: Nicomachus of Gerasa (ca 100 AD), author of an introduction to arithmetic

1972 *Apuleius*: Apuleius of Madaura (b ca 123 AD), more famous as the author of the *Golden Ass*; he also wrote an *Arithmetica*, now lost.

Boece: Boethius; see line 1677n above. The name is spelled 'boys' in P (line 2079; line 1972 is missing in P), which suggests the monosyllabic pronunciation required to make lines 1972 and 2079 scan.

1975–2016 The section on geometry is too general to assign to any definite source, although some of the terms are made clearer by comparing it with the account in Isidore, III x–xiv, or with the little treatise on geometry ascribed to Boethius.

1978 *plumbe*: the leaden weight attached to the end of a plumb-line

1979 *fygures queynte*: 'ingenious or skilful diagrams.' Both Boethius and Isidore begin geometry by defining the different figures with which it is concerned, such as the triangle and quadrilateral in line 1983 below.

1982 *spyres*: 'spheres'

1989 Isidore (III xii 1) explains that the centre of a circle is called the 'point' ('punctum') of a circle in Latin.

1994–5 Isidore derives 'geometry' from the Greek words for 'earth' and 'measure.' See the account of the origin of geometry, line 2010n below.

1996–2009 These two stanzas are, as Bühler points out, taken directly from Balbus, sv *terra*. Aristotle records that mathematicians put the cirumference of the earth at 400,000 stades (*De caelo* II xiv; 298b), which appears as 24,000 miles in the Latin text used by the scholastic philosopher Albertus Magnus (d 1280). Albertus thinks that this figure must either be a scribal error or is simply incorrect, because at the time of Aristotle the diameters of the sun, the moon, and the earth were not correctly known (*Commentarium in De caelo* II, tract iv, ca 9, in *Opera Omnia* ed A. Borgnet, 4 [Paris 1890] 234–5).

2003 *Tholome*: Ptolemy, who wrote on geography as well as astronomy. See also lines 1888n, 2199n.

2008–9 Balbus ascribes this maxim to the fifth homily of the *Hexaemeron* of St Basil the Great (see above, line 1257n); I have been unable to find it there. In Latin it runs: 'Que utiliora sunt mandari memorie principalius meruerunt.'

2010–11 Isidore (III x 1) explains that the Egyptians discovered geometry (or 'earth-measure') because of the necessity of replacing their boundaries every time the Nile flooded and covered everything with mud.

2012 *Theodosius*: Theodosius of Bithynia (150–70 BC?), Greek mathematician and astronomer; see Sarton i 211. A Latin version of his work on the sections of the sphere had been made by Gerard of Cremona in the twelfth century; see Sarton ii 341.

2015 *Euglyd*: Euclid; see above, line 1884n. His work had become available to the West in a Latin translation made from the Arabic in the later twelfth century.

2019–27 Dame Musyk's three ladies are the three parts of music listed by Isidore (III xviii). Dame Armonyca is 'harmonica, quae decernit in sonis acutum et gravem' ('harmony, which distinguishes high and low sounds'). Rethmica is 'rythmica,

quae requirit incursionem verborum, utrum bene sonus an male cohaereat'
('rhythm, which takes care of fitting in the words, and whether the sound blends
well or badly' ['measured dyte with the note': 'put the words to music,' line
2025]). Metrica, the third, deals with metres; in the *Court* she writes down the
song (*OED, prick* v 13: 'to set down music in writing') in notes of the appropriate
length.

2029–30 Isidore (III xv): 'Musica est peritia modulationis sono cantuque consistens'
('Music is skill in melody and it consists of sound and song').

2032 *Tubal*: the founder of music according to several medieval authorities, including
Isidore (III xvi). The basis for this assertion was Gen 4:21–2, where it is said that
Jubal was 'the father of them that play upon the harp and the organs,' and his
half-brother, Tubalcain, was the first smith. Medieval writers thought that this
was the true version of the story about Pythagoras, mentioned here in lines
2036–7. The Jubal/Tubal confusion is not explained. It goes back at least as far as
Isidore; see A.G. Rigg 'Gregory's Garden: a Latin dream-allegory' *Medium
Aevum* xxxv (1966) 34.
Linus Tibeus: Linus Thebaeus, also mentioned by Isidore in the same chapter.
Linus of Thebes was a legendary classical musician and singer mentioned by
Virgil, *Eclogues* iv 56.

2033 *Zetus, Amphyon*: Zethus and Amphion, both mentioned by Isidore (III xvi),
were, in classical mythology, the twin sons of Antiope and Zeus. Amphion was
famous for having built the walls of Thebes by drawing the stones after him with
the music of his lyre. Zethus has no claim to musical fame: he must have found
his way into Isidore by association with his brother. This line has too many
syllables in all witnesses; perhaps 'as' could be omitted.

2034 *Orpheus*: the most famous mythological musician, who brought his wife back
from the underworld with the music of his lyre. Isidore (III xxii 8) tells how he was
given his lyre by Mercury.

2036–7 This was a famous story of the invention of music, mentioned briefly by
Isidore (III xvi) and given in more detail by John of Affligem, *De musica cum
tonario* iii (see line 2081n). The philosopher Pythagoras of Samos (see above, line
1676n), passing by a forge, noticed that the hammers made different sounds. He
entered, weighed the hammers, and discovered the musical scale and the
mathematical relationships between sounds. Pythagoras then taught the Greeks
music, and Boethius transmitted the art to the Latin West. The story is also given
by Macrobius, *Commentary on the Dream of Scipio* trans Stahl, 186–8.

2040–4 *monycord*: a monochord, 'a contrivance consisting of a single string which is
stretched over a lengthy wooden resonator to which a movable fret is attached, so
that the vibrating length of the string can be varied' (*Harvard Dictionary of
Music*). It was used to teach the mathematical proportions of the musical inter-

vals. Dame Musica demonstrates in lines 2052–8 how the fret ('gyn,' line 2042) is used to lengthen and shorten the string to produce low and high notes.

The monycord in line 2092 is perhaps the more elaborate instrument that evolved from the primitive one-string monochord.

2041 *holowe*: See line 1573n.

2045–50 *sex syllabes*: the names of the six notes of the hexachord. The hexachordal system was a method of teaching students to sing; it had been invented by Guido of Arezzo (see below, line 2082n). He worked out a way of memorizing a sequence of six tones (with a semitone between the third and fourth notes) by using a verse from a well-known hymn, *Ut queant laxis*, in which each phrase begins on a note higher than the preceding phrase. The opening syllable of each phrase became the name of a note of the hexachord: '*Ut* queant laxis, *resonare* fibris, *mira* gestorum, *famuli* tuorum, *solve* polluti, *labii* reatum.' See D.J. Grout *A History of Western Music* rev ed (New York 1973) 59–60. The author of the *Court* may well be using the lucid explanation of John of Affligem at this point (*De musica* i 49–50; see below, line 2081n).

2047 *ympne*: disyllabic in Middle English; see Chaucer *Legend of Good Women* prologue F 422.

2057–8 *dyscencyon, ascencyon*: These two terms appear in reverse order in PT, who are probably correct.

2059 *gamma-ut*: the note G on the lowest line of the bass scale; the lowest note in the medieval scale. The note itself was given the Greek name 'gamma'; 'ut' is its title as the first note of the first hexachord, the basis for the medieval method of singing. See *OED*, *gamut*; Grout 60.

2061 This line refers to 'Guido's hand,' the invention of Guido of Arezzo (line 2082n). He taught his pupils to associate each of the twenty notes in the medieval scale with a different joint of the hand. When the master held up his hand, palm outwards, and pointed to the different joints, the students would sing the appropriate notes and intervals. There is a reproduction of Guido's hand in Grout, page 61.

2066–9 *tunes parfyte, tunes inparfyte*: These terms refer to the temporal relationships between notes in mensural music. Unlike modern notes, the notes of the mensural system could have different time values depending on whether they were in a 'perfect' or 'imperfect' tune. For example, a semibreve in perfect time was equal to three minims; in imperfect time it equalled two minims.

2070 *Proporcyon*: Proportion, in mensural notation, is 'the diminution or (more rarely) augmentation of the normal note values in arithmetic ratios' (*Harvard Dictionary of Music*).

2071–2 *Dyapason, dyapente, dyatesseron*: the medieval names of the more common intervals. A diapason is an octave, a diapente a fifth, a diatesseron a fourth.

2073–4 These lines contain the names of the notes in the mensural system. The mensural system was a new (thirteenth-century) method of musical notation that gave each note a strictly determined value, thus making music more 'scientific' in the view of its exponents. The 'large' is the Latin 'maxima,' the note with the highest time value; the 'long' ('longa') was the next longest, equal to either two or three 'breves'; the breve ('brevis') was in turn equal to two or three semibreves; and the 'semybreve' was in turn equal to two or three minims. These five notes are all discussed by Jean de Muris, *Libellus cantus mensurabilis* i, in E. Coussemaker *Scriptorum de Musica Medii Aevi* nova series III (Paris 1869; reprinted Hildesheim 1963) 46. The 'crochet' developed later: there are no English examples of the word before the fifteenth century. See also Johannes de Muris *Notitia artis musicae* ed Ulrich Michels, Corpus Scriptorum de Musica 17, American Institute of Musicology (1972) II i, iv, vii–xii; *Harvard Dictionary of Music* 'Mensural or mensurable music.'

in rule and eke in space: on the lines and in the spaces of the musical staff

2079 *Boece*: Boethius (see above, line 1677n) also wrote a textbook on music (*De institutione musica*) that was widely revered during the Middle Ages.

2080 *Berno*: Berno, Abbot of Reichenau (d 1048), wrote a short treatise on music.

2081 *Johan de Muris*: Jean de Muris of Normandy (fl 1321–51), a teacher at the University of Paris and an exponent of mensural music. He was the author of several treatises on music, mathematics, and astronomy; see Ulrich Michels *Die Musiktractate des Johannes de Muris* Beihefte zum Archiv für Musikwissenschaft 8 (Wiesbaden 1970) 1–14.

John de Musica: John of Affligem, author of a treatise entitled *De musica* (written ca 1100–21). He was known at one time by the erroneous name of John Cotton. He mentions Boethius, Berno, and Guido at the beginning of his treatise. See Johannes Affligemensis *De Musica cum Tonario* ed J. Smits van Waesberghe, Corpus Scriptorum de Musica 1 (Rome 1950).

2082 *Guydo*: Guido of Arezzo (fl ca 1023), author of the *Micrologus*, a famous authority and teacher of music, inventor of the hexachord system. See J. Smits van Waesberghe, *De musico-pedagogico et theoretico Guidone Aretino eiusque vita et moribus* (Florence 1953). The corruption of the title of his work in C may have been intentional: there is a commentary on the *Micrologus* entitled *Metrologus*, which seems to originate in thirteenth-century England; the author of the *Court* or the scribe of the manuscript behind C may have known this better than the *Micrologus* itself. The *Metrologus* has been printed by J. Smits van Waesberghe in *Expositiones in Micrologum Guidonis Aretini* Musicologia Medii Aevi 1 (Amsterdam 1957) 61–92; the text contains the quotation from Isidore on harmonica, rythmica, and metrica (68).

2091 *pype*: any kind of flute or oboe

trump: a trumpet

ribibe: a rebeck, an early form of fiddle with three strings.

sautry: a psaltery, a stringed instrument resembling a zither

2092 *rote*: a stringed instrument resembling a harp

orgons: the organ, a musical instrument with pipes, much smaller than the modern organ. The plural form of the word was common in medieval writers; see OED, *organ* 1b.

2093 *gyterne*: a gittern, an instrument strung with wire like a guitar

clavycord: This instrument appears to have come into use in the later fourteenth century; there is only one recorded use of the word before the *Court* in MED.

2094–205 *Astronomye*: The whole of this account is taken from Isidore's chapters on astronomy, III xxiv–lxxi. The author may also have consulted Bartholomaeus' book VIII.

2098–107 The distinction between astronomy and astrology is made by Isidore, III xxvii. Astronomy deals with the stars in general; astrology, when lawful, describes the courses of the stars and planets, but it becomes unlawful when it attempts to predict the future (line 2106), or to demonstrate the influence of the stars and planets on man, or to relate the signs of the zodiac to different parts of the body.

2109 *the world*: 'the universe' (Latin 'mundus'), containing heaven and earth and the stars (Isidore III xxix)

2110 *heven*: Latin 'caelum,' used in this sense to mean the outermost sphere of the universe, which contains the fixed stars and has within it all the circuits of the planets and, at its centre, the stationary earth. Isidore devotes separate chapters to the position ('situs') of this celestial sphere, its poles, its course, its parts, its motion, and its two 'gates' ('januae'), east and west, out of which the sun emerges and to which it returns (III xxxi–xl).

Line 2110 is metrically deficient as it stands, and the repetition of 'cours' in 2113 is a problem. P reads 'site' for 'cours' in 2110, but this only duplicates 'syhte' in 2113 and does not improve the metre. 'Courses' would improve the metre, but properly speaking the heaven has only one course: a revolution from east to west every twenty-four hours. Isidore III xxxiv: 'De eiusdem sphaerae cursu' ('On the course of the same sphere'). It is tempting to assume that another disyllabic term, such as Isidore's 'axis' (III xxxvi), perhaps originally stood in 2110.

2114 The only witness for this defective line is P; C has a feeble substitution. It could easily be made regular by adding 'both' before 'oeste.'

2115 *hemyspery*: The hemisphere of the heaven is the half of the sky that can be seen from any one spot. The five circles in medieval astronomy are those which define the zones of heaven: the arctic and the antarctic zones (those regions of the sky where the sun never goes), the equinoctial zone (where the circle the sun describes makes days and nights on earth equal), and the two zones which lie between, bounded by the circle the sun makes at the summer and winter solstices. Isidore (III xliv) says 'how they cleped bene' (line 2116) in Greek.

2117–21 Isidore III xlv–lix

2125 *Lucina*: a classical name for the moon, especially with reference to her function as goddess of childbirth; mentioned by Isidore, III lxxi 2

2126–8 Isidore (III lxxi 3) derives 'star' ('stella') from 'standing' ('stando') because the stars are fixed in the heaven. Hence he adds that 'shooting stars,' which seem to be falling from the sky, are not really stars but portions from the region of 'aether' that have been disturbed by winds.

2130 This does not seem to mean unlawful divination: what Isidore says is that mariners and others can often make a weather forecast by studying the positions, brilliance, and clarity of known constellations (III lxxi 4–5).

2132 *Arcton, Ursa*: Isidore (III lxxi 6) says that 'Arcton' (properly, Greek 'Arctos') is the Greek name of the first of the constellations, which in Latin is called 'Ursa,' or 'the Bear.' As the author of the *Court* observes, the Bear is a double constellation, called the Greater and the Lesser Bear: 'the more eke and the lesse.'
This line has an extra syllable in both witnesses.

2134 *Tryones*: The Triones are the seven principal stars in Ursa major.
Boetes: the constellation Bootes, or the Wagoner
Yades: the Hyades, a group of seven stars in the head of the constellation Taurus

2135 *Arcturus*: the name of the brightest star in Bootes
Oryon: the constellation Orion
Plyades: the Pleiades, a group of stars (usually seven) in the constellation Taurus

2136 *Lucyfer*: 'the morning star,' the name given to the planet Venus when it appears before sunrise
Cometes: a comet. (Isidore uses this Greek spelling as a singular.)
Vesperus: Hesperus, or 'the evening star'; early identified with Lucifer or the planet Venus

2144 *Ramme, Bul, Gemelles*: the signs of the zodiac Aries, Taurus, and Gemini. (Gemelles is from Latin 'gemellus': 'twin.')

2145 *Crabbe, Lyon, Mayd*: Cancer, Leo, and Virgo. (The reading in C is 'the streyt Mayd'; the emendation 'sterell' has been accepted from P because Bartholomaeus (VII xv) explains that the sign Virgo is so named because a virgin is sterile, like the scorched ground in the height of summer: 'Virgo sterilis est et sine fructu, sic Sol intrans illam partem zodiaci ... suo calore humorem consumit, et sic terram a fructu sterilem facit' ('Virgo is sterile and without fruit, for thus when the sun enters this part of the zodiac ... he consumes the moisture with his heat, and thus makes the earth sterile of fruit').

2146 *Balaunce, Th'Archer, Scorpio*: Libra, Sagittarius, and Scorpio

2147 *Gote, Water-syre, Fysshe*: Capricorn, Aquarius, and Pisces

2148 *this*: 'these'

2157–63 This stanza is obscure in the *Court*, but it is clearer in Isidore, who reverses the two statements. Discussing the superstitions of the pagans, who put these images of beasts in the sky, he says: 'Aries ... they named thus on account of Jupiter Ammon, on whose head the image-makers feigned the horns of a ram. For this reason the gentiles put this sign first, because they say that in the month of March, which is the beginning of the year, the sun makes his way into that sign' (III lxxi 23–4).
Mars: the month of March

2257 A syllable seems to be missing from this line in both witnesses.

2259 This line, like others containing the word 'cours' (492, 2110), seems to be one syllable short. I have accepted Spindler's emendation to 'courses' in line 492, but a plural sense seems unsuitable both here and in line 2110. Perhaps (a desperate solution) the author used the Latin form of the word, 'cursus,' in all three places; this form is both singular and plural and would account for the unanimous readings of the witnesses. Compare the poet's use of a Latin word, unparalleled elsewhere, in line 484.

2164–5 Isidore repeats the classical tradition that the bull, the constellation Taurus, was set in the sky in honour of Jupiter, who, disguised as a bull, abducted Europa to Crete.

2166 *Castor, Pollux*: the brothers of Helen of Troy, Greek heroes. They were frequently identified with the constellation Gemini: Isidore explains that after their death they were put among the stars.

2169–70 The constellation Leo was thought to represent the giant Nemean lion, killed by Hercules as one of his twelve labours (Isidore III lxxi 27).

2176 *Hound*: the constellation Canis
Swanne: the constellation Cygnus
Egle: The constellation Aquila, which the pagans 'placed among the stars of heaven on account of the tale of Jupiter, in his memory' (Isidore III lxxi 32). This is all Isidore says; the reference is to the story of the shepherd-boy Ganymede, abducted by Jupiter in the shape of an eagle. Ganymede became cup-bearer to the gods, 'Joves chyef squyer,' but it is the eagle that was set amongst the stars.

2178 *fatall*: 'decreed by fate, predestined'

2181 *hym*: 'them' ('hem')

2183 *Socrates*: The metre requires a disyllable here: Spindler reads 'Socrate.' Isidore has the name 'Plato' at this point (III lxxi 39).

2190 *Isodore*: *Etymologiae* III lxxi 40

2192–8 The founders of astronomy are given by Isidore, III xxv. The Egyptians first discovered astronomy, the Chaldeans, astrology. 'But the author Josephus asserts that Abraham [who was from Chaldea] taught the Egyptians astrology'; 'whom' in line 2195 therefore refers back to 'Astrologye' in line 2193. Josephus (b 37–8 AD) was the author of *Antiquitates judaicae*, a history of the Jews from the creation onward; it was very influential throughout the Middle Ages as a historical authority.

Athlant: Atlas (the Latin genitive is 'Atlantis'), whom the Greeks claimed as the inventor of astronomy, was a Titan who held up the sky; this was rationalized by saying he was the first astronomer.

2199 *Syre Tholome*: Ptolemy, or Claudius Ptolomaeus (fl 121–51 AD) of Alexandria, the classical astronomer and geographer whose work on astronomy (known to the Middle Ages as the *Almagest*) was enormously influential. 'Sir' was frequently added to classical names as an honorific (see above, line 1886), but it may be used here because the author of the *Court*, like many medieval writers, confused Ptolemy the astronomer with Ptolemy the King of Egypt (all the Macedonian kings of Egypt bore this name).

2200 *John de Hispayn*: Joannes Hispalensis, John of Seville (fl 1135–53). He was an important translator of texts from Arabic to Latin, among them several astronomical works; see Sarton ii 169–72.

Mysaleth: Māshā'allāh, whose name is corrupted to Misalath or Miselat in Bartholomaeus. Māshā'allāh was an Egyptian Jew (d ca 815), a famous astronomer and astrologer, whose works were translated into Latin by John of Seville and Gerard of Cremona in the twelfth century. See Sarton i 531. He is one of Bartholomaeus' authorities on astronomy (VIII xxii).

2203 *ho*: 'to stop,' 'to cease'; see *MED, ho*.

2204–5 The idea that the seven arts led men onward and upward, ending in the contemplation of the heavens, is frequently mentioned in Christian writers; Isidore repeats it at the end of his chapters on astronomy.

2211–12 This refers to the common medieval tradition that the twelve apostles compiled the Apostles' Creed by each contributing an article of faith. Balbus, *Catholicon* sv *fides*, records the story and lists the articles, each with an attribution to its apostolic author. See also Curt F. Bühler 'The Apostles and the Creed' *Speculum* XXVIII (1953) 335–9.

2213–40 There were three definitive statements of faith or creeds current in the later Middle Ages. The briefest, the Apostles' Creed, was required knowledge for the laity and was recited (in Latin) daily at morning and evening prayer (matins, prime, and compline) by the clergy. The slightly longer Nicene Creed was recited at mass, and the Athanasian Creed (see line 2247 below) was recited by the clergy every Sunday at prime, or daily at prime in the Sarum Use. The creed given here in the *Court* is a blend of the Apostles' Creed and the Nicene Creed. Lines 2215, 2217–20 ('He cam from heven': 'descendit de caelis') and 'baptysme' in line 2235 are taken from the Nicene Creed, and the other articles are from the Apostles' Creed, with some influence from the wording of the Nicene Creed. See *The Sarum Missal* 211; *The Annotated Book of Common Prayer* 17–19; J.N.D. Kelly *The Athanasian Creed* (London 1964), especially page 44.

2226 *watry woundes*: perhaps an allusion to John 19:34: 'One of the soldiers with a spear opened his side; and immediately there came out blood and water.'

2227 Perhaps, 'Because he was buried, he brought man out of hell.' The reference is to the Harrowing of Hell, which was believed to have taken place between Christ's burial and resurrection. The phrase 'descendit ad inferos' ('he descended into Hell') occurs in the Apostles' Creed only.

2235–6 *communyon / Of sayntes*: the medieval (and Catholic) doctrine of the spiritual unity of all members of the Christian church, in heaven, purgatory, and earth. The phrase is in the Apostles' Creed but not in the Nicene Creed.

2247 *Quicumque vult*: 'Whosoever wishes [to be saved],' the opening words of the Athanasian Creed, the definitive statement of orthodox belief on the mystery of the Trinity

2249 *Mary Magdalene*: identified with the sinful woman of Luke 7:36–50 during the Middle Ages. She is in Dame Feyth's parlour because Christ said to her, 'Thy faith hath made thee safe' (Luke 7:50).

2252–3 Martha's faith is emphasized in the story in John 11:1–45.

2254 *Regulus*: This refers to Christ's miracle in healing the ruler's son, John 4:46–54. The Latin 'ruler' is 'regulus,' which has been misunderstood to be a proper name. The author of the *Court* is probably following pseudo-Bonaventura, *Meditationes* xxii, where the same mistake occurs.

2255–6 *Canane*: similarly taken to be a proper noun when in origin it is an adjective. 'Canane' is the Canaanite woman of Matthew 15:22–8 to whom Christ said, 'O woman, great is thy faith.' Her daughter, whom Christ cured, was 'grievously troubled by a devil.'

2262–4 *confessours, Doctours, martyrs*: different classes of saints. A confessor is one who maintained his faith under persecution but did not suffer martyrdom. A doctor is a saint renowned not only for holiness of life but also for his learning and teaching.

2271–4 Eph 6:16: 'In all things taking the shield of faith, wherewith you may be able to extinguish all the fiery darts of the most wicked one.'
The 'thre enemyes' of man are the Devil, the World, and the Flesh. 'Enemyes' is here disyllabic, as 'enmye' in line 1770.

2274 See line 110n.

2275 Mark 11:24: 'All things, whatsoever you ask when ye pray, believe that you shall receive; and they shall come unto you.'

2276 'She is ay for as the clerke sayth' C; 'She ay one is for as a clerke seith' P. Both versions of the line are defective.

2276–7 Eph 4:5: 'Unus Dominus, una fides' ('One Lord, one faith')

2281–2 James 2:20: 'Faith without works is dead.'

2283–6 Compare lines 1506–12 and notes above.

2292 'He has the power to preserve and love whoever believes in Him.'

2295–6 John 11:25: 'Jesus said, ... "He that believeth in me, although he be dead, shall live." '

2306 *as lowe as lede*: a proverbial phrase; see Whiting L125. The expression is similar in sense to 'as heavy as lead,' 'as dull as lead.'

2311–73 This section of the poem exists in only one manuscript; Caxton ends with Dame Feyth. The text in the manuscript is not good: the metre is often doubtful (see lines 2315, 2327?, 2334, 2346, 2354, 2359?), and one rhyme is clearly wrong (line 2350), but emendation is impossible without another witness.

2313 *table long*: a painted tablet, sometimes, as here, with words and captions accompanying the pictures. The next four stanzas of the poem comprise the inscription on this table.

2316–17 Balbus *Catholicon* sv *spes*: 'Spes est certa expectatio future beatitudinis' ('Hope is the sure expectation of future bliss').

2324 *Go were he go*: 'wherever he may go'

2325–6 'Few people want what reason requires: the particular thing that would sustain them best.'

2343–5 Perhaps, '[Willingly endured] suffering, which always serves Hope, is so powerful with its pains in this life that Hope's reward is eternal happiness.' That is, hope enables one to endure suffering, and hope will be rewarded in heaven.

2350 *also*: should perhaps be amended to 'al sure' in order to preserve the rhyme scheme

2357 'What man may have more abounding grace than to nourish in thee, O Lord, his temporal condition with good hope.' See MED, *cost* 3; *feden* 5.

2360–1 Perhaps, 'What spirit so cowardly as to find reason to despair of doing possible things?'

2369–72 Modern English requires another negative: 'No trespass so great that the sinner may not be forgiven, if Hope ask for mercy.'

Here endith ...: See introduction, pages xiii, xvi.

APPENDIXES

TEXTUAL NOTES

BIBLIOGRAPHY

GLOSSARY

INDEX OF PROPER NAMES

Appendix 1

The following lists of things Christians should know are taken from the printed editions of the *Court*; see introduction, pages xiii, xvi.

These thynges folowyng is every Crysten man and woman holde and bounde to lerne and to conne to theyr power in waye of theyr salvacyon:
The *Paternoster*, the *Ave Maria*, and the Crede.
The Ten Commaundementes:

Have one God in worshyp. (In this is forboden al maner mawmetrye, wytchecraft, enchauntement, redynge of dremes, and al mysbyleve.)

Take not his name in vayn. (In this is forboden al heresyes, al mysmenyng, unworshyp of God, forsweryng, takyng his name in vayne, and suche other.)

Halowe thyne holy day. (To this belongeth heryng of thy servyse, kepynge the oute of dedely synne, vysytyng of thy powre neyghbours, accordyng them that ben at debate, and suche other.)

Worshyp thy fader and moder. (God thy fader, holy chirche thy moder, the ghoostly faders, thy flesshely fader and moder, al men of age and worshyp, and prelates of holy chirche.)

Slee no man. (With hond smytyng, with mouthe bacbytyng, herte cursynge, ne wyllyng evyl ne vengeaunce.)

Do no lecherye. (Here is forboden alle spousebreche, alle flesshely dedes, and al mysshedyng of mannes seed.)

Doo no thefte. (Here is forboden stelyng, wronge purchacyng, dysherytyng of heyres, trecherye, usurye, wronge amersementis, false mesure and weyghtes, and suche other.)

Bere no false wytnes. (Here is forboden false lyeng, bacbytyng, accusyng, appayryng of good loes, and suche other.)

Desyre not thy neyghbours wyf. (In this is not onely forboden the dede but also the desyre and wyl of herte.)

Desyre not thy neyghbours thyng. (Hows, londe, beest, servaunt, ne nothyng that is his.)

The seven dedely synnes:

Pryde (Herof comyth boostyng of proude beryng, dysplesyng, scornyng, hyghe herte, gay array, pryde of rychesse, fayrenes, cunnyng, strengthe, vertue, goodnes, pryde of kynne, unbuxomnes, vayne glorye, dispyte of thyne neyghbour, ypocrysye, and suche other.)

Envye (Glad of thy neyghbours evyl fare, hevy of his welfare, backbytyng, sownyng [probably 'sowyng'] of dyscord, scornyng, and suche other.)

Wrath (Fyghtyng, chydynge, hurtyng, betynge, waryeng, cursyng, grutchyng, desiring of vengeaunce, cruelnes, manslaughter, and suche other.)

Covetise (Falsehode in wynnyng, in beyeng, in sellyng, in metyng, in weyeng, gyle, trecherye, sacrylege, simonye, usurye, thefte, receyvyng of stolen goodes, extorcion, wrong withholding, withdrawing of servauntes hire, withholding of tithes and dutees of hooly chirche.)

Glotonye (Etyng or drynkyng over moche, to erly, to late, oute of mesure, brekyng of fast, usyng of delycate metes and drynkes, or in usyng them to strengthe thy body to synne, and suche other.)

Slouthe (Therof cometh ydlenes, delite in sleepe, neclygence of thy bileve, unlusty to Goddes servyse, foryetefulnes of shryfte, myspendyng of tyme, dyspayer, wanhope, and suche other.)

Lecherye (In thoughte, wylle, werke, syght, felyng, dede doyng; with sengle, with comune, wydowes, maydens, wyves, gossybbes, goddoughters, relygyous, or ony other oute of wedlok; synne ayenst kynde or suche other.)

The fyve wyttes: syght, heryng, smellyng, tastyng, feelyng.

The seven dedes of mercy bodyly: fede the hungry, yeve drynke to the thursty, clothe the naked, herberowe the howseles, vysyte the syke, delyver the prysoners, and burye the poure that ben dede at her deth.

The seven dedes of mercy ghoostely: Teche them that cannot, yeve good counseyl to hym that asketh it, chastyse thy subgette that offendith, comforte the sory, foryeve hym that trespaceth to the, have routhe on the synnar, and praye for thyne enemye.

The seven pryncypal vertues:

Fayth (This is ground and begynnyng of oure salvacyon, and it standeth in thre thynges: in the unyte of the godhede in thre persones, in the manhode of Cryst, and in the sacramentes of the chirche.)

Hope (This is a trust by the mercy of God to be saved, and it standeth in the grace of God and good werkes.

Charyte (This is the ende and perfectyon of al the commandementes of God, and it standeth in the love of God above al thyng, and thy neyghbour as thyself.)

Ryghtwysenes (This is a payeng of deute of eche thyng that it duly longeth to, as to God praysyng and thankyng, to thy neyghbour love and charyte, and to thyself besynes to fulfylle Goddes wylle.)

Wysedom (That is a vertu to departe good fro evyl, and it stondeth in chesyng of good and in refusyng of evyl.)

Strengthe (Thys maketh a man myghty and hardy to doo grete thynges for the love of God, and it stondeth in suffryng pacyently adversyte, and mekely takyng prosperyte.)

Mesure (This is a mene bytwene to moche and to lytel, and it stondeth in takyng suffycyently that nedeth, and in refusyng utterly that is to moche or to lytel.)

By these thynges shal eche man and woman knowe God.

These that folowen brynge a man to heven: good perseveraunce, pacyence in adversyte, obedyence of the commaundementes of God, ryghtwysenes in dedes, penaunce in the lyf, contrycyon of synne, knowlege of thyself, and charyte.

These bryngen one into helle: desperacyon, wodenes in adversyte, unryght-wysenes of dedes, love of synne, malyce, obstynacyon in synnes, despyte of the commaundementes of God, hate of good thynges, and ignoraunce.

The fyve wyttes ghoostely: mynde of the kindenes of God and of thy last ende, understondyng of his benefettys and of his lore, wylle to wor-shyppe hym in thought, worde, and dede withoute ony werynes, reson to rewle with thy wittes both inward and outward withoute ony blynde-nesse, ymagynacyon of vertuous lyvyng, nedeful werkes, and dredeful dedes of joye and of peyne.

Here endeth the Court of Sapyence. Enprynted at London in the Fletestrete at the sygne of the sonne, by Wynkyn de Worde, the yere of Our Lorde a MCCCCC and x. Wynkyn de Word.

GLOSSARY TO APPENDIX I

accordyng making peace between
amersementis amercements, arbitrary fines
appayryng of good loes taking away someone's good name
comune common women, prostitutes
cunnynge knowledge
dysplesyng offensiveness

ghoostely spiritual
gossybbes 'gossips,' baptismal sponsors
herberowe harbour, give shelter to
heryng of thy servyse hearing Mass
loes name, reputation
mawmetrye idolatry
mesure temperance
metyng measuring
mysmenyng misinterpretation
mynde memory
shryfte sacrament of confession
spousebreche adultery
unbuxomnes obstinacy
unlusty slothful
unworshyp dishonour
wanhope hopelessness, despair of salvation
waryeng cursing, blaspheming
wodenes rage
worshyp *n* dignity, honour
worshyp *vb* honour

TEXTUAL NOTES TO APPENDIX 1

p 157 Commaundementes] W; commandentis C
    Worshyp] W; Worspyp C
    loes] C; name W
p 158 sacrylege] sacrrilege C
p 159 Here endeth ... Wynkyn de Word] W; *there is no colophon
    in Caxton.*

Appendix II

The interlinear glosses found in TH are listed below by line number; see introduction, page xvi.

91 ie nobilis regina *over* other my
 ie infirmi *over* seke
98 ie gouerner *over* reygne
 scilicet partes policie *over* dyuerse
963 id est reformeth loue *over* adamant
1144 equidistancia a centro terre *over* distaunce
1148 id est quattuor elementa *over* natures foure
1189 aceciam in libro suo xiii° *beside* booke
1581 sustres *under* persones
1712 scilicet dei nature naturantis *over* nature
1814 Ortographia *over* furst
1815 Ethymologia *over* second
1818 Diasintastica *over* thryd
1819 Prosodia *over* last
1829 in grecisme *over* Eborard
1830 helias qui compilavit memoriale minor *over* Petyr
1831 Achos pictariensis *over* lambard papy
1834 Januens compilavit *over* Catholicon
 Aristotylles compilavit *over* pariarmonise
1853 the sonnes [somies?] of art *over* comone tretyse
1854 what qualis *over* Euery quatkyn
 quanta *over* what is
1856 id est proposicio *over* predicate

162 Appendix II

1914 id est ad librum qui incipit papa stupor mundi *beside* sunt
1932 de planctu *over* Alayne
    Silvestris *over* prudencius
1960 Arsmetryk *over* lady

Textual Notes

The textual notes contain all departures from the copy text (C) and all significant variant readings in T, H, and P. Wynkyn de Worde's later print (W) is cited occasionally to show where corrections of C were thought to be necessary. Most of Spindler's emendations are given for their interest.

Each reading is given from the witness listed first; the sigla after the first letter indicate that the witnesses agree in sense, but not necessarily in spelling, with the reading given. For emendations I have chosen the text whose spelling most nearly resembles Caxton's; on a few occasions I have slightly adjusted the spelling of an emendation to conform with Caxton's usual practice (eg line 764).

C is the only independent witness for lines 1–56.
The Courte of Sapyence] W; no title in C
Prohemium] Here begynneth the proheme of this present boke W; *om.* C
  19 and] Spindler's emendation; *om.* CW
  23 illumyne] Spindler's emendation; illumynyne CW
  47 more] Spindler's emendation; *om.* CW
  49 subtylte] subtylyte CW
  50 O] Spindler's emendation; *om.* CW
  57 *P begins here.*
  57 love] C; lawde P
  61 to] P; for to C
  62 herte] C; eere P
  64 or] C; and P
  70 conserve] P; conferme C
Explicit Prohemium] C; *om.* P
  71 *TH begin here*
  74 lete youthe have] TH; telle youthe hath C; lete thought haue P

77 thought] CP; youth TH

80 and quene, aulfyn, knyght, roke and] or quene aulfyn / knyght or C; and quene
   alphyne knyght and TH; *and* quene alfyn roke *and* P

81 in] PTH; in his C

85 Fyrst] CTH; For P

87 I had espyed] C; espied I had P; aspyed I haue TH

90 and] C; the TH; *om.* P

96 man conne hymself] CP; on hymself T; oon hymself H

101 whoso] PTH; who C

105 I thought me] T; I me thought C; me thought me PH

106 bord] C; brode PTH

107 forth put] furth put H; put forth PT; fyrst put C
   or] PTH; or to C

108 Forth] PTH; Fyrst C

113 thus to me] C; to me thus PTH

116 any] PTH; enuy C

117 a] C; oo TH; one P

120 to God abone] a bone C; God aboue T; God aboone H; to God abowne P

121 weye unto] C; the weye to PH; way to T

122 lerne] C; leue PT; leene H

124 insuffycience] insufficience THP; insuffycence C

125 Fer from al help for] CP; For help of TH

126 upon a] CP; ageyn in H; apon in T

128 in] TH; in a CP

133 iwys] PH; *om.* C; I was T

137 encomerous] C; encombrouse T; encomberous HP

139 throng] PTHW; thorugh C

141 unto] C; on to PTH

145 watres name asked I] C; water I askyd TH; wateres name I askid P

148 vertues] C; vertue PTH

152 heven and erthe] C; heven and in erth P; erthe and heuene TH

158 thyng ... thyng] CTH; thyng*is* ... thyng*is* P

162 The] C; This PTH

164 me] CP; vs TH

166 lyf hele] lyf hele and C; lif hele P; and lyfe TH

167 have al daye] C; hath alway PH; haue alwey T

170 ful] CP; *om.* TH

176 myghty] CTH; worthy P

181 maundement] PTH; commaundement C

184 Bad one hym put in bitter] Bad one hym to put in C; Bad on hym put in bitter P;
   And oone hym put in bytter TH

185 Another] PTHW; And other C
187 The] CP; These TH
191 sawe she] CP; she sy TH
192 to] PTH; *om.* C
193 dysteyned] CP; disteyneth TH
199 inmensurable] C; immesurable P; incomperable TH
200 benyngne] CPH; myghty T
202 Of] C; On PTH
206 thy gemme] CP; the gemme] TH
208 sustenaunce] THP; substaunce C
211 my] P; *om.* CTH
212 theyr] C; they TH; the P
214 bemed] CP; beauteuous TH
215 tery ryver] CP; chery rud TH
216 swannysshe] C; snowish PTH
217 al is] CP; as I H; as hit ys T
220 al myn] al this myn C; all my PTH
221 al] HPT; *om.* C
222 restrayne] C; refrayne PTH
228 in] CTH; on P
229 as proude] H; as a proude CT; as a P
238 any sute] HT; euery fute CW; any maner sute P
242 vycyate with] viciate with P; vnyat with C; vycyate thorough TH
243 is lawe] CP; thy lawe TH
246 Fro thy godhede] P; For thy godhede TH; For thy godlyhede C
247 and] CP; *om.* TH
249 for brekynge] PTH; forbrokyn C
251 For] PTH; For sauns doute C
253 Knowe] C; Wote PTH
257 myghty] CTH; myght and P
258 yone] PH; than T; releue C
261 strong] CP; straunge TH
263 Nor hole ne herne the playne] Nor hoole ne herne the playne P; Neyther hoole ne
    herne the playne TH; Nother in herne ne in hole trouth C
269 ye] CP; he TH
273 that better were] C; at bettyr were TH; which were bettyr P
281 I] PTH; that I C
285 I not than] C; I than nat TH; not I then P
294 was anon] CP; anone was TH
297 spareth] PTH; spared C
298 for lowe for to] CH; ne for lowe forto P; for low to T

300 and] CP; all TH
303 what] PTH; *om.* C
304 how] TH; *om.* CP
306 to] PTH; unto C
308 fulfylled] THP; fulfylleth C
309 couthe] CP; cowde THW
310 rest and] C; lust or PTH
311 the] P; *om.* CTH
312 made hym] CTH; to hym did P
313 all] PTH; *om.* C
324–9 *missing in T*
324 and] CP; the H
326 Gan] PH; Saue C
327 ful] HP; ful iust C
329 rede] PH; dede C
330 the] CPH; that T
331 of portature] C; of pictature P; promptratoure TH
332 Her] CP; With HT
333 kyssyng unto] CP; kyssyng*is* to TH
338 sayd O] sayd to C; seyde O THP
    what] PTH; how C
339 Is it] H; It is PT; Is C
341 to ordeyne deth for to] C; for to ordeygne deth to TH; to ordeyne deth to P
342 were no more but to] P; were no more but for to TH; wold no more but for to C
343 of] PTH; and C
348 thenne] CTH; ther P
350 Than] THP; That CW
357 Stryf] Chyef stryf C; Stryfe THP
    and al aquayle] and all aquayle TH; and all batayle P; in al batayle C
359 this] CTH; his P
361 Leve youre debate and cese] TPH; ben youre debate and rees C
368 is to Mercy] CP; to Mercy ys TH
372 physyk] phisike do PTH; be syke C
374 where] PTH; there C
376 be] PT; by C; were H
378 yet] C; yet sure P; yift H; thyef T
379 as] PTH; as a C
381 injure] CP; rumour TH
384 Without] PTH; Withouten C
385 hyr] TH; theyr C; *om.* P

389 thynge] PTH; thynges C
    bere] CP; can TH
390 thynge] P; thynges CTH
391 Wyteth awey] C; Wastith alwey P; With whiche alwey HT
    therfor lete] CPT; late therfor H
392 to] CTH; in P
396 of sothfastnes] P; O sothfastnes TH; of stedfastnes C
400 said] PTH; sayth C
    knelyd] PH; knelyng T; and kneleth C
405 if] PTH; om. C
407 recordyng] PTH; reseruyng C
408 the to] PTH; to the C
409 fals cruell] PTH; cruel fals C
410 attend] CP; entende TH
407 and] CP; in TH
424 in a swonyd] in a swoune HTP; a swonyd C
425 in] PTH; om. C
428 see] THP; for C
429 Lieth in a swouned] Lythe in a sowne T; Lyeng in a swoune HW;
    Lieth in sowne P; Leyng in a swoued C
430 Right unrightwisly] HT; vnryghtwysenes C; vnrightwisly P
431 hath] HCP; haue T
433 retourne] PTHW; retourned C
434 thy] C; this HT; that P
441 man is] CTH; is he P
442 yeve up] TH; yeue C; leue P
444 al your] C; al HT; youre P
445 dysteyned] CP; discryued T; disceyved H
446 Mercy] P; om. CTH
448 pouer] C; pore P; pure TH
450 ye Vertues and O ye] vertues and ye C; virtutes and O ye P; ye virtutes and H; ye
    Vertues and T
452 O] PTH; with C
454 and] CTH; O P
455 nyne] CP; now TH
460 and] CP; nor H; ne T
    for hym no grace may] for them no grace may CH; for theym may no grace T;
    no grace for hym may P
465 that] CH; which PT
466 jugement] HT; that jugement CP

468 gilty] PTH; gylt C; gylte W

472 thou] CP; the TH

474 tempestouse] P; tempestuous H; tempestious T; temrestes C

476 rayne] C; reigne H; ring PT

479 and I not] H; and I wote nat T; and not P; I wote neuer C

484 rydeth] CP; lawgheth TH

485 than mayst thou] CP; thow mayst than TH

486 june in] June in C; Jvne in P; june and H; in T

492 courses] Spindler's emendation; course PTW; cours CH

504 With reuth] PTH; Thorugh C

506 Without] P; Withouten CTH

507 thys] CTH; the P

512 O soverayne myghty] C; souerayne O myghti P; O myghty souuerayn TH

516 save] CTH; haue P

517 *H breaks off at this line*

519 wil no wey] C; will no wise P; no wey wyl T

520 hit is incomerous] C; that is encomberous P; hit ys encombrouse T

523 solen] PT; sole C

527 hir] P; theyr CT

528 the] C; yone P; thow T

535 Of] CT; And P

blessyd hevenly] CT; hevenly blessid P

537 ben] PT; both C

539 treuse] C; trewis P; trewes T

542 lyeth in] C; lyth in T; light on P

545 for] PT; om. C

550 reuth] PT; trouthe C

553 thyself of this] CT; of this thy selfe P

558 For whiche] C; Wherfore PT

561 These] CP; Thy T

564 than thynk I] that thynk I C; thinke I than P; than thynke I T

565 one] PT; to one C

566 that] CT; than P

571 ye] T; I CP

576 godenesse wyt and myght] godenesse myght and wyt C; wit goodnes and might P; goodnes wyt and myght T

579 that] C; as T; om. P

582 name] CP; man T

584 name] C; man PT

587 and] CT; of P

mayst] TP; may C

590 ful of all] ful of C; full of all P; of all T
591 of] CT; his P
592 in kynd is] CT; is in kynde P
596 now] TP; *om.* C
598 so] C; full PT
602 nere but disporte] C; nere but a sporte P; were but dysport T
603 he conclude] T; he concluded C; concludid P
605 deth for lyf] CPT; lyfe for dethe: Spindler's emendation
606 make] CT; take P
608 mannes] mannys T; manes P; mans C
609 among] TP; *om.* C
614 the carybde] CP; thys caryld T
615 hym had] C; had hym P; had T
622 of] CP; to T
625 oure] PT; *om.* C
629 unto] C; after PT
631 or yet] T; or P; *om.* C
636 the shap of it] PT; of it the shapnesse C
637 sit] PT; *om.* C
639 of] CT; on P
640 ones] PT; *om.* C
644 come] PT; comyn C
654 thy] T; thyn P; the C
655 this] CP; the T
660 voyd shal they] CP; shull they wyde T
664 Soo] CT; Go P
665 in] C; at PT
666 and more] PT; *om.* C
672 is] PT; *om.* C
673 The archangels] Tharchangel C; The Archaungelles T; The angele P
674 adoune] Spindler's emendation; doune CPT
677 the lust us to] and as thou lyst C; and as the lyst T; ye lust us to P
678 Withyn] P; Us in CT
683 beshent] C; to shent PT
686 byfore] C; to fore P; afore T
689 unto] P; to CT
691 God] CT; lord P
695 Of] C; On PT
696 we] PT; I C
710–14 *missing in T*
716 thurgh] CT; for P

719 His ... hys] C; His ... the P; The ... hys T
721 al lust and] CT; lust and all P
722 doune] CP; *om.* T
    of] CP; full of T
726 lord] C; kynge PT
731 the lyst] CT; ye lust P
735 bandes] C; bondis P; penaunce T; handes W
736 fader] PT; *om.* C
737 and lust] C; with lust PT
745 pryncesse] C; empris P; emperyce T
748 that] CT; the P
751 lyf ... lust ... love] C; love ... lust ... spouse PT
752 shal] CP; *om.* T
753 Become a man] CP; Shalt become man T
755 hym whiche was] whiche was C; hym which is P; hym that was T
757 Thus] C; This PT
761 Doo feete] T; Do fight P; To fyghte C
763 you at lust to] C; yow at lust T; at youre lust to P
764 Revygure gan] Reuyue gan C; Refigire gan P; Reuyguryd than T
767 swete] CP; swythe T
771–7 *missing in T*
777 eyther other] C; eche other they P
779 Conclude] T; Concluded CP
781 her to] C; hir thoo P; hyr so T
785 herte lust] C; hert loue P; loue hert T
795 Rent] CP; Reuyd T
    flayn] slayn C; fleyne P; flown T
796 Dye] CP; Dyed T
797 Suffre] CP; Suffryd T
798 Hard was this payn] CP; Here was the payne T
800 Flayne] PT; Beten C
    a] CP; the T
801 the] C; his P; *om.* T
802 of] CT; with P
803 to life] PT; *om.* C
807 the blessyd mayd] C; the maide blessid P; that blessyd mayde T
809 commended] commendid PT; commaunded C
812 eft wold with man] T; with man wold CP
813 he] PT; she C
817 I] PT; *om.* C

821 that] PT; *om.* C
822 deme] CT; done P
829 is] PT; is eke C
830 Mercy thy suster] PT; thy moder C
831 man] CT; he P
836 wight] PT; *om.* C
    erthe or heven yet] C; heuen or erth it P; erthe or heuen hyt T
844 and] CP; or T
850 Thy] PT; the C
851 hym] P; *om.* CT
852 it dere is bought] C; it is dere y bought P; ys dere bought T
854 mow] C; now T; *om.* P
855 more strong the] more straunge the C; the more strong P; most strong the T
857 these] CT; the P
862 of] CP; on T
863 have hym] T; haue them C; hym haue P
871 I] TP; *om.* C
    to] TP; for to C
872 shal hold] C; will shew P; shall hole T
873 they] CT; ther P
879 ofter syth] after syth C; aftyr syth T; oft P
880 Than] P; That CT
881 to] PT; for to C
883 than] C; tho TP
886 trewe] PT; trouthe C
887 eke is] CP; ys eke T
896 Ryght and] CP; ryghtyng T
898 Thou] PT; *om.* C
    a] C; the PT
899 I] PT; *om.* C
Explicit … osculate sunt] T; Explicit … obstulate sunt C; Explicit primus liber P
905 And to] And I C; And P; To preche and T
907 feete ben] feete byn T; cyte is CP
909 for] PT; *om.* C
914 nyl] TP; wol C; wyll W
915 to] C; and TP
    manere] PT; matere C
916 thynges] CT; thyng P
917 refrendary] PT; referendary C; ferendary W
920 sonne in] CP; sonny T

922 Soo done alday these wyse men fooles lere] C; So done allwey wyse men thorow
   foolys lere T; And hur doth geue hir light and all hir chere P
923 Wherfor] C; Therfore T; Sowe P
   thou lust] C; thou list PT
prohemium] W; *om.* C; prohemium libri secundi T; prohemium secundi libri P
Incipit liber secundus] T; Sequitur secundus liber P; *om.* C
928 with her she] CP; she wyth hyr T
931 mote] C; shalt PT
932 thens] C; tho TP
937 a wyse] a wise P; auys C; wyse T
941 prospect] TPW; prospet C
946 on] C; in PT
948 Come in] C; Come T; Come on P
952 is] C; thyk TP
953 alabastyr the] C; alablauster and P; alabaustre and the T
956 adamante] admante C; adamonte P; adamant T
957 amatyst] T; admatyst C; amatise P
   amatyte] admatyte C; amacite T; amatite P
959 no spyryte myght] C; no spirit couth P; none spyryt cowde T
962 sayd] C; seid P; sad T
963 adamant] TP; admant C
969 wit lost] PT; with lust who C
970 old] CP; all T
976 seke] PT; *om.* C
977 corall] PT; gyral C
979 calcophan] caleophan C; calcophane P; calciphane T
   sore] CP; hoorse T
980 The cabiate that techeth elloquence] The cabiate that tellith Eloquence P; The
   Cambrace that techeth elloquence T; Al these doon bote without offence C
982 whiche] PT; whiche that C
983 womans] TP; wombes C
993 excolycerose] excolyterose C; excolicerous P; excolicors T
999 Were] PT; Where C
   she shold anone uryne] she shold anone ruyne C; anone shulde she vryne P; she
   wold anone vryne T
1000 galachyte] salachyte C; galachite P; gagachite T
1004 men] PT; *om.* C
1005 telleth] TP; telle C
1006 thynke] T; thynk ye C; thyng P
   of] C; in TP

1007 feverous] PT; feuours C
1008 There sawe I lye ful of al lustynesse] Ther for I lye ful of al lustyness C; Ther
     sawe I ly full of all lustynes P; As clerkis wyse in wrytyng done expresse T
1010 in] PT; in the C
1012 another stone full] P; ouer other stone C; another stoone T
1014 do] P; *om.* CT
1015 do] PT; *om.* C
1018 techeth] CT; tellith P
1019 sad] CT; said P
1020 idropsy] P; idropesy T; drapcy C; dropcy W
     I] CP; we T
1022 *missing in T*
1027 myght] CP; lyght T
1028 abisate] T; abistist P; abatystus C
1030 bryght] CP; good T
1032 grace and] CP; gret T
1033 soveraynly] PT; soverayne C
     attractyf] attractatyf C; attractive P; actractyf T
1034 exceptyf] C; acceptive PT
1037 memphyte] TP; menysyte C
1041 medus] TP; medrys C
1042 noset] TP; neset C
1044 that] CP; whyche T
1045 in] P; *om.* CT
1047 Optallyus] CT; Optallus eke P
     straunge] PT; strong C
1055 whiche hath a] CT; the whiche hath P
1059 quandras] T; quadrans P; quanydras C
1062 reben] T; ruben P; Rebe C
     the] TP; *om.* C
1067 Causer] P; Comforte C; *missing in T; supplied from C in margin in a later hand*
1068 is] P; and CT
1071 He] CP; Hit T
1076 sardius] T; sardyns C; badius P
1077 gemme] PT; gemmes C
1081 is eke to men] C; is also to men P; eke ys to man T
1085 man in his mynd] CT; manes mynde P
1091 whoso] PT; who C
1093 cleped] clepyd TP; cleped the C
1094 Isodore] Isidore T; Isidrie P; Isodre C

1096 please] CT; best please P
1097 natures] CP; Nature T
1098 my] PT; comyn C
1100 the seme] Spindler's emendation; thou seme C; ye seme P; ye see T
1102 the] thou C; ye PT
1106 and for] P; and for the C; for the T
1112 thyng] C; best PT
1115 tempreth welle also] C; tempreth also well P; tempereth also T
1117 geveth] PT; greueth C
1118 as] T; is C; om. P
1121 swete] C; wete PT
1122 conjunctyf] TP; commyttyf C
1127 al] CT; eche P
1129 diffusyon] diffusioun T; effusyon C; discension P
1130 partes of the] C; parties of the T; portyse of P
1131 taken] PT; take C
1134 dyssolved] CP; dysseueryd T
1138 there declareth] C; that declareth T; ther declared P
1141 erth] PT; hym C
1142 without] PT; withouten C
1145 ryght] TP; lyke C
1148 The] CP; That T
1149 general] gene ra C; generall PTW
1152 had] C; hath PT
1158 hym] PT; them C
1162 joye] C; ioie it P; thyng T
1163 sownes] C; sowne T; sownde P
1164 murmour] CP; myrrour T
1166 sapour] CP; vapour T
1167 On] CT; in P
1171 floodys] TP; flood C
1175 moysty] P; moyst CT
1178 many] CP; many a T
1180 of] P; om. CT
1181 is not] PT; I snote C
1184 and O] P; and C; o T
1186 Ye ar] T; ye art P; Were C
     no poyntes] C; no poynt P; nothyng T
1190 he goo and] ye goo and C; he goodly PT
1195 As Isidore] As Isidre P; And Isidore T; As I rede C
     this] CP; these T

1199 oores] P; *om.* C; course T
1200 lere to] bere and T; lerne to P; lere C
1205 a] T; all P; *om.* C
1208 on] PT; of C
1210 ne hooke ne deceyte were they aferd] ne hooke of deceyte were they aferd C; and
   hooke ne deceyte were they aferde T; ne hoke ne disseite yet they ferth P
1211 a joye] C; on heven P; an heuen T
1212 escaryus] escarius PT; estaryus C
1213 effimeron] effuneron C; effymoron P; efemerion T
1214 uranoscopus] vratynstopus C; vrounscopus P; *om.* T
1215 fascolyon] fastolyon C; fascalion PT
1216 fleith] P; fleteth CT
1217 hamio] Spindler's emendation; hamo CPT
1219 myllamur castor ypotamus] P; millamur castor ipotaneus T; myllanne gastor
   ypocamus C
1220 serra] PT; ferra C
1221 eke the] PT; eke C
   corus] CP; cocus T
1225 fele] PT; selle C
1228 trowte] TP; rouche C
1231 may hym] C; myght hym P; myght he T
1232 in blysse] C; and in blis P; and blysse T
1235 Fro he] P; Fro that he T; For her C
   in] P; in to T; from C
1236 tastid] PT; *om.* C
1240 I nede] C; it nedith PT
1242 for] PT; *om.* C
1247 Whosoo] And whosoo CPT
   knowe] PT; to knowe C
1249 fede] PT; fed C
1253 thou] CT; ye P
1255 Ysydore] Ysider P; Ysydre C; Isidore T
1256 Barthylmewys] Bathylmewys CW; Bartilmew T; Bartholomewes P
1260 goo] CT; to P
1266 I wol] C; I will P; wyll I T
Incipit descripcio prati] T; *om.* CP
1269 moder the fresshe] CP; modyr of the T
1271 enormentes] C; honourment T; enorment P
1275 it] P; *om.* CT
1276 herbe floure] C; floure herbe PT
1277 thryfty] T; thursty C; trusty P

1280 art not now but as] P; art not now but C; nart now nought but as T
      feyned] CP; feynt T
1281 hath dysteyned] CP; doth dysteynt T
1282 and] Spindler's emendation; *om.* CPT
1284 and] CT; *om.* P
1285 In] PT; *om.* C
1286 there was] C; was ther PT
1287 colours and] T; coloure and P; colours C
1290 laughyng] PT; langyng C
1291 payne] C; hete PT
1296 laughyng] PT; longyng C
1299 gendren flour or sede of fresshe] gendreth floure or sede of fresh P; gendren
      seede or flowre or ryche T; gendreth flour or fresshe C
1302 The] PT; Of C
1306 eke] PT; *om.* C
      is good] CP; good ys T
1309 dok the] TP; dok thre CW
      and the] TP; and eke the CW
1313 hound] C; houndes TP
1314 ther] PT; eke C
1316 hath] PTW; hast C
1317 to] PT; for to C
1325 that] C; the P; a T
1331 good] CP gret T
1332 ryse] TP; ryse and C
1333 frute] PT; *om.* C
1337 ne hete myght not] P; nede not to C; ne heete myght T
1340 In] PT; The C
      in appels] and appels CP; in appulles T
1342 gumme from his bole] gumme from his hole P; gom from hys boolle T; come
      from his hole CW
1344 The amonum] P; The cinamom T; To Amoune C
1346 marugh] CT; marche P
1347 balsamum] PT; balsom C
1352–4 *are very confused in C: 1352 and 1354 seem to have exchanged positions;
      subsequent attempts to make sense of them have garbled them further.*
1352 With grapes hony with thure and herbes digne] PT; The vyne tree beryng
      clustres grete and huge C
1353 Thys wood wax moyst gan flow refleyre and sprede] Thys wood wax moyst gan
      flowre refleyre and sprede T; This wode wox moyst gan flow refleyre and sprede
      P; In this wood whiche largely dyd sprede C

1354 The first two bene in sapoure right benygne] The first to bene in sapoure right
     benynge P; The furst two byn in sapour ryght benygne T; With grapes hony
     swete and herbes duge C
1355 The other] PT; Whiche C
1357 ben] be C; bene P; byn T
     for] PT; unto C
1359 and in] P; and CT
1360 of] CP; ouer T
1361 bole] PT; hole C
     the bark] CP; and the barke T
1364 The byrd in] TP; In brede and C
     the bee] T; they ben C; they be P
     bole] TP; hole C
1365 in] PT; out of C
1366 above] PT; om. C
1367 bole] PT; hole C
1368 benethe] TP; fyndeth C
1371 of] CP; and T
1372 the] C; that PT
1375 frutes] C; frute PT
1379 vyne] TP; wyn C
1381 as] PT; and C
1383 gan] P; can C; gomme T
1385 casia to] TP; tasia gan C
1388 anone] PT; om. C
1389 aungelyk] TP; Anglyk C
1391 Gan perse] TP; Gaue pryce C
1393 thy] P; om. CT
1395 blosome] P; blossom T; blosme C
1396 fethers and clene] CP; federes shene T
1399 pure] PT; om. C
1401 foule] PT; foules C
1404 hertes] hertis PT; om. C
1405 Debate ne] PT; Debate no C
1407 supported] supporte C; supportid PT
1412 hym] PT; heuen C
1414 fed] TP; fode C
1416 fresshe] CP; gentyll T; gerfaucoun: Spindler's emendation
1421 in blysse] C; and blis PT
1423 sparowes] CP; sparow T
1424 roke] C; coke PT

1425 for] PT; *om.* C
1429 nought] PT; not C
1431 gyler] C; gyldyr T; *om.* P
1435 above] PT; among aboue C
1436–63 *missing in* W
1439 rest and pees] C; pees and rest PT
1441 eke her] C; eke the PT
1443 hynde] C; lyon TP
1445 and brest] CP; in breste T
1451 the lynx] T; and the lynx C; and the P
1454 the whelpe] PT; *om.* C
       bryght and whyght] C; whit and bright PT
1455 the myse] C; the mule P; the mowlle T
1457 wryte] TP; wyte C
1458 mede] PT; *om.* C
1461 To stert to synge swymme laugh and refleyre clene] To stere to swymme, synge laugh or flene C; To styrt to swyme to syng lawgh and refleyre clene T; To stirt to syng swym laught & refleyre clene P
1462 the] CP; in T
1466 floures] PT; floure C
1469 Enspyryng] Enspiryng PT; Enspyred C
1470 Depaynted new] Depayntid new PT; Hit to seen was C
1471 that] PT; the C
       solempne soverayne] CP; souuerayn solempne T
1472 lyte] Spindler's emendation; lytel CPT
1475 vawtes] T; rances P; wantes C
1477 hyght] lyght C; high P; heyghte T
1479 Quyete] PT; comete C
1482 a wall] PT; one as C
1487 kirnell] P; Corner C; *om.* T
1491 thys wryten was] thys wrytyn was T; this writyng was P; thus y wryte C
1494 that] PT; the C
1495 storme ne stryfe] PT; scorne ne thirst C
1499 toures seven] PT; heuen C
1501 names] PT; name C
       wol I] C; will I P; I woll T
1502 did] PT; *om.* C
1505 hyr] TP; to C
1506 Clennes] PT; Clemens C
1508 Lowlynes] PTW; lowlmesse C
       maide] PT; dame C

1509 thre] ther C; iii PT
1514 Pacyence] pacience PT; sapyence C
1526 Sobrenes] CT; sikirnes P
1528 Sylence] T; silence and P; scyence and C
1529 withouten] PT; withoute C
1531 for] CP; for non T
1534 Dame] PT; dyuyne C
1536 salewyd] TP; folowed C
1537 to] C; hir PT
1539 ful of grace] CPT; full of lust and grace: Spindler's emendation
1541 scyences] sciencis T; scyence CP
1542 knowyng] CT; connyng P
1544 wise] P; scyence C; was T
1550 the] CT; that P
1551 as] C; whom PT
1552 the way she took] CP; she toke the wey T
1555 who lust to] C; whoso lyst TP
1557 the] P; om. CT
1558 governaunce honest] CP; honest governaunce T
1561 As in as moche] P; As moche as C; In as moche T
1564 is] P; om. CT
1567 uncertaynte] T; certaynte CP
1569 As] P; And CT
1573 massy] PT; moysty C
1577 Within] C; Whiche in PT
1584 Grece] PT; grace C
1586 eke clepe] P; eke clepyn C; clepyn eke T
1587 Logyca] logica PT; Loyca CW
1591 His ... his] PT; Her ... hir C
1592 thrifte] P; trust C; thryst T
1593 and of] PT; and C
1594 vertues] CP; vertew T
1596 dyscrecyoun] dyscrecioun TP; discrypcyoun C
1600 thyng] PT; om. C
1601 of] C; and TP
1605 founde for] PT; founder of C
1606 knowe] PTW; knewe C
1612 vertu] CP; vertues T
1614 clene] PT; chene CW
       strengthe] CP; art T
1615 vertu] CP; vertues T

1617 serven] Spindler's emendation; serue CPT
1620 other speketh] CP; speketh owther T
1622 Proverbiis] T; prouerbes C; proverbis P
1624 Cantycles] TP; Cantycle C
1625 Philosophicall] TP; philosophye called C
1629 Dame] PT; *om.* C
1630 dyscrecyoun] discrecioun PT; discrypcyoun C
1636 the] PT; *om.* C
1637 geteth] CT; gevith P
1639 servauntes] CT; ladies P
1640 Arsmetryk] T; Arysmetryk C; arsmetrike P
1648 bounte] CP; beawte T
1649 on] T; of CP
1651 doutaunce] PT; dystaunce C
1652 all] PT; of C
Incipit processus de prima curia] supplied by Spindler; *om.* CPT
1656 With] PT; Whiche C
      loyal] C; roiall PT
1662 Of] PT; And C
      in lythe or yet in lym] in lythe or yet in hym T; in lith or yet in lyme P; he in
      lyeth or yet in hym C
1668 And] CP; As T
1671 there was] TP; *om.* C
1672 They] PT; The C
1674 Averous] Averous and CPT.
1675 Galyene] Galien PT; Galyene and C
1677 Cato] PT; Crato C
1679 Theophyl] theophill PT; cleophyl C
1681 serven] Spindler's emendation; serue CPT
1683 hir] P; *om.* CT
1686 Whyles] CT; Till P
1689 of] PT; of the C
1700 and] PT; *om.* C
1704 yeve us than] C; yeue then us P; haue yeue us that T
1706 hand] PT; *om.* C
1708 us] CT; we P
1709 Denyse] P; Dionyse T; Dapys C
1711 With eyne] P; Within C; Whyche yow T
1713 a] CT; that P
1721 thyng] P; thyngis T; *om.* C

Explicit processus de secunda curia] PT; *om.* C
1724 good godly] goode godly P; good C; goodly T
1726 a] C; an T; the P
1730 Hit] CP; That T
1735 was] P; ys T; *om.* C
1736 a maystry] TP; mayster C
1737 aras] T; ares P; auys C
1738 stories] PT; sterres C
1743 declare gan] gan declare P; declare can T; clare gan C
1744 And on] C; Amyddes T; Amyd P
1745 all] PT; *om.* C
1747 enarmed] PT; enourned C
1748 bound and] TP; *om.* C
1754 thre] PT; there C
1761 Jupyteres] Jupyters C; Jubiters P; Jupiteris T
1762 To] C; That T; The P
1763 commeth] TP; come C
1764 and] C; or PT
1767 honour] T; of honour CP
1770 enmye the fende] enemy the fende PT; enuye C
1771 must] TP; mote C
1773 and] PT; and of C
1775 sylence] silence PT; lycence C
1783 hym] CP; eke T
1786 gloryous] CP; gracyous T
1787 the] CP; thys T
1791 to] C; at PT
1796 Gregor] T; Gregory CP
1797 thynges] CP; thyng T
1798 aboute] PT; al aboute C
1804 The] PT; To C
1805 one] CP; *om.* T
      clerk] CP; clerkis TW
Explicit processus de tercia curia P; *om.* CT
Incipit brevis tractatus de gramatica] P; Incipit processus de gramatica T; *om.* C
1807 foure] PT; *om.* C
1809 grene] C; clene PT
1811 Dyasyntastica] Diasentestica P; Diasintastica T; Dyasynstastica C
1814 write] PT; them write C
1815 partes] C; partyes TP

1817 nowne ... verbe ... which pronowne] PT; nomen ... verbum ... pronomen C
1818 parfyte] TP; party C
1819 accent] TP; accident C
1829 Ferryn] Ferrun PT; Ferryn and C
1835 auctors] TP; auctor C
        tractatus] TP; tractacio C
1843 clerk and] clerke and P; clerk of C; a clerk and T
1845 theyr] CP; hyr T
1851 full depeynted was] full depaynted was PT; depeynted ful al C
1852 *desinit*] T; desynith P; dyffynytyf C
1853 therwith] PT; ryf C
1854 is] PT; is a C
1860 Indefinite singler] T; Indiffinite singuler P; Infynytyf syngulere C
1862 by] PT; be C
1863 eke] PT; *om.* C
1867 dysputen] Spindler's emendation; dyspute CPT
        comonyng] T; connyng CP
1868 strong] T; *om.* CP
1871 the] PT; *om.* C
1872 The] CP; The syx T
1873 many] CP; other T
1876 was] P; was a CT
1878 court] PT; towre C
1880 concours] concourse PT; contours C
1882 Demostene] P; Demoscene C; Demostene T (1883)
1884 Euclide Rufus] euglide rufus P; Euclides Rufus T; Euclido Rusus C
1886 Syr Theoprasse] C; Sir theoprassus P; And Theofrast T
        Tytus and Cipio] Tytrus and Cypro C; Titus and Cipro T; titus and cipio P
1887 Conches Zeno Johannycus] Concles peno Johanneus C; Conches Varro and plun-
        ius T; conches yeno Johannycus P (1888)
1888 Varro and Plinius] P (1887); Zeno Johanucius T; and Nero and plunius C
1890 names] PT; name C
Explicit brevis tractatus de dyaletica] Explicit breuis tractacio de Dyalecica C; Explicit
        breuis tractatus de dialetica P; *om.* T
1897 myght ravysshe] CP; mowth rauysshyth T
1898 many] CP; many a T
1903 of] PT; as C
1904 Cacephaton] PT; Catephaton C
1905 all] PT; *om.* C
1909 poynted] CP; peyntyd T

1911 coma colym periodus] Coma Colym perydus C; colum cola periodus P; Coma
    Colon Periodus T
1912 But whoso thynke] PT; Who so thynketh C
1917 fourth] TP; fyrst C
1919 In] CP; To T
1921 This] PT; His C
    of glorye is] of glory is PT; and glorye in C
1922 thinges] C; thyng PT
    the lust] thow lust CP; ye lust T
1924 eke] TP; *om.* C
1927 had] C; hath PT
1928 de Pophis] P; de paphys T; pophys C
1929 Farrose] C; Pharas hys T; Ferros P
1930 metres] T; maters CP
1933 the] CP; these T
1934 As] PT; As a C
1935 Echone] Ichone PT; Eche C
1937 by] CP; of T
1939 Withouten] C; Withoute PT
1940–2009 *The leaf containing these lines in P is separated from the rest of the*
    manuscript; see introduction, p oo.
1940 and] TP; and the C
1943 aboune] C; aboven PT
1944 conteyneth] TP; contenteth C
1945 and how] C; and PT
1953 be] C; were PT
1954 wryten] Spindler's emendation; wryte CPT
1956 he] CP; we T
1957 lyst have] TP; hath C
1958 or yere there is unsure] yere there is sure C; or yere ys vnsure T; and yere is
    vsure P
1960 trew] TP; haue C
1961 odd] old C; odde T; ode P
1966 dymynew] T; to mynue C; deviue P
1967 taught us craftely] P; tolde us craftyly T; taught truly C
1968–74 *The corner of the leaf is torn in P, and the whole stanza is damaged. The last*
    three lines are missing entirely
1970 set] C; sate T
1972 Apuleius] Apulenis C; Apuleyus T
1973 and in] T; and C

1975 Dame] TP; And C
1976 in] TP; *om.* C
       as] CT; a P
1978 many] CP; many an T
1981 was her craft] T; craft was P; her craft C
1983 y-wrought] j wrought P; wrought CT
1986 to] PT; the C
1987 lowe] C; depe TP
1989 or] C; and TP
1991 y-cut] cut C; kyt T; j knyt P; y-kyt: Spindler's emendation
1998 myle] TP; *om.* C
1999 cercle] CP; circuite T
2000 is] CTP; *om.* Spindler
2001 they] T; there CP
2003 other clerkes sewyng Tholome] other clerkys sewyng Tholome TP; another clerk
       shewyng Theolome C
2004 that the] T; that C; the P
2006–7 *damaged in P*
2008–9 *cut off at bottom of page in P*
2010 clerkes of Egypte] C; of Egipte clerkis PT
2012 in] CP; on T
2017 lyte] lite P; lytel CT
2020 Rethmica] PT; Rethenica C
2022 trewe] PT; newe C
2023 Theyr] CP; That T
2024 her in tunes mete] C; hur in toones swete P; in hyr tewnys swete T
2028 with them] CP; whyche of theym T
       clerkis that thus] C; clerkis which this P; thus clerkis T
2030 syngynge] CP; lyuyng T
2032 some] PT; somme sayd C
2037 musyk ganne to] musike gan to PT; ganne Musyk C
2038 on] T; or P; *om.* C
2041 An] PT; On C
2042 with] PT; in C
2043 wrought] C; brought PT
2045 syllabes] T; syllables CP
2051 syllabes sex useth] syllables sex used C; sillibles sixe usith P; syllabes useth T
2052 the] C; these PT
2053 gan it] P; gon T; *om.* C
2055 which lowe] which law P; whyche lowe T; lowe C
       which sharp] which is sharpe P; whyche sharpe T; or sharp C

2057 dyscencyon] C; ascencioun PT
2058 ordre] PT; ordres C
     ascencyon] C; discencion PT
2059 *gamma-ut*] Spindler's emendation; Gammoth C; gamvt P; Gammuthe T
2061 on] C; in PT
2063 knowe] C; knewe PT
2066 than] PT; *om.* C
     tunes] CT; tone P
2068 tunes] CT; tones P
2071 and] C; with PT
2073 which long] PT; long C
     or] C; which PT
2076 trace] CP; pace T
2079 Boece] CT; boys P
2079 *T concludes at this line, adding, 'Explicit processus de Musica. Explicit hic trac-*
     tatus qui vocatur Curia Sapiencie.' 'John Lydgate' has been added in a later
     (Stowe's) hand. 'Here lackethe 33 staves and more' is written in the margin in
     the same later hand.
2082 Guydo] guyde C; gwydo P
     Metrologo] C; mycrologo P
2083 There mayst thou] C; Thou maist ther P
2084 Rethmica] Rethinica C; Rithmica P
2087 And] C; All P
2088 provynce with] C; pronownce P
2091 ribibe] P; ryuyls CW
2092 the orgons] orgons C; the organce P
2094 see] C; sawe P
     of] P; of al C
2101 is kyndely] C; kyndely is P
2105 which seke] P; seke C
2110 cours] C; site P
2111 poles] P; paleys C
2114 His yates twoo whiche ben oeste and vest] P; With al other partyes most and lest
     C
2118 effectes] effect C; effectis P
2120 her dyvers] C; and diuerse P
2121 eclypse] eclips P; Eclypses C
2124 her] here P; their C
2126 that] C; the P
     the heven] P; heven C
2127 y-sene] j-sene P; sene C

2128 thyng] P; *om.* C
2130 come men] C; comen P
2131 for] P; *om.* C
2132 Arcton] P; Arctur C
2133 Thus] C; These P
2135 Arcturus] Aricturus CW; Arcturas P
2141 al] alle P; *om.* C
2144 eke] P; *om.* C
2145 sterell] P; streyt C
2147 the Fysshe] the fyssh P; and the fysshe C
2148 to] C; do P
2149 So is] P; Suche C
2150 sygne] signe P; fygure C
2151 to] *om.* CP
2153 honour with worshyp] C; worship with honoure P
2160 howe] P; *om.* C
2162 do paynte] do paynt P; depaynte C
     Jubyteres] Jubyters CP
2164 Europe] P; Europa C
2173 bestyal] C; beestis that P
2175 Bull] P; bore C
2178 fatall] P; batayl C
2185 For] P; Or C
     man] a man CP
2186 actes] P; artes C
2190 Isodore] Isodre C; ysidre P
     his] P; *om.* C
2194 Caldee] P; Calde C
2196 withoute] P; withouten C
2197 they of Grece] P; grekes C
2203 the] P; *om.* C
2206 led us to] led vs vnto C; had vs to P
2212 feith] P; trouthe C
2213 had] C; bad P
2216 Jhesu] P; *om.* C
2219 of] C; by P
2222 was] P; he was C
2229 up] P; *om.* C
2234 had] C; bad PW
2236 eke and] P; eke C

2239 ay] P; *om.* C
2245 ought] P; *om.* C
2246 pryvate] C; preue P
2251 and] C; she P
2256 brought was] P; was brought C
2257 that of] that of ony C; of that P
2259 and leprous] leprous C; and lepres P
2263 here] P; *om.* C
2266 to] Spindler's emendation; *om.* CP
2271 whoso] P; who C
2272 victoure reverent] P; vnto reuerence C
2273 entent] P; pretence C
2276 one] P; *om.* C
      the clerke] C; a clerke P; the clerkes W
2281 good] P; quyk C
2290 It] PW; If C
2291 any] P; in many C
2294 as] P; a C
2299 defe] P; deth C; deef W
2301 sorow] P; sour C
2303 yet] *om.* CP
2306 as lowe] P; lowe C
2309 set] P; beset C
      et cantus familie sue] et cantus famule sue C; *om.* P
C breaks off at this point; 2311–73 and the Latin notes at the beginning and end of
      this passage exist in P only.
2314 was] now P
2335 blis] and blis P
2336 Rest] Best P
2364 grace] grace and P
2365 shalt] shat P
2372 without] withouten P
Rhyming summary: *4 and 5 appear in reversed order in P.*

Bibliography

Abbreviations of standard reference works have been incorporated in the bibliography. The bibliography contains only works mentioned in the introduction and notes.

Abelson, Paul *The Seven Liberal Arts: a Study in Mediaeval Culture* Columbia University Teachers' College Contributions to Education 11 (New York 1906; reprinted 1965)

Albricus Philosophus *De deorum imaginibus*, in *Fulgentius Metaforalis* ed Hans Liebeschütz, Studien der Bibliothek Warburg iv (Leipzig 1926) 117–28

Ashby, George *George Ashby's Poems* ed Mary Bateson EETS ES 76 (London 1899; reprinted 1965)

Balbus, Joannes *Catholicon* (Mainz, Johan Gutenberg 1460; reprinted Gregg International, Westmead, Hants 1971)

– *Catholicon* (Strasbourg, Adolf Rusch 1475?)

Bartholomaeus Anglicus *De rerum proprietatibus* (Nuremberg, Fridericus Peypus 1519)

– *De rerum proprietatibus* (Frankfurt 1601; reprinted Minerva, Frankfurt 1964)

– *Bartholomeus de proprietatibus rerum* trans John Trevisa (Westminster, Wynkyn de Worde 1495?)

– *On the Properties of Things: John Trevisa's Translation* ed M.C. Seymour and others, 2 vols (Oxford 1975)

Berchorius, Petrus *De formis figurisque deorum* ed Instituut voor Laat Latijn der Rijksuniversiteit Utrecht, intro J. Engels (Utrecht 1966)

Bernard, St *Sancti Bernardi Opera* v *Sermones* ii, ed J. Leclercq and H. Rochais (Rome 1968)

Bible *Biblia Sacra juxta Vulgatam Versionem* ed Robert Weber OSB, 2 vols, 2nd ed (Stuttgart 1975)

– *The Holy Bible: Douay Version* translated from the Latin Vulgate (London 1956)

Blades, William *The Life and Typography of William Caxton* 2 vols (London 1861–3)
– *The Biography and Typography of William Caxton* (London 1877)
Bloomfield, Morton W. '*Piers Plowman* and the three grades of chastity' *Anglia* LXXVI (1958) 227–53
pseudo-Bonaventura *Meditationes vitae Christi,* in *Opera Omnia S Bonaventurae* ed A.C. Peltier (Paris 1864–71) vol 12
– *The Mirrour of the Blessed Lyf of Jesu Christ* trans N. Love, ed Lawrence F. Powell (Oxford 1908)
– *Meditations on the Life of Christ: an Illustrated Manuscript of the Fourteenth Century* trans and ed Isa Ragusa and Rosalie Green, Princeton Monographs in Art and Archaeology 35 (Princeton 1961)
Book of Common Prayer The Annotated Book of Common Prayer ed John Henry Blunt (London 1869)
Bracton, Henry de *De legibus et consuetudinibus Angliae* ed G.E. Woodbine, trans S.E. Thorne, 4 vols (Cambridge, Mass 1968–77)
Brown, Carleton (ed) *Religious Lyrics of the xvth Century* (Oxford 1939)
Brown-Robbins Index Carleton Brown and Rossell Hope Robbins *The Index of Middle English Verse* (New York 1943)
– Rossell Hope Robbins and John L. Cutler *Supplement to the Index of Middle English Verse* (Lexington 1965)
Brunner, Karl 'Bisher unbekannte Schluszstrophen des *Court of Sapience*' *Anglia* LXII (1938) 258–62
– *An Outline of Middle English Grammar* trans G.K.W. Johnston (Oxford 1965)
Bühler, Curt F. *The Sources of the Court of Sapience* Beiträge zur englischen Philologie 23 (Leipzig 1932)
– 'Notes on the Plimpton Manuscript of the *Court of Sapience*' *MLN* LIX (1944) 5–9
– 'The Apostles and the Creed' *Speculum* XXVIII (1953) 335–9
Burleigh, Walter *De puritate artis logicae tractatus longior* ed P. Boehner, Franciscan Institute Publications, text series 9 (St Bonaventure, NY 1955)
Cassiodorus *Institutiones* ed R.A.B. Mynors (Oxford 1937).
The Castle of Perseverance, in *The Macro Plays* ed M. Eccles EETS OS 262 (London 1969)
Caxton, William *Caxton's Mirrour of the World* ed O.H. Prior EETS ES 110 (London 1913; reprinted 1966)
Chaucer, Geoffrey *The Works of Geoffrey Chaucer* ed F.N. Robinson, 2nd ed (London 1957)
Chaundler, Thomas *Liber Apologeticus de Omni Statu Humanae Naturae* ed Doris Enright-Clark Shoukri (London and New York 1974)
The Court of Sapience ed Robert Spindler, Beiträge zur englischen Philologie 6 (Leipzig 1927; reprinted New York 1967)

Creek, Sister Mary Immaculate *See Rex et famulus*

Curtius, Ernst Robert *European Literature and the Latin Middle Ages* (1948) trans W. Trask (New York 1953)

Denholm-Young, N. *Collected Papers on Mediaeval Subjects* (Oxford 1946)

DNB *Dictionary of National Biography* ed Leslie Stephen and Sidney Lee (London 1885–1909)

DOST *A Dictionary of the Older Scottish Tongue* ed Sir William A. Craigie and A.J. Aitken (Chicago 1931–)

EDD *The English Dialect Dictionary* ed Joseph Wright (Oxford 1878–1905)

EETS OS The Early English Text Society, Original Series

EETS ES The Early English Text Society, Extra Series

Evans, Michael W. *Medieval Drawings* (Feltham, Middx 1969)

Friedberg *Corpus Juris Canonici* ed Aemilius Friedberg 2 vols (1879; reprinted Graz 1959)

Fulgentius metaforalis See Ridevall

Gesta Romanorum ed Hermann Oesterley (Berlin 1872)

Glossa Ordinaria Bibliorum Sacrorum Glossa Ordinaria ed Franciscus Fevardentius OFM, 6 vols (Venice, apud Iuntas 1603)

Gratianus *Decretum See* Friedberg

Grout, D.J. *A History of Western Music* rev ed (New York 1973)

Harley Catalogue *A Catalogue of the Harleian Manuscripts in the British Museum* 4 vols (London 1808)

Harvard Dictionary of Music Willi Apel *The Harvard Dictionary of Music* 2nd ed (Harvard 1969)

Hawes, Stephen *The Pastime of Pleasure* ed W.E. Mead EETS OS 173 (London 1928; reprinted 1971)

– *The Minor Poems* ed Florence W. Gluck and Alice B. Morgan EETS OS 271 (London 1974)

Hodnett, Edward *English Woodcuts, 1480–1535* Bibliographical Society Illustrated Monographs 22 (London 1935; reprinted with corrections 1973)

Holcot, Robert *M. Roberti Holkoth Angli, O.P. ... in librum Sapientiae regis Salomonis praelectiones CCXIII Moralizationum liber est adjectus* (Basel 1586)

Hugh of St Victor *De sacramentis Christianae fidei* PL 176, cols 176–618

– *On the Sacraments of the Christian Faith* trans Roy J. Deferrari (Cambridge, Mass 1951)

– pseudo-Hugh of St Victor *De fructibus carnis et spiritus* PL 176, cols 998–1006

Isidore of Seville *Isidori Hispalensis episcopi Etymologiarum sive Originum Libri xx* ed W.M. Lindsay, 2 vols (Oxford 1911; reprinted 1962)

Jacobus a Voragine *Legenda Aurea* ed Th Graesse, 3rd ed (1890; reprinted Osnabrück 1969)

Jacobus de Cessolis *Libellus de moribus hominum et officiis nobilium ac popularium super ludo scachorum* ed Sister Marie Anita Burt, PhD dissertation, University of Texas 1957

James, M.R. *The Western Manuscripts in the Library of Trinity College Cambridge* ii (Cambridge 1901)

Jean de Muris *or* Joannes de Muris *Libellus cantus mensurabilis*, in E. Coussemaker *Scriptorum de Musica Medii Aevi* nova series III (Paris 1869; reprinted Hildesheim 1963)

– *Notitia artis musicae* ed Ulrich Michels, Corpus Scriptorum de Musica 17, American Institute of Musicology (1972)

Joannes Affligemensis *De Musica cum Tonario* ed J. Smits van Waesberghe, Corpus Scriptorum de Musica 1 (Rome 1950)

Justinian *Digestum vetus* (Lyons 1549)

– *The Institutes of Justinian* trans T.C. Sandars (London 1934)

Kelly, J.N.D. *Early Christian Doctrines* 5th ed (London 1977)

– *The Athanasian Creed* (London 1964)

Langland, William *Piers the Plowman* text B, ed W.W. Skeat EETS OS 38 (London 1869; reprinted 1964)

Lewis, C.S. *The Allegory of Love* (London 1936; reprinted 1961)

Lewis and Short *A Latin Dictionary* ed C.T. Lewis and C. Short (Oxford 1879)

Liebeschütz, Hans *See* Ridevall

Logica Modernorum, a contribution to the History of Early Terminist Logic ed L.M. de Rijk (Assen, Neth 1962) vol 1

Ludus Coventriae ed K.S. Block EETS ES 120 (London 1922 [for 1927])

Lydgate, John *The Troy Book* ed H. Bergen EETS ES 97, 103, 106, 126 (London 1906–35; reprinted 1973)

– *The Life of Our Lady* ed J.A. Lauritis, V.F. Gallagher, and R.A. Klinefelter (Pittsburgh 1961)

MED *Middle English Dictionary* ed Hans Kurath, S.M. Kuhn, and John Reidy (Ann Arbor 1952–)

Mirrour of the World See Caxton

Murphy, James J. 'Caxton's Two Choices: "Modern" and "Medieval" Rhetoric in Traversagni's *Nova Rhetorica* and the anonymous *Court of Sapience' Medievalia et Humanistica* 3 (1972) 241–55

Murray, H.J.R. *A History of Chess* (Oxford 1913; reprinted 1969)

OED *The Oxford English Dictionary* ed James A.H. Murray, Henry Bradley, W.A. Craigie, and C.T. Onions, 12 vols (Oxford 1933)

Orme, Nicholas *English Schools in the Middle Ages* (London 1973)

Peter of Spain *or* Petrus Hispanus Portugalensis *Tractatus, called afterwards Sum-*

mulae logicales ed L.M. de Rijk, Philosophical Texts and Studies, Uitgaven van het Filosofisch Instituut der Rijksuniversiteit te Utrecht 22 (Assen, Neth 1972)

Pevsner, Nicolaus *The Buildings of England: Derbyshire* (London 1953)

PL Patrologia Latina (Patrologiae cursus completus, omnium SS Patrum, Doctorum, Scriptorumque ecclesiasticorum) ed J.-P. Migne (Paris 1878–90)

Rex et famulus, in Bede *Homiliae subdititiae* PL 94, cols 505–7

– edited in Sister Mary Immaculate [Creek] 'The Four Daughters of God in the *Gesta Romanorum* and the *Court of Sapience*' PMLA LVII (1942) 951–65

Ridevall, John *Fulgentius Metaforalis* ed Hans Liebeschütz, Studien der Bibliothek Warburg IV (Leipzig 1926)

Rigg, A.G. 'Gregory's Garden: a Latin dream-allegory' *Medium Aevum* XXXV (1966) 29–37

Rivière, J. *Le Dogme de la Rédemption au début du Moyen Age* Bibliothèque Thomiste, section historique XVI (Paris 1934)

Sajavaara, Kari *The Middle English Translations of Robert Grosseteste's Chateau d'Amour* Mémoires de la Société Néophilologique de Helsinki XXXII (Helsinki 1967)

Sarton, George *Introduction to the History of Science* Carnegie Institution of Washington Publications 376, 3 vols (Baltimore 1927–48)

The Sarum Missal ed J. Wickham Legg (Oxford 1916; reprinted 1969)

Schubert, Grace M. 'The Court of Sapience: a collation of the Plimpton Manuscript with introduction and notes' MA thesis, Columbia 1937

Seznec, Jean *The Survival of the Pagan Gods* trans B. Sessions (1953; reprinted New York 1961)

Sir Gawain and the Green Knight ed J.R.R. Tolkien and E.V. Gordon, 1st ed (corr) (Oxford 1930)

Smalley, Beryl *English Friars and Antiquity in the early fourteenth century* (Oxford 1960)

SND *The Scottish National Dictionary* ed William Grant and David D. Murison, 10 vols (Edinburgh 1931–76)

Spindler *See Court of Sapience*

Spurgeon, Caroline F.E. *Five Hundred Years of Chaucer Criticism and Allusion* (Cambridge 1925)

STC *A Short-Title Catalogue of Books Printed in England, Scotland, and Ireland, and of English Books Printed Abroad 1475–1640* compiled by A.W. Pollard and G.R. Redgrave (London 1946). A revised edition of the second half (I-Z) of this volume appeared in 1976; the *Court* is still listed under Lydgate.

Thorndike, Lynn *A History of Magic and Experimental Science* (New York 1923) vols I, II

Thorndike, Lynn and Pearl Kibre *A Catalogue of Incipits of Medieval Scientific Writings in Latin* rev ed (Cambridge, Mass 1963)

Traver, Hope *The Four Daughters of God. A study of the versions of this allegory with special reference to those in Latin, French, and English* Bryn Mawr College Monographs 6 (Bryn Mawr 1907)
– 'The Four Daughters of God: a Mirror of Changing Doctrine' *PMLA* XL (1925) 44–92
Tuve, Rosemond *Allegorical Imagery* (Princeton 1966)
Webb, Geoffrey *Architecture in Britain: the Middle Ages* (Harmondsworth 1956)
Whiting, B.J. *Proverbs, Sentences, and Proverbial Phrases* (Cambridge, Mass 1968)

Glossary

The glossary contains only those words that might cause difficulty to those unfamiliar with Middle English. Line references are given when a word occurs only once or is used in that particular sense only in that context; a line reference followed by an 'n' indicates that the word is discussed in the notes. The letter y has been included in i throughout.

abisate   1028n   a precious stone (Latin: abisatus)
abone, abonne, aboun, aboune   above, on top of, in heaven (northern form)
accesse   attack of fever
acordeth unto   agrees with
adachyte   1011n   idachytes, a precious stone
adamante   956n   loadstone
adequate   equal in distance
adnychylate   annihilated, destroyed
adnull   annul, obliterate
aferd   afraid
affectuous   eager, earnest
affyle   polish (one's tongue), improve (one's speech)
ageyne   821   in return for
agnus castus   1300   a shrub, agnus castus
ay   always, forever
ayenst   against
al oute   altogether
alabandine   1027n   almandine, garnet
alabastyr   953   alabaster
alday   all the time
aller   *gen pl of* al   of them all

aloes 1345 aloe, an aromatic tree
amatyst 957n amethyst
amatyte 957n a precious stone
amonum 1344 amomum, an aromatic plant
annys 1305 anise
anon, anone soon, at once, straightway
appropred is an attribute of
apryce excellence, value
aquayle 357n destroy? ruin?
aras-werk tapestry
argeryte 954n a precious stone
arystologye 1304 aristolochia, birthwort
aromatyke fragrant, spicy
ascaunce as if to say
asketh 464 requires, demands
asper bitter, cruel
assent opinion, formal endorsement of an opinion
assessours legal advisers to a judge
assoylle disprove (an argument), absolve (a sin)
asteryte 956n asterite, a precious stone
asteron 955n astrion, asteriated sapphire
astyed climbed, mounted
asure 1285 lapis lazuli
attend 1206 to be present, near
attractyf having the property of drawing out or towards
auctor author, source
aulfyn bishop (in chess)
aurypygment 954n auripigment, orpiment
auronnea 1220n a fish
avaunt boast, promise, merit

balsamum 1347 balsam shrub, balm
beauperlaunce lovely speech
beel fair, good
behest 730 request, command, promise
beldame title of respect used to an aged woman
bele fair, good
belyve at once
bemed emitting rays of light, shining
benyngne gracious, gentle, kind

besene, bysene   equipped, furnished with, arrayed; wel besene   beautiful
beshent   ruined, shamed
besy   diligent, attentive
besought   afflicted
best, at the best   most excellently (tag)
best   1112   beast
bestyal   animals, livestock
bet   better
bete   1305   beet
byhest   command, promise
byrdes   young birds, song birds, birds
byrel   967   beryl
bysene   *see* besene
blysse   *vb*   glorify, praise gratefully
blysse   *n*   delight, blessedness
blyve   delightful, pleasant
blont   dull, stupid, unskilful
blowe   breathe out, utter
bone   request, prayer
boost   outcry, threatening
bounte   excellence, good condition
brenneth   burns
brent   shone, blazed
brere   1309   briar
briddes   birds
brocke   1450   badger
bure   1311   burdock
burgyn   burgeon, grow
but, but if   unless, except that

caas (law)   a suit, a cause; situation
cabiate   980n   a precious stone
cacephaton   1904   cacophony
cakodryl   1214   crocodile
calcophan   979n   calciphane, a precious stone
calcydone   974n   chalcedony
calendres   1964   mathematical tables
camen   1019n   cameo-stone
canne   1345   sugar cane
carabo   1213   crab

carbuncle   971n   carbuncle, a precious stone
carybde   Charybdis, engulfing danger
cast, kest   plot, decide upon, deliberate
castor   1219   beaver
cease, cees, cese   put an end to, allay, stop, bring to a stop
century   1308   centaury
ceranne stone   978n   thunderstone (Latin: cerauneus)
certayn, in certayn   surely, indeed (tag)
chattes   1374   ash-keys
chaunce   1699   fate; 313   fortune
chere   face, bearing, spirit, mood, feeling
cherubynte   1377   terebinth
chyef   supreme, best
chylder   children
chrysopasse   975n   chrysoprase
cyrcumstaunce   existing aspects
clare   explain
clence   heal
clene   *adj*   clean, pure, bright, excellent
clene   *adv*   chastely, wholly
clepe, clepyn, cleped, clepest   call, name
clere, for clere   clearly, perfectly (translates Latin 'perfecte')
clerk, clerke   scholar, learned man
clyppes   eclipse
coeterne   coeternal (of members of the Trinity)
collage   fellowship, assembly
collatural   less important
combuste   burnt, scorched
comfortable   invigorating, strengthening
comfortatyf   strengthening, cheering
comyn   *see* comune
comonyng   talking together, discussing, debating
complacence   delight, pleasure
complement   fulfilment
comport, comporte   bear, endure, suffer; 2271   carry
compromyt in   agree to refer (a matter) to (an arbiter)
computacyon   arithmetical calculation, reckoning
comune, comyn   common, ordinary
comunte   common or general knowledge, common use

conclude   come to a decision, resolve; resolved
conclusyon   end, purpose; in conclusyon   in the end, finally
concordaunce   harmony; daunte unto concordaunce   harmonize
condescend   assent, give consent
conger   1221   conger eel
conjunctyf   producing cohesion, solidifying
conne   know how to, be able, learn how to
connyng   knowledge
conserve   preserve, keep
constaunce   stability
constytucyon   law, ordinance
consubstancyal   of the same essence, coessential (of the Trinity)
contencyon   quarrel
contene   1512   continue; 1577   contain
content, conteyned   contained
contrarious   opposing, antagonistic
contreved   devised, managed
converce   live, be in company with
conversacion   behaviour, mode of life
conversaunte   having lived and grown up (in a place), brought up
corall   977   coral
coryandre   1313   coriander
corus   1221   a fish (Isidore: aphorus)
counterfete   imitate
countre   engage in a battle   (at chess)
courage   spirit, boldness
couthe   could, was able, knew
covert   thicket, underbrush
craft   art, branch of learning, skilful method
craftely   skilfully, according to the rules of a craft or art
craveys   1226n   a crayfish or crawfish
crisolyte   972n   a precious stone, chrysolite
crystal   976n   crystal
cost   2358   temporal condition
cubyculers   chamberlains, attendants
cure   effort, achievement, care, office
curyous   fine
currycles   courses of time, recurrent periods
cut, y-cut   intersected

damecyne 1374 damson
dampned (law) condemned to death, declared guilty
darted pierced
daunt harmonize
debate (law) quarrel, suit, or action; ben at debate be engaged in a dispute
degoute sprinkle
degree rank, order; in al degree in every respect
dele, every dele every part, in every respect
delycacye delightfulness, pleasure
delycate pleasing
delycately pleasantly
delyver answer, give judgment
deme (law) to pass judgment, sentence; to think, suppose
denseth makes thick
departed divided, subdivided
depose make a statement
depure purify, define
depured polished, clear
dere harm, injury; do dere wound
descryve describe
despyte, holden in regard with contempt or hatred
destroyed of deprived of
determyne to define, describe
detray, detraye 60 disparage, abuse; 64 take away
devyse, at devyse perfectly, neatly, clearly (tag); to devyse to one's liking or wish
devyse vb compose, declare
dyadek 981n diadocus, a precious stone
diffinid defined
dyffyntyve (law) decisive, conclusive
dyghte dressed, adorned
digne noble, worthy, pleasing
dyke moat
dymynew subtract
dyonys 982n dionise, a precious stone
dysceverd scattered, separated
dyscencyon lowering of pitch
dyscrecioun discernment, judgment
dyscryve describe
dyscusse examine (for judgment), determine (the truth)
disgressyon digression

dyspyte   injury
dystaunce   discord, conflict, affliction
dystayn, dystayne   deprive of beauty, put in the shade, stain
dysteyned   stained, marred
dystylle   fall in drops, trickle
dystyllyng   dropping
distraynte, in distraynte   216n   in torment?
dyte   words, song
dyten   1306   dittany
dyvyne   *adj*   learned in divinity
dyvyne   *vb*   tell, ponder, think; 2106   prophesy, practise divination
do, doth, dost, done   make, makes, made
dok   1309   dock
dome   judgment
dome   2259   dumb
dongeon   1548   donjon, castle keep
doughtful   mighty
doutance   uncertainty
dragaunce   1309   dragonwort
drawe, drawen   78, 84   to make a move (at chess)
draught   a move (at chess)
drenched   overwhelmed, plunged
dresse   911   correct; 1233   set out in order
drew   1974   added up, calculated? wrote about?
drewe of   2202   wrote about
dulcor, dulcour   sweetness

eche   35   eke out, amplify
echone   each one
eclippes, clyppes   eclipse
effect, effecte   purpose, intent; in effect   in force, actually, really (tag)
effimeron   1213n   an ephemeral fish
eft, efte   again, a second time; 834   afterwards
egal   equal
eyen   eyes
eke   also, moreover
electorye   953n   a precious stone (Latin: allectoria)
electuarye   1372n   a compound medicine
elytrope   986n   a precious stone, elitrope; *see also* ilytrope
elumyned, ellumyned   adorned; 1657   decorated (as a manuscript) with paintings

emachyte 985n haematite, iron ore
enarched constructed with arches
encense waft perfume
encomerous difficult
endelong and overthwert in all directions
endyte compose, write
enydros 988n a precious stone
enlumyned decorated
enourne decorate, embellish
enornement, enormentes adornment, decorations
enspyre blow upon, breathe on
entencyon 1132 intensity (Latin: intensio)
entent meaning, purpose; wish, desire
entone sing
epystyte 992n a precious stone (Latin: episterus)
equyte 466 moderation
erde earth (northern form)
ere plough
ergo therefore (term from Latin logic)
erratyk wandering
escaryus 1212n an unknown fish (Latin: escarius)
eschek! Check! (at chess)
eschekker chess-board
eschyte 983n echites, a precious stone
eterne eternal
evanysshed disappeared, vanished (a late and northern word)
even 1552 straight
every dele in every way
exceptyf 1034n acceptable? pleasing?
excolicerose 993n excolerius, a precious stone
execucyon the carrying out or realization of a design, power to act; doothe execucyon
  enforces a law, carries out a sentence
expresse fully, quickly, at once (tag)
exuberaunt over-abundant, abounding

fable, withouten fable without falsehood, truly (tag)
facund eloquence
facundyous eloquent
fayne joyful, fond

falle to   come into agreement with
familitees   households
fantasy   delusion
fascolyon   1215n   fuscaleon, a fish
favour   469   mercy, leniency
feete in armes   knightly exploit
feyne   423   hold back, restrain oneself
feyned   1280   feeble, pale
fele   *adj*   many
fele   *vb*   1225   taste
felle upon a slepe   fell asleep
fellid   are overthrown, have succumbed to temptation
fenyx   1420   phoenix
fere   companion; in fere   together, in a flock
ferful   awe-inspiring
ferme   faithfully
fyne   end, purpose
flayn, flayne, flene   skinned alive, scourged
flee   *vb*   flay, skin
flee   *vb*   1429   fly; fleyng   flying
fleen   *vb*   973   flee, fly from
flees   *n*   fleas, insects
flete   1200   float; 1348   flow
flouke   1225n   flounder, fluke
fomyng of blode   wet with blood, covered with blood
foo   enemy
forbete   wounded with blows; beaten severely
force, of force   of necessity
forge   fashion, make
foryeve   forgive
forthynketh, it forthynketh me   I repent
fowles   birds
fragraunt   pleasing, delightful
free   noble
freel   weak, sinful
frendful   friendly, beneficial
frenetyke   delirious, crazed
fresshe   eager, vigorous
fro   from; 1235   from the time that

fructuous   fruitful, beneficial
fulfylleth   fills up
fumytere   1308   fumitory

gadred   gathered, collected
gagates   995n   jet
galachyte   1000n   galactite, a precious stone
gan   began, did
gentyl   noble
gentyles   2172   gentiles, pagans
gentylnesse   excellence
geratycen   1002n   geraticen, a precious stone
gesse, as I gesse   I suppose (tag)
gest   guest
gestys   writings
y-gete   begotten
gyler   a snare for birds, trap
gylofur   1279   gillyflower, clove-scented pink?
gylted   adorned, decorated with gold, precious
glad   make joyful
glose, withouten glose   truthfully, truly (tag)
godely   excellent, virtuous
goo forth   Be off! Get away!
gooshauk   1416   goshawk
governaunce   moral discipline
grave   engrave
graven   2227   buried, entombed
greynes   1382   grains of Paradise, a spice
grene   youthful, lively, new; woundes grene   unhealed wounds
greves   groves, thickets
grones   murmurings
grounde   grounding, fundamental principles
groundely   firmly, fully
grutchyng   complaining

habound   abound
had   805   took
half, on every half   everywhere, on all sides
hamio   1217n   a fish
hastyf   rash, quick

held   715   incline
hele   recovery, restoration, healing
hepe, upon an hepe   all together; brynge to hepe   bring together
herberd   harboured, gave shelter to
herbergage   house, lodgings
herne   corner, hiding-place
hevynesse   sorrow
hygh   exalted, lofty; heinous, dire
hyght, on hyght   loudly, raised (of voices)
hyght   *vb*   called, is called
hyght   *n*   587   pride, haughtiness
ho   stop
hold   398   uphold, keep; 2236   believe
hole   *adv*   wholly
hole   *adj*   whole, healthy, supreme
holt   wood; thorugh holt and heth   through woods and heaths, far away
hows of offyce *pl?*   store-room, room for domestic use, such as a pantry or
   brewhouse

yafe, yave   gave
yate   gate
idropsy   dropsy
yeve, yeveth, yeven   give, gives, given; yeve for   exchange
illumyne   enlighten
ilytrope   1310   calendula, pot-marigold
ymagery   carved figures or decorations
ympne   hymn
include   contained
incluse   shut in, shut up, surrounded
incomerous   difficult
inconsonaunt   at variance with, out of harmony with
incorperacyon   1116–18n   substance, bulk
inforce   strengthen
infortune   misfortune
injure   injustice (northern form)
inmedyate   next, close, nearest in order
inmensurable   innumerable, vast, not to be counted
inmortal   immortal
inscyence   ignorance, foolishness
insuffycience   insufficiency, inadequacy

insygnyte   distinguished, eminent
interupte   halting, impaired
invariaunt   unchanging, unchangeable
yode   went
yongly   young, youthful
ypyphanye   1697n   epiphany, showing forth; name of the first hierarchy
ypotamus   1219   hippopotamus
yrous   wrathful, angry
irys   1016n   iris, a prismatic crystal
iwis, ywys   certainly, indeed (tag)

jacynct   1009n   jacinth, a precious stone; 1296n   hyacinth
japed   frolicked
jardyns   1341n   Jordan almonds
jaspre   1006n   jasper
jena   1018n   hyena, a precious stone
jerarchye   hierarchy, rank of angels
jerachyte   1014n   the irachite, a precious stone
june   come into conjunction with (northern form)
juste   fight, tilt

kepe   protect, sustain
kest   229   plot; *see also* cast
kynd, kynde   nature, the natural world, natural history
kyndely   natural, according to nature
kirnell   notch or embrasure in a battlement, battlements (northern form)
knyghthode   military service, prowess, courage
knyt   attached to, united with

laberous   difficult, onerous
lake   658   pit, lion-pit, prison
lamperey   lamprey
langours   sicknesses, diseases
late, lete   let, cause to, allow; lete be, late be   give up, cease
laugh on   smile at
leche   physician
lede   1019   overlaid, inlaid
lees   lies; withouten lees   assuredly (tag)
lere   teach, learn
lerne   teach

lete   *see* late
lette   hinder
leve   live
lyef   dear, beloved
lygurius   1021n   ligure, a precious stone
lipparia   1023n   a fabulous stone
list, lyst   *impers vb*   923n   to want, to choose
lyst   *n* desire, wish; at theyr owne lyst   by their own wish
lyte   little
lith, lieth   lies
lythe   joint; lythe and lym   joints and members, all the body (tag)
litteral   of letters
loke on   gaze upon, look at; unto loke   to gaze on
longeth   2242   pertains to
lordshyppes   realms, territories, estates
lorne, y-lorne   ruined, destroyed
lose   834   to lose, fail to keep
lose, losed   free, set free
loth   hated, hateful
love   57   praise
lowte   bow, make obeisance to, honour
lust   *impers vb*   923n   it pleases, to wish
lust, luste   *n* pleasure, happiness; at lust   according to wish or pleasure
lusty   pleasant, beautiful, bright, vigorous
lustynesse   pleasure, delight

magnes   1032n   magnet
maystry   wonderful work, marvel
makers   poets
makyng   poetical composition
malve   1309   mallow
mametrye, maumetry   false gods, idols
mandement, maundement   commandment
mandrage   1314   mandrake
maners   659   estates
maners   1622   morals
margaryte   1030n   pearl
marygold   1310   calendula or pot marigold
marugh   1346n   pith, marrow
mastyk   mastic, resin

mater, matere   subject matter
mede   meadow
mede 2359   reward
medus   1041n   Median stone
medytacyon   preoccupation, meditation
mellanyte   1034n   melanite, a precious stone
melochyte   1037n   malachite
memphyte   1037n   Memphian stone
mercy, have mercy of   have mercy upon
mercyable   merciful, compassionate
meryour   mirror
merveylous   wonderful, marvellous
meschyef   distress, calamity
mete   2024   meet, suitable, fitting
meve   move
mile   1898   miles
myllago   1216n   flying fish?
myllamur   1219n   melanurus, a fish
mynysse   reduce, compress, abridge
mynyster   dispenser, agent
mynystre   *vb*   furnish, supply
myryte   1036n   myrrhite, murrhine stone
myslyvers   persons of evil life
moble   movable, unstable, fickle
moysty   moist, wet
moo   more
moral sense   1762   allegorical meaning, moral interpretation
more   1376   mulberry tree
mow, mote   may, must, be able to
must   1708   it behooves

naked   bared
nas = ne was   was not
ne   not, nor
negheth   draws near
nere but = ne were but   would be nothing but
netheles   nevertheless
neven, nevene, nevened   name, named
nyce   1447   foolish
nyl = ne will   will not

nys = ne is   is not
nyst = ne wyst   know not
nitrum   1040n   natron or washing soda
noy   trouble, harm
nones, for the nones   for the purpose (tag)
noset   1042n   toadstone
not = ne wot   479, 774   do not know
note   1671   famous, noted
numeracyon   the arithmetical skill of reading numbers; calendres for numeracyon-
   lists or tables by which to teach the value of figures
nutrytyf   nourishing

obeysaunce   obedience, deference
object   put in front, exposed to sight
oblygacyon   a binding argument
obloqucyon   obloquy, slander
observaunce   duty, rule, custom
occyan   the ocean encompassing the known world
occult   hidden, secret
occupacyon   business, employment
offyce, hows of   building(s) for domestic purposes
ofter   more often
ofthyrst of   athirst for
olybanum   frankincense
ones   once for all
onychyne   1044n   onyx
onyx   1045   onyx
oores   oars
operacyon   working, manner of working
oppynacyon   opinion, conjecture (Latin: opinatio)
optallyus   1047n   opal
or   before
oryte   1049n   orites, a precious stone
other ... or, outher ... or   either ... or
overthwert   athwart, crosswise; overthwart and endlong   crosswise and lengthwise,
   in all directions

paced   stepped, walked
payn, payne, peyn   penalty, suffering, effort
pantere   1450   panther

parfyte   faultless, complete, perfect
parfyte   *adv*   perfectly, completely
paryus   1051n   Parian marble
party   part, division, portion
patron   331   model, pattern; 1048   protector
pease   *vb*   appease, reconcile
peyn   *see*   payn
penaunce   punishment, penalty
peramour   lover, beloved
perce, perse   pierce, penetrate, move deeply
percele   1311   parsley
peregal   fully equal
permute   exchange one for another
pertryche   1422   partridge
phager   1220   a fish (Latin pagrum)
physyk   372   medicine; 1924   natural science
pye   1423   magpie
pyrryte   1053n   pyrites, fire-stone
playse   1225   plaice
plesaunce   pleasure
poynt   *vb*   to write, jot down
poynt, in   on the point of; in no poynt   in no respect; in eche poynt   in every
   respect
polocye, polycye, polycy   polity, an organized state; political science
ponyte   1055n   pumice-stone?
portature   portraiture
portrature   1736   appearance?
poudred   sprinkled, decorated with
pouer, power   poor, deficient
prassyus   1051n   prase, quartz
preche   proclaim, speak out seriously
preygnaunt   weighty, cogent
presence, in   in attendance (on a superior)
prevely   secretly
pryce   reward, bribe; of pryce   of great value, highly esteemed
prycked   set down music by means of 'pricks' or notes
processe   the proceedings in an action at law; by processe   in due course
pronounce   declare, report
properte   383   special character or nature, attribute, characteristic nature; of propyrte, properte   of right

proporcyon   musical harmony, melody
propre   one's own
propre   587   in the strict use of the word? exact, proper
provynce   2088   area of study, subject
puerly   clearly, without blemish
punycyon   punishment
pure   spotless; 439   complete, absolute, total
purperate, purpurate   shining, brilliant, beautiful (Latin: purpurare)
purpoos, to purpoos   to the matter in hand, effectively
purveaunce   provision for the future, providence
put forth, put the forth   come forward

quadraunt   square, rectangular
quandras   1059n   vulture stone
queynte   skilful, wise, ingenious
quyck, quyk   alive
quyrryne   1058n   a precious stone (Latin: quirinus)
quod   said

rayne   rain, let fall
rampe   1376n   buckthorn?   restharrow?
rasyne   1377   resin
raveyn   ravin, act of seizing prey
ravyssyng   1731   enchanting, delightful
reame, royalme   realm
reben   1062n   a stone found in a crab
recomforte   console, relieve of distress
record on   think about, remember; relate in words
red   taught
rede   *vb*   advise, counsel, say
rede   *n*   counsel, decision
rede   1344   reed
redolent   fragrant, sweet-smelling
refectyoun   refreshment
refleyr   *vb*   distil perfume, shed scent
refleyr   *n*   scent
refrayne, refreyn   check, hold back
refrendary   reporter, one who furnishes news or information
refuyte   1368n   refuge
refuse   *vb*   avoid, keep clear of

refuse *n* 441 outcast, reject
regnaunt ruling, exercising influence
reygne 98 kingdom, realm
rejoysed have full use and enjoyment of
relygyon 1510 religious conduct of life
remewe, remeved to remove, persuade one out of a promise or resolve
remyt forgiven
renne run
repeyre strengthen
replete filled, imbued with
represent give back
repressyf repressive, able to check
repreve reject, condemn, disprove
reson 2190 argument, premise; 1815 sentence
resort unto revert to
respect hath has regard to, considers
restauracyon restoration
reuth compassion, pity
reveste to clothe again, dress
revygure to recover vigour, revive
reward 642 regard, consideration; 773 recompense
reward *vb* requite, repay
rewe show pity
riall splendid, excellent
rydeth laughs (Latin: ridere)
ryght *n* justice
ryght 1772 lawful; 1992 straight
ryght as just as; right in specyal just on this point
roche 1224 roach
roche 1485 rock
rode rood, cross
royalme, royame realm, kingdom
roke rook (in chess)
ronge, oute ronge sounded clearly, proclaimed?
rosyn 1350 resin
rote 703 root, source
route a troop, retinue; on a route in a large number
route *vb* move
rudeness lack of education

ruynous   destructive, pernicious
rumoure   report

sad, sade   settled, firm, earnest, constant, serious; heavy; dark-coloured
sad   *adv*   firmly, seriously
salewe   salute, greet in words
saphyre   1065n   sapphire
sapour, sapoure   taste, savour
sardius   1076n   cornelian
scole   schooling, training
scripture, scrypture   writing
seche unto   resort to
see   88   position, territory
sees, seceth   stop, puts an end to
see-swyn   1215   sea-swine, a fish
seke   to seek, look for; she had it not to seke   she did not have to look for it
selydon   969   celidony, a precious stone (Latin: celidonius); 1307   celandine
sempyterne   eternal
sentement   personal experience, perception
sequestracyon   banishment, exile
serenyte   1078n   selenite or moonstone, a precious stone
serra   1220n   sawfish
set   1970   sat
sewe, sewen, sewynge, sewed   follow, followed, following
shap   form, likeness
shold   372   profits
shoures   showers
syght   1334   place, position
sykernesse, sykernes, sikernes   security, assurance
syllabe   syllable (northern form)
symple   48   simply
syn   since, since the time that, considering that
syngulere   1420   unique
syth   since; syth   879   times
sytte on knee, syt on kne   to go down on one's knees
sklaunder   slander, malicious statement
sleeth   destroys, extinguishes
slough   slew
smaragde   1072n   emerald

solempne   serious, grand, famous, awe-inspiring
solempnyte   due order or ceremony
solen   unique, singular
sonnes gemme   1077n   sunstone
sonnysshe   sunny, golden
sope   sip, mouthful
soth   truth; soth to sayne   truth to tell (tag)
sothfastnes   truth, truthfulness
soverayne   superior, lord, mistress; supreme, excelling
soveraynte   supremacy, pre-eminence
sowne, soune   sound
sparkyng   sparkling
speculer   having the reflecting property of a mirror
specyal   individual, particular
spille, spylt   perish, destroy, put to death
spyres   spheres
spyryte   586   emotional part of man as the seat of hostile or angry feeling; pride
stable, stabled   make firm, confirm, ratify
starf   died
started   capered, jumped, sprang
sterve   die
stewe   fishpond
stye, styed   mount up, ascended
style   353   title
stirt   spring about
stok and stone   (gods of) wood and stone
store   376   value
stout, stoute   splendid, magnificent
streyte   strait, narrow
strondes   rivulet, stream (northern form)
strong   855   strongly
studyous   requires study
subjecte to   under the rule of; subjecte   vassal, dependant
subjectyon   obedience; doth him subjectyon   pays him homage
subtyl   1164   winding?
suerte   security, certain knowledge
superfycyal   on the surface
superne   above, on high
superstyous   superstitious
sustene   sustain, support, maintain

sustenaunce   sustenance, food
sute   461n   (legal) case?
swageth   assuages, appeases, relieves
swannysshe   swanlike
swete   *vb*   sweat, exude in drops
swete   *adv*   sweetly
swete   *n*   sweat
swyth   quickly
swoune   swoon

table   2313   tablet
telle   name in order
tempestous   tempestuous, stormy
temporatyf   having the quality of tempering; mitigating
termes gay   elegant language
tery   teary, tearful
thank   *n*   favour, grace
thanked of   gave thanks for
tho   then
thought   anxiety, distress of mind
thral   enslaved, captive, in bondage
thryft, thrifte   management, economy
thryfty   flourishing, vigorous, becoming
throng   force one's way
thure   frankincense   (Latin: thus, thuris)
thwyte   whittle, shape by paring
tofore   in front, before
tood   toad
topacius   1079n   topaz
to-rent   torn in pieces
touche   lay hands on, hurt; to pluck (a string)
trace   follow, discover, search out
travayled   laboured
trespassure   sinner, wrongdoer
tressyd   braided
trest   trust, confidence, hope
tretes   books, handbooks
treuse take   to undertake to make the peace
trone   throne
trowe, troweth, trowith   believe, believes

turkoys   1082n   turquoise
turtyl   1420   turtle-dove

umbre   shade, shadow
ungentylnesse   ungratefulness, unnatural behaviour
unhele   sickness, trouble, infirmity
unyverse, in   97   in general, in the universal scheme of things
unkynd   unnatural, ungrateful
unkyndely   unnatural, bad
unleful   illicit, unlawful
unneth   scarcely, hardly
unrest   trouble
uranoscopus   1214   a one-eyed fish
ure   1154   ore
uryne   urinate
us   1708   we
usurpe   914   make pretensions

vacuate   made empty
vayne   worthless, useless
varrye   to undergo change; pass from one to another
vawtes   vaults, arched roofs
veray, verray   true, full, exact
vertuous   2319   strong, potent
vyce   defect of character, imperfection, vice
vycyate   to make imperfect
volunte   will, pleasure
vouchesauf   grant, permit, deign
vulgare   vernacular, native tongue

wage   reward, recompense
wake   stay up at night (to study), be alert, vigilant
ward   part of a castle, either a guarded entrance or an area within the inner walls
ware   aware
wax, wexe, waxeth, wox   grow, grows, grew
weleaway, weleawey   welladay, alas for
wend   go
werne   refuse, deny
werre   382   war
wexe   grow

whereso   wheresoever
while   time, period of time
whyles   until, while, as long as
wight, wyght   creature, person
wyse   way, manner; on thre wyse   in three ways
wyst   knew
wyt   wisdom
wyte   *vb*   lay the blame on
wyte   *n*   blame
wyteth   perishes, vanishes away
wold, wolt   would, wanted to; wolt   wouldest, wilt
wondre   marvellous
wondre   *adv*   wonderfully
wonderly   marvellously
wonnyng, wonyng   dwelling a
woo worth   a curse upon, may evil befall
wood, woode   ferocious, fierce
worshyp   source of honour, distinction, credit
worshypped   honoured
worthynesse   worth, value, credit
wote   know, knew; thou wost   thou knowest
wox   grew

Index of Proper Names

Lightning Source UK Ltd.
Milton Keynes UK
UKHW012354200722
406167UK00001B/415